Seoul

A Window into Korean Culture

To: Professor Mark Watson
with respect
Dec 17. of
Joon Sik Choi.

$Seoul$ A Window into Korean Culture

Copyright © 2009 by Choi Joon-sik

First Published 4ᵗʰ March 2009.

Author Choi Joon- sik
Proofreading and partial translation Sandra Choe
Publisher Shin Young- mi
Company HER ONE MEDIA

Address Room 1104, World Officetel, 65-1. Unni-dong, Jongno-gu,
           Seoul, Korea 110-350
Tel 82-2-766-9273
Fax 82-2-766-9272
website www.herone.co.kr
E-mail dayonha@hanmail.net

ISBN 978-89-92162-15-9 03980

Price 25,000 won

CIP 2009000609 http://www.nl.go.kr/cip.php

＊Damaged books can be exchanged.

A Window into Korean Culture

Seoul

Choi Joon-sik Ph.D.

Proofreading and partial translation Sandra Choe

허원미디어
HER ONE MEDIA

Acknowledgements

Seoul, the current capital city of South Korea, is an ancient city that boasts more than 600 years of rich history. There are few books written in English that are concerned with the traditional culture of Seoul. Of course, there are several of them that tell the history of Seoul in fragments. However, it is not easy to find a serious study written in English that explains to foreigners the cultural meaning behind the city that is Seoul. I felt that this situation needed to be amended, so the Korea Foundation graciously gave me an opportunity to write a book for foreigners on this subject.

I would like to make clear that this book is not merely a translation of a previously published book of mine. I wrote the original version of this book in Korean, my native language with the anticipation that foreigners would like to know more about Korean traditional culture. Obviously, there are differences between Korean and foreign readers; I plan to publish a separate Korean edition of this book. The Korean edition will contain some sections that are not found in the English edition while lacking other sections that are part of the English edition.

The Korea Foundation provided financial assistance to have this book translated professionally. No publisher in Korea could have provided the generous support that was given by the Korea Foundation. I am once again very grateful to the Korea Foundation.

Secondly, I would like to thank HER ONE MEDIA for their decision to publish this book. This book contains many photographs, which initially made the manuscript quite dense, but HER ONE MEDIA CEO Dr. Eunsil Yu allowed me to include them nonetheless. I also thank Chief Editor Ms. Shin Young-mi and thank Professor S. Capener for my first introduction to the translator. Also, my former student Sandra Choe has provided invaluable assistance in wresting the manuscript into its final form. A certified translator as well as a native English speaker, this book reads with more consistence and clarity thanks to the efforts of Ms. Choe and I again wish to express my gratitude. Another person who deserves my genuine thanks is my assistant for this project, Minseo Sim. Her help in making documents and communication with the Korea Foundation was dispensable.

Finally, I extend my thanks to my nephew Dr. Paul S. Lee for a general proofreading this book. With an undergraduate degree in English Language and Literature, Dr. Lee provided helpful comments and finishing touches that I greatly appreciated. I also thank the many people and countless organizations which provided me with the wonderful photographs found throughout this book.

I hope that this book offers something valuable to those who want to learn more about Korean traditional culture.

Choi Joon-sik Ph. D.

Contents

Millions of foreign visitors seek Korea every year for a multitude of reasons; the legal foreign resident population is almost 900,000 as of May 2008. One place not to be missed when visiting Korea is Seoul, the capital city for over six centuries since 1392. Because the population is so heavily concentrated in the Seoul metropolitan area alone, the saying goes that nothing can be done without visiting Seoul—a phenomenon that sets Korea apart from its neighbors. When traveling in China or Japan, it is not necessary to visit Beijing or Tokyo to say 'I have been to China' or 'I have travelled to Japan.' However, it is virtually impossible not to visit, much less to stop by, Seoul, as all resources are concentrated here. All international flights arrive and depart from Seoul except for a few close routes to China and Japan; even if a business meeting is held in a provincial city, there is no way to avoid Seoul.

There is a common saying—half-jest, half-serious—that Korea is made up of two to three separate states. When we say there are 'two states,' it refers to the 'Republic of Seoul' and the 'Rural Republic,' 'three states' further divides the Republic of Seoul into the 'South Han Republic (Gangnam, the area of Seoul south of the Han River)' and the 'North Han Republic.' It satirizes the large development gap between the capital and rural areas as well as within the capital between the haves and have-nots; such demarcation clearly reflects the resulting sociocultural differences of an economic divide between the two regions separated by the Han River. All of the above shows the extent to which everything is centralized in the capital: most government offices and the headquarters of major companies are all located in Seoul, and it is also home to almost all the highest quality cultural and educational facilities. The saying, "You have to send your kids to Seoul if you want them to succeed," is not a product of mere happenstance.

Such an abnormal tendency toward centralization has predictably resulted in a population explosion. The population of Seoul is just below 11 million, and with the total population of South Korea at 50 million as of November 2007, approximately one in every five Koreans lives in the capital city. However, this in itself is hardly an accurate estimate. When we include those living in satellite cities on the outskirts of Seoul, the total population of the larger Seoul metropolitan area increases to 48 percent of the country population. The human congestion level of Seoul is probably among the highest in the world, and this alone largely accounts for why it is impossible for visitors to bypass this city.

A person's face is considered to be representative of the entire body. With so many faces within its borders, Seoul cannot help but be the 'face' of Korea. Consequently, I believe that there is no better way to introduce Korea than through a close exploration of Seoul. Seoul has served as the capital for more than six centuries, and therefore boasts countless relics and historical sites from its rich and varied history that can satiate avid travellers. During the Joseon Dynasty (1392~1910), Seoul was the center of political, cultural and economic affairs. However, it might not be fair to say outright that Seoul represents the whole of Korea— especially the more traditional aspects—as there are other cities that have served as the capital city of previous dynasties. When we take a different perspective on what defines 'tradition,' we can conclude that Seoul plays no small role in representing Korean traditional culture. In order to reach such a conclusion, we must first ask ourselves the question — when were 'things Korean' first formed? In other words, what is the origin of what we consider Korean? Many would probably guess that most of what they know as 'tradition' dates from a very long time ago. Tae Kwon Do, the most representative martial art of Korea, is generally known to have its roots in the ancient Three Kingdoms Period (6th century A.C.E.). However, contrary to popular assumption, the history of this sport is much shorter. Tae Kwon Do has its origin in the Japanese martial art Karate. Karate was imported to Korea after Korea's liberation from colonial rule in 1945, and it evolved within the Korean setting into what we know today as Tae Kwon Do. Now Karate and Tae Kwon Do are two completely different martial arts. If this example seems too contemporary, let us look at another case that dates a bit further back.

No Korean would object to selecting *kimchi* as the most representative Korean food. Like pasta sauce in Italy, there are many types of *kimchi* and it is made differently in each province and household; of these, cabbage *kimchi* is the most popular and widely loved. Many would be surprised to discover that this seemingly traditional food was in fact first developed in the late 19th century. Also, the most important ingredient of *kimchi*, red pepper, was first introduced to Korea in the early 17th century through either China or Japan. The import of cabbage in the late 19th century from China explains the rather late emergence of cabbage *kimchi*. Many similar such cases exist—let us look at one more. The fan dance is almost always on the program when introducing traditional Korean performance art to foreign tourists. Even the world-famous travelguide series, *Lonely Planet*™, chose a picture of the fan dance as the cover image for its book on Seoul. But not many people know exactly when the fan dance was created; most vaguely guess that it was danced in the Joseon royal court, but it is actually a far more recent creation that was made in the 1950s exclusively for stage use.

Thus, it is important to keep in mind that a lot of what we perceive as Korean tradition is in fact relatively recent, most of it from late-19th century Seoul. Therefore, there is no better place to go than Seoul to experience what we call 'tradition.' This book is not a Seoul travel guide; there are many of them, including *Lonely Planet*™, available in bookstores. Because travel guides often focus on tourist attractions and are written to cater to foreign travelers, they do not delve deeply into the fundamentals of Korean culture and often neglect explanation on traditional culture, knowledge of which is vital to thoroughly understand Korean society.

Seoul *Lonely Planet*

On this note, the editorial stance of this book does not intend to introduce places in Seoul that foreign tourists would love to see. Instead, this book has attempted to shed light upon the aspects of traditional culture that Koreans would love to introduce to foreign visitors. Although there may be some overlap between these two approaches, I have tried to create this book so that it not only sponsors a Korean perspective but also accomodates information that is of interest to foreign visitors as well. Here, a 'foreign visitor' refers to someone who is interested in traditional Korean culture and is trying to understand the history and culture of Korea in greater depth than the ordinary tourist. I hope this book can enable readers to gain a better understanding of the history of Seoul and its culture, and in this process become able to approach Korean culture with more sensitivity.

Korean Culture Through Relics in Seoul

Many Koreans and foreigners alike think that Seoul is limited to a six hundred-year history as a capital city and are shocked to learn that it is actually more than 2,000 years old. The beginnings of Seoul date back to 1st B.C.E., when it was made the capital city of the ancient kingdom of Baekje (18 B.C.E.~660 A.C.E.). We will not cover the ancient history of Korea in detail, but a brief explanation of Baekje is necessary for a better understanding of our subject. Baekje was one of the three kingdoms that occupied the Korean peninsula during the Three Kingdoms Period (57 B.C.E.~668 A.C.E.). The first king of Baekje came down to the Han River area from Manchuria, and built his capital city along the Han River. He built two castles, Monchon and Pungnap Fortress, which are located side by side in Olympic Park in southeastern Seoul and still stand today. A group of archeologists and historians recently discovered that Pungnap Fortress was the seat of government for Baekje's first capital city. Pungnap Fortress is located along the riverbank and is easily accessible by subway (close to Cheonho Station on subway line 5). The only six-star hotel in Korea, W Hotel, is right across the river. There are also prehistoric settlement sites in the nearby Amsa-dong, so this general area is highly recommended for anyone who is interested in the ancient history of Korea.

The Kingdom of Baekje lasted for more than 400 years with Seoul as its capital. However, the era of Seoul came to an official end in the 5th century when Baekje could no longer withstand pressure from the Goguryeo Kingdom to the north. Baekje eventually retreated southward, and moved its capital to Gongju in South Chungcheong Province. Seoul had to wait until the founding of Joseon at the end of the fourteenth century to reappear in history as the capital city, but there were numerous attempts made before then to make Seoul the capital city by other dynasties and it was always specially regarded due to its strategic and geographic advantages. One king from the Goryeo Dynasty (936~1392, the dynasty that directly preceded Joseon) even devised a concrete plan to relocate the capital city to Seoul. This indicates how important Seoul has been throughout Korean history. Seoul makes a celebrated comeback to the forefront of Korean history with the birth of the Joseon Dynasty in 1392.

Before we take a look at the significance of Seoul within Korean history, we will first review how the name 'Seoul' was created. Seoul was called by different names before the modern Republic of Korea was founded on the heels of liberation in 1945. During the Joseon Dynasty, the capital city was called 'Hanyang(漢陽),' meaning 'north of Han River' and was called 'Gyeongseong(京城)' during the Japanese colonial period. Hanyang and Gyeongseong are each a combination of two Chinese characters; after 1945, the patriotically-imbued leaders of newly independent Korea wanted to give the capital city a Korean name to make a break with past Chinese tradition. They decided on the name Seoul, the name of the capital city of the ancient kingdom of Silla. Silla's capital was and still is called Gyeongju, but it was also called 'Saebeol,' meaning 'new land' in Korean or 'Seorabeol' in Chinese characters. In

Mongchon Fortress

other words, Seoul is a modified form of the name 'Saebeol.'

As I already mentioned, Seoul emerged to the forefront of Korean history upon the establishment of the Joseon Dynasty in 1392. Thereafter, it became the center of everything from political and economic affairs to education and culture. This is why the saying goes, "If you know Seoul, you will see Korea." As we have seen thus far, many cultural relics can be found in Seoul today because it has been inhabited from the prehistoric era to the present. It is impossible to review such cases in this single volume, and there is no need to do so. Because it is impossible to do everything about all things, selectivity is crucial; this book will focus on artifacts that make Seoul truly 'Seoul' —artifacts that are important because they are places that cannot be found anywhere else in the world. Of course, focus is not given exclusively to the past; the concluding chapter will also attempt to portray the unique culture of Seoul as found within the vibrant nightlife of young Seoulites. The majority of this book will deal with the Gangbuk (north of the Han River) area, the region of Seoul that was demarcated by the four original city gates. Gangnam, the prosperous and bustling region south of the river, possesses few representative historical sites because of its relatively short history. Therefore, it is the Gangbuk area that deserves the attention of those who are interested in traditional Seoul.

Seoul is home to many of the entries that are included on the UNESCO World Cultural Heritage list. Two of them are Changdeok Palace, the second palace of the Joseon Dynasty, and Jongmyo, the National Royal Shrine dedicated to holding memorial services for deceased kings and queens of Joseon. The main palace of the Joseon Dynasty, Gyeongbok Palace, failed to be named a UNESCO World Cultural Heritage because it endured too much damage throughout the

Japanese colonial period and the Korean War. North Village, the area between Gyeongbok and Changdeok Palaces, is also intriguing. North Village used to be the residential area of high-ranking Joseon government officials and for this reason is famous for having the best-preserved *hanok* (traditional tile-roof house). There is a smaller palace next to Changdeok Palace called Changgyeong Palace, built mainly for the royal family women. Although this book will not cover Changgyeong Palace, it will discuss the attached facility known as Sunggyungwan. Sunggyungwan was the Joseon Dynasty equivalent of a state university, where Confucian classics were taught and prospective state officials were carefully selected. But Confucianism was not the only ideology alive in Joseon. We will also visit institutions related to Buddhism and Shamanism, two other religions that were also close to the heart of Joseon people.

The places that have been mentioned thus far are clustered around old Seoul. They are best viewed from Mt. Nam, a mountain in the center of Seoul that is neither too big nor too small at little over 200 meters high. From its peak, one can see Seoul's natural landscape as well as the principles that formed palaces, institutional buildings, and residential houses. Evidence of the Japanese role in modern Korean history can also be seen. Foreign tourists visit Seoul Tower to view the nocturnal skyline of Seoul, but Mt. Nam contains many more stories that lie underneath the glittering lights. Mt. Nam will be the first destination of our journey in Seoul, and from there, we will explore more of Seoul by themes and places.

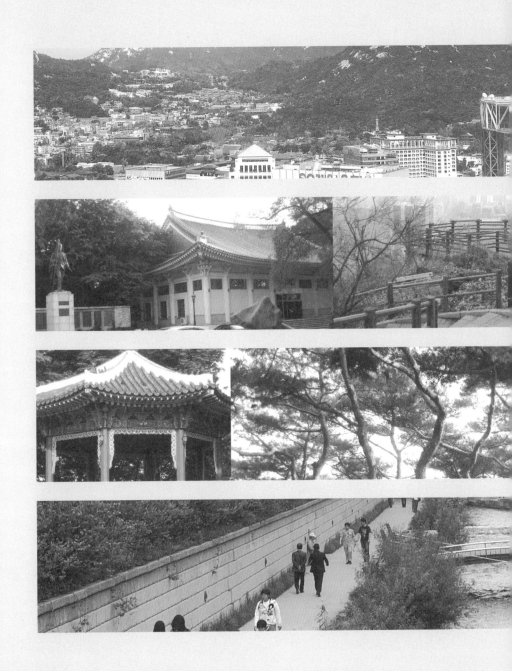

Seoul and the Life of Koreans

Chapter **1**

1. Nature in the City, the City in Nature

We must first understand the guiding principles by which Seoul was created when attempting to understand Korean culture through Seoul. While location is a basic characteristic of capital cities regardless of East or West, Joseon in the East was particularly concerned with geomancy (*Fengshui*). Within Northeast Asia, China and Korea adhered to *Fengshui* principles when building palaces, but the latter was undoubtedly more faithful in its application of *Fengshui*. This point becomes quite obvious with a comparison of the main palaces of both countries—Gyeongbok Palace of Korea and the Forbidden City of China. A more detailed explanation will be provided later in this chapter, so let us keep in mind for now that both Seoul and Gyeongbok Palace were constructed after long deliberation and detailed planning in strict accordance to *Fengshui* principle.

Fengshui is the guiding principle that determines the two most important sites for any person—the lot for a home, and the ground to be used for burial. It is certainly an important theory because of its role in deciding the locations of living and dying. It would be a huge undertaking to explain all the complex background principles of geomancy, but the basic underlying worldview is simple—nature is not dead, but alive. According to *Fengshui*, there is an energy, *Qi*, that flows in nature the way it flows in the human body. A basic tenet of Chinese medicine, *Qi*, the energy of life, flows in our body along special veins, and the points where this energy converges are called *hyeol* in Korean. To use a more simple analogy, veins are equivalent to railroad tracks, while *hyeol* would be equivalent to train stations. In Chinese medicine, sickness is the negative result of poor circulation of *Qi* in the veins, and it is cured by performing acupuncture on *hyeol* spots to redirect the flow of *Qi*. Therefore, these converging spots of *Qi* occupy an extremely important position. This same philosophy is directly applied to nature. In nature, there are 'earth veins' similar to those in the human body as well as *Qi* that flows through these earth veins; the point where the energy merges is called an auspicious site. It is said that a person can absorb propitious energy by building a house or family burial site on such an auspicious spot.

From the viewpoint of modern science, this type of reasoning sounds unscientific and superstitious. Consequently, it may also seem as if people no longer believe in such superstition; in actuality, geomancy still exerts a considerable influence on modern-day Koreans. There are many anecdotes about determining the family burial site, and the most representative of these is linked to the presidency. Many former Korean presidents and presidential candidates have relocated the burial site of their ancestors, thinking that moving the tombs of their ancestors to an auspicious location would bring the good energy necessary to become president. This clearly shows the unconscious belief of most Koreans toward geomancy despite outward denial of it. I personally do not believe that ancestral remains, with or without *Qi*, can help a descendant become president, but on the other hand I am also opposed to the bashing of *Fengshui* as groundless superstition. While an obsession with geomancy is problematic when choosing a burial site, I find this very useful in deciding the lot for a house.

According to geomancy, the most important condition in choosing the site for a home is a mountain in the back that can 'anchor' the lot and provide protection, as well as flowing water in the front of the house. The technical term for this concept is *'Jang Pung Deuk Su,'* meaning 'control the [energy of the] wind and allow water to flow [in front].' Many houses in Korea face south. This is to prevent houses from directly facing the cold Siberian wind that comes from the northwest, and to receive as much warm sunlight as possible in the meantime. It is important to note here that the goal is not to completely block the movement of wind, as this would impede the flow of *Qi*. The key is to not block but instead to save some of the cold northwesterly wind and store it. When this is accomplished, energy can then flow from north to south without being disrupted. When the north side is blocked, the south side must be opened to achieve balance. In geomancy, it is called *'Bae San Im Su,'* which means having 'a mountain in the back, and a river in front.' There are two main reasons for a river to be placed nearby. The first is for practicality; it is useful to have easy access to a water source, a vital element in sustaining life. The second reason is related to geomancy principle; a river serves as a natural barrier that prevents positive energy from flowing out to other places. In this way, people live comfortably on an auspicious site under the protection of nature, backed by a mountain in the back and nourished by a river in front.

Seoul was constructed by faithful adherence to *Fengshui* principle. As mentioned previously, *Fengshui* is a set of theories that sound rather superstitious. But one thing that is certain is that when a lot has been staked out in accordance to these principles, you can count on both a beautiful view as well as a comfortable lifestyle. For this reason, I have chosen to focus on the practicality rather than the scientific legitimacy of

Fengshui. Fengshui is useful because it can assist our daily lives! Let us take a look at Seoul from Mt. Nam. Had Seoul been able to avoid the series of thoughtless and reckless development schemes that have pervaded its modern history, it could have been one of the most beautiful cities in the world; the extent of its 'development' becomes instantly obvious with a view from atop Mt. Nam. The beauty of Seoul lies in its natural endowments—it has many beautiful mountains and a majestic river that runs across the city from east to west. Few capital cities in the world are similarly equipped with these two gifts of nature. Mt. Bukak sits behind Gyeongbok Palace and the current presidential residence Cheong Wa Dae with much dignity and grace. Its nicely-cut triangular shape gives the mountain a more stately air. Unfortunately, the beauty of Mt. Bukak had been closed from public viewing for nearly 40 years until very recently. Access to the mountain had been restricted ever since 31 North Korean commandos reached the foot of Mt. Bukak close to the presidential residence in January 1968 to assassinate then-President Park Chung Hee. Park, who felt his livelihood was under great danger, immediately blocked all public access to the mountain. Very recently, the government has temporarily opened some parts of Mt. Bukak to the public, but access is still very much limited.

To the north of Mt. Bukak, a series of larger mountains is connected to one other to form the Mt. Bukhan sub-range that dominates the northern part of Seoul. In a country in which 70 percent of the land is mountainous, Mt. Bukhan is touted as one of the four best mountains in Korea. One can conclude that it is good enough to defeat a lot of competition. Interestingly, Mt. Bukhan is within a 15-minute drive from Gwanghwamun Intersection, the center of Old Seoul. From the entrance of the mountain, a ten-minute walk will reveal dense forests and a ravine

Mt. Inwang

Mt. Bukak

bordered by a clear stream. Every time I visit here, I find it remarkable to find myself deep in the mountains when I am so close to the city center. Seoulites can take refuge in this wonderful nearby natural shelter when they feel exhausted from the hectic pace of city life. There are not many capital cities in the world that can boast similar qualifications, and people who travel widely seem to be of the same opinion. I believe that the secret of this success lies in *Fengshui*. By defining the perimeters of the most optimum living space, *Fengshui* allows people to do their daily work and return to nature whenever they feel like it. There is a sense of belonging to both human society and the larger subcategory of nature. There are other such mountains in Seoul that serve similar purposes. Mt. Nam and Mt. Inwang, which both face Cheong Wa Dae, are other examples that will be covered in this book. Although they are not as great in stature as Mt. Bukhan, they still provide good resting places for the people of Seoul.

Speaking of Mt. Bukhan, there is a great travel course that offers spectacular views and leads us to many hidden historical relics in the surrounding area. A bus from in front of the Kyobo Life Insurance

S e o u l

Mt. Bukhan range

North Seoul

building on Sejongno will take you to the entrance of Mt. Bukhan National Park. At the entrance, there is a sign that directs visitors to a Buddhist temple called Seungga Temple, which can be reached by a 30-minute hike. The path leading to the temple provides a beautiful view of dense forests and clear flowing streams. However, once you arrive at the temple, you might be disappointed by what you see. This is because a pagoda was recently built inside the temple in a way that does not at all agree with its surroundings. The overall first impression is gaudy and unsettling, an attempt at outward finery that reflects the cruder side of capitalism. The shoddy outer appearance set aside, you can discover that the temple houses two National Treasures. National Treasures are designated by the government, and thus imply great value. One of them is Treasure No. 215, a seated rock-cliff Buddha. You can reach the Buddha after climbing up many stairs behind the main hall of worship. As it is located high in the mountain, both the rock-cliff Buddha itself and the distant view of Seoul are spectacular. It was made about 700 to 800 years ago, before the decline of Buddhism began in earnest in Korea, which probably explains the exquisite and high-quality level of

Rock-cliff Buddha at Seungga Temple

craftsmanship. On the way back to the temple, you can find Treasure No. 1000, Stone Statue of Monk Seungga, in a small cave. Although it is not as artistically refined as the rock-cliff Buddha, it appears to have been designated as a treasure in consideration of its origins in the 11th century.

Because mountains are so prevalent in Seoul, Koreans love to go hiking. Weekends see hoards of visitors at mountains near Seoul. Seoulites should be grateful to the benefits of *Fengshui* for being able to enjoy such easily-accessible natural surroundings. But as previously mentioned, *Fengshui* is not all about mountains; it also emphasizes the need for a river. Of course, Seoul has the Han River that runs from the east and flows into the Yellow Sea. Rivers provide people with many benefits; they provide drinking water, a basic necessity for survival, and a means of transporting goods and people. For these reasons, a good city must have a river nearby. However, the Han River used to be much more beautiful before development projects on it began in the 1960s. There used to be beautiful pavilions, ferry points and villas of the nobility built along the Han River in harmony with the surrounding nature. Now, however, the river seems to function only as a large waterway, due to reckless development schemes that covered the entire embankment with cement and replaced the pavilions with tall apartment buildings that are entirely lacking in character. The old charm of the riverside has completely disappeared, and many foreign tourists who tour the river by boat complain that there is nothing to see but apartment buildings. One foreign visitor once remarked that all he could see in Seoul's cityscape was boring apartment buildings. He had expected to see a lot more greenery, having learned prior to coming to Korea that over 70 percent of the land is mountainous. Korea, one of the most impoverished countries in the world merely half a century ago, was swept up by a blind obsession to modernize itself, and chose to ignore paying attention to the preservation of historical and cultural heritages. Fortunately, the Seoul Metropolitan Government, dreaming of the age of a Han River renaissance, decided to restore the Han River and its original surroundings. Only time will tell how the cityscape of Seoul will change within the next few years.

According to *Fengshui*, a city must have a river inside as well as outside the city limits. When the outside is *yang*, the inside becomes *yin*; to balance the two polar energies, when there is a river outside, the city must have a river inside. For this reason, Seoul has a water source inside the city called *naesu*, otherwise known as Cheonggyecheon (It has been fully renovated as of 2007). During the Joseon Dynasty, the size of Seoul was much smaller than present-day Seoul, and the Han River was situated

Grand Han River

outside the city limits. Therefore, Seoul needed a river running through the city as well. Cheonggyecheon was artificially made to fill this specific need 600 years ago right next to Seoul's main street Jongno in order to attract *yin* energy. However, it was covered up 40 years ago as part of the ambitious post-war reconstruction plan, including plans to build a road while President Syngman Rhee was in office. Later, an elevated highway was constructed by President Park Chung-hee to maximize transportation efficiency. Administrators blind to all else but economic development were probably unable to bear the thought of leaving a river to run right through the city. They would have wanted to cover it up to allow automobile travel. Eventually, a highway was built over the cement cover, which did increase the efficiency of traffic and transportation. At the time, political leaders and the general public alike hailed the construction effort as a great achievement of industrialization. However, as Korea became better-off as the decades passed, Koreans gradually began to feel ashamed of this particular piece of construction. In other words, people started focusing on the quality of life. Under the shared impression that the Seoul cityscape was too bleak, it was decided that the stream would be returned to its former condition. The restoration project began in July 2003 and was completed in just three years on September 2005, transforming a collective eyesore into a beautiful work of art. Because it was a rare type of construction that is difficult to witness in developed countries, many architects from abroad came to Seoul as a field trip to watch the stream reveal its original form. It must have been very unusual to the eyes of foreign architects to see this kind of large-scale construction be completed in just three years. Among other things, this massive restoration project required the evacuation and resettlement of countless stores and 'road shops' situated along the stream, tearing off 5.84 kilometers of roads, and the construction of a green zone in its place. Finishing this type of project in three years must have been a shock to foreigners. A German architect who witnessed the construction allegedly said that such a project would take more than 10 years in his country, and found it hard to believe how driven and focused Koreans were to be able to do it so quickly.

From the perspective of geomancy, the role of Cheonggyecheon is to collect negative energies floating around the city and drive them out. Nobody has elaborated on exactly what constitutes negative energy, but one

Old Cheonggyecheon in the 1970's   New Cheonggyecheon

Current inside view of New Cheonggyecheon

thing certain is that Cheonggyecheon carries the sewage and waste water accumulated inside the city out into the Han River. Although Seoul's economic scale used to be miniscule compared to what it is today, it was nevertheless a community of people living together and thus inevitably produced waste. The role of Cheonggyecheon is to take away the filthy water from the waste. From the example of Cheonggyecheon, we can see that *Fengshui* is not only a theoretical idea but has a solid foundation in real life that can serve very practical purposes.

So far, we have briefly talked about the natural landscape of Seoul. The best place to see all of this is Mt. Nam, a required stop on any tour of Seoul. It has served as a shelter for Seoul citizens and is the source of many historical anecdotes, especially related to the Japanese colonial period. We will begin our journey of Seoul by first visiting Mt. Nam.

2. Looking at Seoul from Mt. Nam

Mt. Nam formed the southern border of Hanyang, the capital city during the Joseon Dynasty. A visit up Mt. Nam today will reveal the still-standing remains of a fortress, the borderline that divided the city from the outside. But when looking at Mt. Nam today, you can see that it lies closer to the north of Seoul. This is because Seoul has excessively developed the region south of the Han River in recent years. There are many anecdotes related to the foot of this mountain, but let us put all these aside for now and climb to the top of Mt. Nam. Basically the only way to go up Mt. Nam is by taking a bus from in front of the Shilla Hotel, which is located near the Dongguk University Subway Station on line 3. There is a cable car that runs between the foot and the top of the mountain, but it is expensive to take and thus is not recommended. I personally think walking is the best way to enjoy Mt. Nam to the fullest, because you miss a lot of the charm of this mountain if you choose to go up by bus. Plus, it takes only half an hour to get to the top even at a slow walk.

The Pine Trees in Mt. Nam

About halfway up the mountain, there is a beltway for pedestrians. This asphalt road was originally built about 20-30 years ago for cars, but the entry of cars to the mountain was soon prohibited due to criticism that cars have adverse effects on the mountain because of the resulting air pollution. This car-free road has thus become one of the most

Pine trees in Mt. Nam

beautiful roads in Korea with cherry blossoms in full bloom in the spring and leaves brilliantly colored red and yellow in the fall. The road has become even more pedestrian-friendly as of 2007 with a special jogging track that has been built along the hiking road. What we really want to see on our way up Mt. Nam are the pine trees. The pine trees on Mt. Nam are so famous that they even appear in the lyrics of the national anthem of Korea. Korean pine trees have peculiar traits that make them easily distinguishable from those of other countries. Korean pine trees almost never grow straight, and twist many times as they grow. Trees with more twists in them are thought to have more aesthetic value and therefore call a higher price. As shown in the picture, these twisted pine trees were one of the most popular objects to be painted by the artists of the Joseon Dynasty; Mt. Nam used to be covered with these pine trees because the government itself planted many of them. However, things began to unfold differently from the start of the early 20th century when

Korea was annexed by Japan. The Japanese colonial administration, seeking to eradicate everything even remotely Korean, was not fond of the pine trees on Mt. Nam. As a counter-measure, they planted large numbers of acacia trees between the pine trees; acacia trees are famous for being easy to breed and can grow well under any circumstances. As a result, many pine trees withered and died, unable to endure the increased competition for sunlight and soil. After liberation, the Korean government executed an all-out campaign to eliminate all acacia trees in order to preserve the remaining pine trees on Mt. Nam. Of course many new pine trees were planted in the process, but a considerable portion of the pine trees found on Mt. Nam today are those that have survived great adversity.

An immortal under the pine tree
by Kim Hongdo(1745~1806)

The pine trees can be found on the left-hand side of the bus path that goes up the mountain. As can be seen in the picture, the pine trees are situated in two or three clusters, and there are viewing facilities that allow you to enjoy the scenery in comfort. A walk on a trail through the pine forest offers the closest possible look at the trees, and the vista it offers is truly magnificent. There is, however, a minor setback in that the trail leads downhill and you are thus forced to walk uphill on the way back. It is also possible to see the pine trees from the bus, but in doing so you will miss out on being able to truly appreciate the beauty of the trees because the bus passes by them too quickly. Because bypassing this wonderful scenery is the same as bypassing one of the most representative symbols of Korea, I strongly advise you to go by foot up the mountain while enjoying a spectacular view of the Han River stretching below the great curving pine trees.

We have spent some time appreciating the pine trees, and will now rush to the top of the mountain. Halfway up Mt. Nam, there are remnants of old fortress walls from the late 14th century, but they have not been properly restored and thus I will refrain from further explanation in this book. The sloppy restoration work on the rampart took place during the mid-1970s, with buckets of cement poured over the 600-year walls without much care. After achieving remarkable economic development within just a few decades, Koreans have restored many damaged historical relics with a sense of renewed self-confidence. However, it seems as if they have yet to turn their attention to restoring the fortress wall on Mt. Nam. Many foreign tourists visit the mountain on the way to Seoul Tower; perhaps it is fine with Koreans to display historical artifacts that have clearly been neglected. Sometimes Koreans appear to have strong pride in their culture, and at other times the very opposite seems true. At any rate, when we reach the peak, you can see Seoul Tower,

N Tower

otherwise called N Tower. From the top of the tower, you can see as far as Incheon on a clear day, but this view must be paid for with a large fee. There is an expensive restaurant at the top which turns 360 degrees at a very slow speed, offering the guests a 360-degree panoramic view while enjoying their meal. It makes a nice place to take your girlfriend or boyfriend out to dinner, but it is not quite appropriate for a student of Korean culture on a tight budget. The top of the mountain also offers an equally great view on how Seoul was constructed.

A view of Seoul Mt. Nam through *Fengshui*

Originally, the best place to get a sense of the *Fengshui* of Seoul was Bongsudae, or smoke-signal station site, on Mt. Nam. The Bongsudae in the picture is not in its original location, but has been recreated in a spot that is easily accessible by the general public. Bongsudae was a communication system of the Joseon Dynasty that used fire in clear weather and smoke in rainy weather to deliver urgent messages between remote cities on the border. It was the Joseon equivalent of a wireless network. Messages from five stations were reported to the king early in the morning every day. Bongsudae used to be open to the public, and I used to visit with my students every time when studying *Fengshui* because of the nice overview of Seoul that is seen from here. But one day it was suddenly closed. I later heard that it had been forcibly closed because of

Bongsudae

excessive scribbling on the walls. The authority said that the scribbling was somewhat bearable, but there was no viable solution for spray-painted graffiti. As access to Bongsudae is no longer permitted, my students and I are forced to find alternative spots—the roof terrace next to N Tower, or an observation booth called Photo Island, located slightly below the peak of the mountain. Of course, the best spot for viewing is the top of the mountain.

It is a well-known fact that Seoul was the capital of the Joseon Dynasty. In the heart of the capital city is the palace. The cityscape is determined by the method in which the palace is built. The main palace during the Joseon Dynasty was Gyeongbok Palace. This will be explained again later in this book, but Gyeongbok Palace is the most frequented place in Korea by foreign tourists. Although only 20 to 30 percent of present-day Gyeongbok Palace has been successfully renovated, the fact that is was the main palace is the reason for the constant stream of visitors. The politicians of Joseon tried to build the palace at the end of the 14th century in accordance with the Chinese principle of Ye(禮), but did not build the entire palace in Chinese style. In China, the palace would have to be built in the exact center of the city, in the way that the Forbidden City was built. This follows the logic that the emperor must always be at the center. But the Joseon Dynasty did not follow this particular Chinese custom, and built Gyeongbok Palace against the northwestern end of the city walls in accordance to *Fengshui* principle. This was done intentionally in order to build the palace at the foot of the mountain. Even when building a village, Koreans prefer a site at the foot of a mountain rather than in the center of open flat land. This is why the administrators of early Joseon followed *Fengshui* rather than *Ye*.

The first task in building a palace is to find the most auspicious site.

Gyeongbok Palace as seen from Mt. Inwang

An auspicious site according to *Fengshui* requires a main mountain to support the north side of the building. This mountain refers to the mountain directly behind the building. In the case of Gyeongbok Palace, as visible in the picture, Mt. Bukak (342 m) serves as the main mountain. In *Fengshui*, Mt. Bukak is represented by *hyeonmu*, the animal in charge of the north. There are four celestial animals in *Fengshui* philosophy, and each is responsible for guarding the four cardinal directions—the black turtle for north, the crimson phoenix for south, the white tiger for west and the blue dragon for east. The black turtle is in fact a mixture of a turtle and a snake intertwined together. It is still unclear why it is a turtle and a snake, but my guess is that people chose animals that seemed mystical. Because the mountain is responsible for protecting the palace, it should not exude an ordinary air. Mt. Bukak, with its neat triangular shape, displays grace and dignity. If the kings of Joseon had actually taken time to look at Mt. Bukak everyday, I wonder whether their hearts would not have come to resemble the quiet dignity of the mountain.

Secondly, there must be mountains on either side of the main mountain—blue dragon on the left and white tiger on the right—in order to absorb and contain auspicious energy. When looking at Gyeongbok Palace from Mt. Nam, there is a large mountain on the lefthand side. This is Mt. Inwang, represented by the white tiger. Although access to Mt. Bukak is limited, technically there are no restrictions on entering Mt. Inwang during the weekdays; it is closed on Monday and after dark on weekdays. Despite relatively free access and the great view of Seoul that this mountain provides, there are not many Seoulites who have actually visited Mt. Inwang. This is probably because of a strong police presence stationed there to protect Cheong Wa Dae, the official residence of the president. From Mt. Inwang, you can see the whole layout of Gyeongbok Palace as well as Mt. Bukak and Mt. Bukhan. For this, I hightly recommend Mt. Inwang to Koreans as well as foreign visitors. At only 338 meters high, it is not difficult to climb. The striking view of Seoul and its

Mt. Bukak   Mt. Bukhan

Mt. Bukhan, *josan*(grandfather mountain) of Mt. Bukak

Cheonji (Heaven's Lake) of Mt. Baekdu

natural surroundings from the heart of Seoul can only be described as incredible. I feel the power of *Fengshui* every time I visit.

Returning to our discussion on the principles of geomancy, *Fengshui* also specifies the need for one more mountain to support the main mountain in the back. This is called '*josan*,' literally translated as 'grandfather mountain' in relation to the main mountain as a father figure. Mt. Bukhan, although the exact name of this mountain is disputed, serves as the grandfather mountain in this case. Such a patriarchal metaphor is not unusual coming from a society heavily influenced by the Chinese-dictated patriarchal system. From a geomantic viewpoint, having many mountains surrounding the palace would help store propitious energy inside the palace. If Mt. Bukhan is the grandfather figure, then what would be the ultimate founding father of this mountain family tree? *Fengshui* scholars of the Joseon Dynasty believed that this was Mt.

Baekdu. Mt. Baekdu is also known as Changbai Mountain in China, and lies on the border between China and North Korea. The highest mountain on the Korean peninsula at 2,750 meters, Mt. Baekdu has been regarded as the most sacred mountain in all of Korea. Koreans believe that the founding father of Korea descended from heaven to this particular mountain five thousand years ago. The volcanic lake at the top of this mountain, Cheonji, or 'Heaven's Lake,' adds an even more mystical air to Mt. Baekdu. *Fengshui* philosophers believe that as true of all mountains in Korea, the mountains behind Gyeongbok Palace are related to Mt. Baekdu; this is not entirely without evidence. The North Korean guerilla fighters who reached Mt. Bukak in 1968 to assassinate then—president Park Chung-hee reached their destination only by scaling other mountains along the way, with no flat land in between. This shows that mountains are that plentiful in Korea.

Mt. Inwang, which is represented by the white tiger, is also home to the most famous shaman shrine in Korea; this will be discussed in the chapter on Korean Shamanism. In any case, Mt. Inwang is definitely worth a visit. The next is the mountain on the east represented by the blue dragon. If there is a weak point in Seoul's geomantic location, it is the blue dragon mountain. Since it is so small in size, you need to take a much closer look to find where it is. There is a mountain, more of a hill, standing about 100 meters high behind Daehanyno, called Mt. Nak. Since it is too small in size to balance its partner Mt. Inwang, the Joseon government attempted various measures to form a balance between the two, such as building an artificial hill near Mt. Nak and a large East Gate. I am not sure how effective these measures ended up being.

I highly recommend a visit to Mt. Nak to any foreigners who are interested in exploring parts of Seoul that are unfamiliar even to most residents of Seoul. The area used to be a slum for a long time before it was completely renovated in the 1990s and transformed into a nice park. The walking trail from East Gate that continues along the fortress walls is especially scenic. The construction of this fortress began immediately after Seoul was designated as the new capital of the newly born Joseon Dynasty in 1392. This 17-kilometer rampart can be seen from Naksan Park, and viewing the fortress from the front and Seoul from the east offers a fresh perspective. Naksan Park is a diamond in the rough, and not many Seoul residents are aware of this. It is an excellent place to explore for those who have a deep interest in Seoul. The experience is enriched when the trail eventually leads us to the residence of the first president of Korea, Syngman Rhee. The house is always open to the public during the day time, and contains many articles and pictures of a man who lived at the center of the most turbulent times of Korean

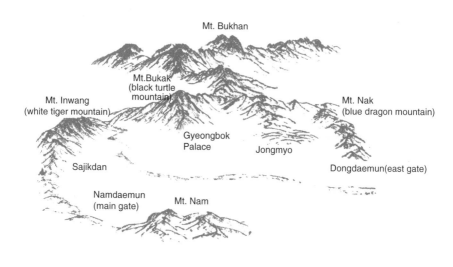

Mountain map of Seoul

An image of phoenix

modern history. This place is a must-see for those interested in modern history of Korea.

We have discussed the three mountains surrounding the palace, so there is one more mountain left. Although it is located quite far down from Mt. Nam, it is relatively easy to find the mountain in the south represented by the crimson phoenix. It stands out with its tall stature and military facilities stationed at its peak, making it easy to see. Mt. Gwanak, 632 meters high, is better known to the public as the campus site of Korea's most prestigious Seoul National University. A phoenix is a legendary bird that looks like a mixture of various birds—It has the head of a cock and the feet of an eagle. Along with the dragon, it is touted as one of the most propitious animals. There are lots of issues to touch upon regarding Mt. Gwanak, but we will leave it at this for the moment in order to not deviate from the topic. I must say that the person who designed Seoul must have been a bold man of large scale. He chose a mountain that is far from the center of Seoul as the phoenix mountain so that the city could expand southward without running into obstacles. It is uncertain whether the geomancer had foreseen the prosperous future of Seoul at the time the layout of Seoul was designed, but there is no doubt that *Fengshui* again played a very practical role.

The next question we can ask ourselves concerns the *Fengshui* of Mt. Nam. What role did Mt. Nam play, and what significance did it hold for the people of the Joseon Dynasty? *Fengshui* theory talks about the need for a small mountain between the larger ones in the north and the south as an intermediary. If Mt. Bukak in the north is a host, Mt. Gwanak in the south is a guest, and Mt. Nam serves as a sort of table in between to let them have a conversation. The solemnity of the two big mountains makes it a bit overwhelming to approach, but there is no such barrier to Mt. Nam. It offers a nice resting place for people to stop by and relax amidst their busy daily lives.

Fengshui is further developed towards the designing of parks in modern times. In fact, Mt. Nam works as the lung of Seoul, taking bad air in and breathing out clean air for Seoulites. Thanks to Mt. Nam, people living in Seoul can enjoy nature in such close proximity to their home. Koreans have been so preoccupied with rapid economic development and industrialization that they have not given much thought to environmental issues and sustainable development. Much of the greenery of Seoul was bulldozed and destroyed during the decades of industrialization, and left much of Seoul bleak and grey. Seoul is also on

Octagonal Pavilion

the list of cities in the world that severely lack green zones. However, when we count in Mt. Nam, Seoul takes a huge leap on the list to the higher group. Again, I cannot help but feel a renewed appreciation for *Fengshui*, which helps people to live in the most humane way possible under the given circumstances. We should acknowledge the validity of this theory and give it just credit for its environment-friendly view of nature.

The last item to cover before we leave Mt. Nam is the Octagonal Pavilion at the peak of the mountain. The building itself is nothing special, but it is significant in that the lot was used to house a shrine for Mt. Nam's mountain god during the Joseon Dynasty. Guksadang, or 'National Shrine,' was built at the end of the 14th century at the order of General Yi (Lee) Seong-gye, the founder and the first king of the Joseon Dynasty. Since then, it has served as the central shaman shrine in Korea. It was the most important and popular shrine in Korea, and therefore hosted numerous shaman rituals. The Japanese colonial administration forcibly moved the shrine to Mt. Inwang in 1925 for reasons that will be discussed in a later chapter. A small sign in front of the pavilion tells only of the existence of the National Shrine. I firmly believe that if Koreans genuinely care about their cultural heritage and take pride in it, the shrine should immediately be restored and renovated. However, this seems to be a hope with slim chance of realization, because Koreans debase Shamanism as superstition and are embarrassed to say that they believe in it. Yet, Shamanism has been closely attached to the life of Koreans throughout history, and has had indelible influence in shaping the mentality of Koreans. On the other hand, a plan to restore Guksadang would undoubtedly provoke massive protests from the Christian population. It is interesting to note here how Koreans and Japanese take different approaches in viewing their indigenous religions, incidentally both of which belong to the category of 'primitive' religion. Koreans should keep in mind that the Japanese take great pride in Shintoism, their indigenous religion. A lot of Shinto shrines are well preserved, and Shinto ceremonies and festivals take place every year in cities throughout Japan. Even without the Guksadang building, several big shaman rituals take place on its lot every year and they are an incredible sight to behold. Scores of shamans participate in a single ceremony, and perform with eclat. Even if there is no shrine to behold, Shamans seem to be trying to revive the glory of the past by holding big ceremonies at least on the auspicious site, if not in the auspicious shrine.

The way down Mt. Nam is easy, as one only needs to come down the stairs. A few minutes into the descent, you will arrive at Photo Island. The view from here is passable, but skyscrapers block the sight of the main historical sites, namely Gyeongbok and Changdeok Palaces. Photo Island

Photo Island at Mt. Nam

offers quite an extraordinary view of Seoul. There is no sense of unity or orderliness in the city, and it becomes obvious that the buildings were built without any consideration given at all to harmony with the surroundings. Some of the buildings were designed by the world's most renowned architects, and they are indeed magnificent pieces of work when viewed individually. One example is Jongno Tower, which stands in the heart of Jongno, Seoul's main street. It was designed by Uruguayan architect Rafael Vinoly, and the building looks innovative and unique on its own. However, it does not match with the rest of the buildings in the neighborhood. This may be my own hasty conclusion, but I fear that northern Seoul is one of the worst cities in the world in terms of urban planning and designing perspective. Whenever I see this area, I witness Koreans' admiration for disorderliness, which plays both for and against Koreans at the same time. One noted architect once said Koreans will be able to find order within the disorderly arrangement of buildings in the end. It seemed as if he believed that 'order within disorder,' a unique

Jongno Tower as seen from Photo Island

feature in Korean aesthetics, could be realized in the cityscape. We will have to wait and see whether his words come true.

To the left of Photo Island, a distant view of the Han River is worth seeing. To the right, there is a small traditional building in the bush where the spirits of legendary Chinese generals such as Liu Bei are enshrined. The fact that these spirits are enshrined in Korea and that there were regular rituals held in memory of them clearly shows the extent to which Chinese culture was fervently worshipped by Koreans. Turning your eyes up to the sky, you will see a dark belt of smog muffling the sky over Seoul. It is the inevitable consequence of too many cars running around on such a small piece of land.

At the Former Site of Japanese Shinto Shrine

Let us leave such ruminations behind and go down the mountain. When we come to the bottom of the stairs, there is a large crater to the left with many trees planted around it. There is no sign to indicate what this place used to be, but during the Japanese colonial period it was the most 'sacred' site in Korea. Before then, it was no more than an anonymous point halfway up the mountain. Upon invasion and

Chosen Jingu as seen in the 1930's   Old site of Chosen Jingu as seen today

annexation of Korea in 1910, Japan tried with all its might to Japanize the Koreans. The best and most convenient way to achieve this goal was the propagation of their native religion, Shintoism. Shintoism epitomizes the roots of the Japanese spirit, and is a polytheistic and animistic religion. The most important deity in Shintoism is Amaterasu-ōmikami, the Sun Goddess, who is believed to have formed the Japanese islands. Temples devoted to worshipping this particular diety are considered higher than ordinary shrines. Therefore, these shrines are called *jingu*, literally meaning 'god's palace,' while shrines that do not worship the Sun Goddess are called *jinja*. One of the best-known shrines of Amaterasu-ō mikami is in the city of Ise, which is built atop 20,000 square kilometers of land, clearly showing the elevated status of this goddess in Japan.

The Japanese colonial administration built such a shrine for Amaterasu-ō mikami in the middle of Mt. Nam and named it Chosen Jingu, the headquarters of Shinto shrines throughout the Korean Peninsula. For the construction of the shrine, the Japanese levelled the lower half of Mt. Nam. The vehicle road that takes us from the foot up to the breast of the mountain is a remnant of that period. The Japanese built the shrine where

384 stairs

we are standing now as well as the 384 stairs leading to the shrine, beginning from the foot of Mt. Nam near the present-day Hilton Hotel. By building a shrine of grand stature, the Japanese leadership hoped to completely brainwash the

Korean people. The logic was that both Koreans and Japanese are in fact descendents of Amaterasu-ōmikami, and thus share the same blood. It was also an indirect order to not even think of independence and to forever live under the yoke of Japan. The Japanese government paid tremendous attention on what to do and what not to do regarding the shrine; when a tram was passing below the shrine, all passengers were forced to rise and stand silently to show respect.

The construction of the Chosen Jingu was completed in 1925, and this was also the period in which Guksadang, the national shrine of Korea at the top of Mt. Nam that worships the mountain spirit, was demolished. The Japanese could not allow another god to stand on top of its most important deity Amaterasu-ōmikami. The shrine was taken down after liberation, and Koreans built a botanical garden on the spot for no apparent reason. The botanical garden was removed in 2007 and was replaced by the trees that are seen today. I personally think that it would be better to make use of this lot as an educational opportunity by putting up pictures and explanations of the former shrine. It is a good way to teach children that a similar deed must never again take place, but Koreans do not seem to be interested in making use of this place.

Instead, there is a plaza on the former site of Chosen Jingu as well as a fountain that has inexplicably been placed in the middle. I will also add that the fountain was built a long time ago, and thus is lacking in design. I do not pretend to understand why Koreans build fountains on important historical sites. However, one building dedicated to a national hero grabs our attention. A look around the plaza will see a statue of An Jung-geun, a famous Korean patriot who was executed for assassinating Japan's leading politician Ito Hirobumi. Ito was one of the most prominent politicians of Meiji Japan, and was highly respected enough to appear on

Patriot An Jung-geun

Japanese currency[1]. When he took the lead in advocating the annexation of Korea in the early 20th century, the fearless An emerged on the scene and assassinated Ito in 1905. The assassination of Ito was big news throughout Northeast Asia at the time, but despite the efforts of such brave Koreans, Korea was annexed just a few years later in 1910 as a colony of Japan. A commemorative museum of An stands next to the statue, and rocks bearing inscriptions of An's statements can be seen in front of the museum.

Although countless attempts were made to assassinate prominent Japanese politicians during 40 years (1905-1945) of Japanese colonial rule, An was the only person who actually succeeded in assassinating a high-profile figure in Japanese politics. Given An's status as one of the most venerated patriotic figures in Korea, the memorial hall seems too shabby to house the memory of such a figure. The layout of the stones in front of the museum also does not seem to be well-aligned. The museum is reportedly suffering from a tight budget; if this is the case, then Koreans have not yet succeeded in liquidating their colonial past. I wonder why Koreans, who are so obsessed about winning a soccer match against Japan, do not care about historical relics like this one. In any case, this is an interesting place to recall the tangled memory of Korea and Japan's

---

[1] Ito Hirobumi was on the 1000-yen bill from 1963 to 1986.

S e o u l

modern history. It is also interesting that one who is praised as a great statesman in one country is castigated as a villainous invader in the neighboring country; another person is revered as a hero in one country and demoted to a fiendish terrorist in another. I wonder if the time will come when both Korea and Japan can be freed from such a tragic past.

This ends our tour of Mt. Nam. Here, we experienced the most harrowing aspects of Korea's modern history by witnessing the violation of the most important natural habitat in Seoul. There are more examples of such humiliation and abuse from the colonial period scattered across Seoul, and we will get to them as they appear along our trip. For now, let us leave behind modern history and return to the past. Here, the 'past' refers to the Joseon period, as the history of Seoul is directly linked to this dynasty. Our next stop is Gyeongbok Palace, the main palace of the Joseon Dynasty.

A Voyage to Joseon
on a Time Machine

You @ Seoul

Hank's Book Cafe

Rio de Janeiro 18,067 km SSW

Johannesburg 12,497 km WSW

New York 11,074 km NE

Toronto 10,621 km NNE

Paris 8,992 km NNW

London 8,882 km NNW

Chapter 2

1. Understanding the Culture of the Royal Court Through the Daily Life of the King — Gyeongbok Palace

In Front of the Gyeongbok Palace

As mentioned before, Gyeongbok Palace endured many tribulations as the main palace of the Joseon dynasty. Visitors will find that it is always noisy inside the palace, unbefitting of a king's residence, because of ongoing construction. This is obvious even before entering Gyeongbok Palace; as of 2008, the main palace gate, Gwanghwamun, is being restored and renovated. Gwanghwamun also has a long history that is full of turmoil. Its first adversity came in 1592 when the entire palace, including the main gate, was completely burned down during the Hideyoshi Invasions. The palace remained sitting in its own debris until the mid-19th century. The reason why Gyeongbok Palace was allowed to remain unrenovated by the administrators of Joseon is because of the existence of a secondary palace. Kings lived in this second palace called Changdukgung, a palace beautiful enough to be a UNESCO World Cultural Heritage. Understandably, kings preferred living among the beauty of Changdeok Palace than Gyeongbok Palace, and this preference likely caused the construction delay. The more probable reason, however, is political. It is said that kings wanted to avoid the bloody power battle that took place in Gyeongbok Palace. At any rate, the royal court of the Joseon Dynasty restored Changdeok Palace first, and lived in the main

The second gate of Gyeongbok Palace

palace for several centuries.

The reconstruction of Gyeongbok Palace finally began in the mid-19th century during the reign of the last king (also the first emperor of the Great Han Empire) of the Joseon Dynasty, King Gojong. More specifically, renovation work began under the direction of the king's father, regent Daewongun. King Gojong was only 11 years old when he was crowned as king, so his father Daewongun served as regent and wielded actual political power for much of the latter part of the 19th century. Daewongun wanted to rebuild the main palace in order to restore royal authority that had been significantly marred by decades of corruption and misappropriation of power by consort clans and a handful of powerful aristocrats. Daewongun managed to finish reconstruction of Gyeongbok Palace in the face of fierce criticism from the opposing faction, but the palace was to endure yet another phase of ordeals. It

Milestone near Gyeongbok Palace

Japanese Government-General
Building before 1995

seems to me that the Japanese colonial leadership tried to undermine Korean morale by defacing the main palace, the seat of royal power of the Joseon Dynasty. They believed that if Koreans were to witness the destruction of the sacred seat of royal power, a major pillar of the Korean psyche might be toppled once and for all. For this purpose, the Japanese administration made a show of tearing down and moving around many of the auxiliary palace buildings, but its most unscrupulous act was the construction of the Japanese Government-General Headquarters right inside the palace. Although it was torn down by the first civilian government of Korea in 1995, it stood between Geunjeongjeon, the throne hall of the king, and the main gate Gwanghwamun to block any chance of people getting a glimpse of the main hall of the palace. It was a calculated act that completely covered Gyeongbok Palace from view and probably aimed to show the people of Joseon that Joseon would never rise again.

During construction of the Government-General Building, the Japanese had planned to get rid of Gwanghwamun, citing the alibi that it would block the view of their own building. The plan was thwarted by intense criticisms from within both Korea and Japan, and Gwanghwamun was eventually moved over to one side of the palace. The checkered fate of Gwanghwamun did not come to an end with Japanese colonial rule. The ravages of the Korean War completely razed Gwanghwamun, leaving only its

View of Gyeongbok Palace right after the Korean war (Source: J. Choi, *SinSeoul Gihaeng*, p.125)

stone foundation intact. Gwanghwamun was finally moved back to its original position in the 1960s, but the Ministry of Culture made the fatal mistake of restoring what used to be a wooden structure with cement. Since then, many scholars and citizens alike have called for the rebuilding of the gate, and the official proposal was finally accepted in 2007. Gwanghwamun is currently under construction, and Gyeongbok Palace has been left standing without its main front gate for the second time since the colonial period.

An all-out destruction of Gyeongbok Palace officially began during the Japanese colonial period, and what little was left after liberation was completely wiped out during the Korean War. As shown in the picture, literally the whole palace was burned down except for a few important buildings. Full-scale restoration of the palace did not begin until the 1990s. Koreans recovered lost pride in their traditions after the country began to achieve remarkable economic development in the 1960s. The Gyeongbok Palace reconstruction project is one example of how this was put into action. However, as the destruction of the palace was rather severe to begin with, it is said that it will take several decades to fully recover the original shape of the palace. The palace is still under construction, but only 20 to 30 percent has been restored as of July 2008. It will be difficult to restore it 100 percent. This is because there are currently facilities within the palace that seem impossible to remove, including a large outdoor parking lot, the National Folk Museum and the National Palace Museum.

Many people compare Gyeongbok Palace to the Forbidden City, the main palace of China. This type of comparison happens frequently because there are so many Chinese tourists who visit Gyeongbok Palace. One common reaction is that Gyeongbok Palace is merely the size of the servants' quarter of the Forbidden City. Just as the picture shows, the foundation of main building of the Forbidden City, the Hall of Supreme Harmony, itself is three stories high, and the entire building is incomparably larger than Geunjeongjeon. The difference in the absolute total acreage of both palaces is almost inconceivable. This may be a fair evaluation for firstcomers to Gyeongbok Palace. However, even when the

Geunjeongjeon

actual size of the palaces is compared, Gyeongbok Palace is not as small as many may think. The exact size of the palace is little over half that of the Forbidden City. When considering how much bigger China is than Korea as a country, this is not a negligible amount at all. Then what makes the Korean palace look so much smaller? The main reason is that there are not as many buildings as there should be to fill in the empty spaces within the palace. Visitors will find that most of the palace grounds are covered by grass—grass indicates that a building used to stand on that site. Because so many buildings have been lost over the last century, the palace looks much smaller than its full size. The grass in the palace can be considered the 'gravesite' of eliminated palace buildings. The second reason has to do with the nature of relations between China and Korea. The absolute size of individual buildings inside Gyeongbok Palace is much smaller than its Chinese counterparts. Since Joseon was a tributary state of imperial China, it was not allowed to build buildings that were larger than those in the Forbidden City; all buildings had to be

Main Hall of the Forbidden City

understated in terms of size. While the foundation of the Hall of Supreme Harmony is three stories high, that of Geunjeongjeon consists of two stories, and all other buildings had to be built even smaller. This explains why Gyeongbok Palace seems so much smaller than it actually is.

The absolute size of each building is not a matter of great importance. I personally think that it is the physical size of the country and not the temperament of its people that was reflected in the size of the palace. China built a large palace because its boundaries are vast, and Joseon built a smaller-scaled palace to match the smaller dimensions of its land. Had China built a palace the size of Gyeongbok Palace, it would have looked rather ridiculous. On the other hand, it would have been wasteful of Joseon to build a palace as large as the Forbidden City, given the size of its land. I do not think it is in people's nature to build a large building on a small piece of land; rather, people built what was best for their own circumstances. Also, when we compare the size ratio of palace to entire country, it turns out that the ratio for Korea is larger. Given the fact that China is a much bigger country than Korea, but the size of Gyeongbok Palace is roughly half of the Forbidden City, it is large indeed. This is why all things need to be evaluated within its particular context, since loss of context can bring about unnecessary misunderstanding.

The influence of Neo-Confucianism, the state ideology of Joseon, was also a significant factor in restricting the size of the palace. Of all Neo-Confucian teachings, the most representative dictum stresses concentrating on the inner mind much more than to outer finery. As a result, unlike its predecessor Goryeo, the Joseon Dynasty did not make great strides in the field of architecture and other areas of visual culture that emphasize aesthetics. A quote from Jeong Do-jeon, an advisor to the founding king (Taejo) of Joseon and an influential Neo-Confucian

Bird's-eye-picture of Gyeongbok Palace

ideologue who laid the ideological foundation of the Joseon state, leaves much to ponder. "Extravagance in the building of the palace will bring about suffering of the people and damage national finances, while too much modesty would lack the charisma and dignity befitting of the royal court. The most beautiful palace, therefore, would be modest yet not shabby, dignified yet not luxurious." Jeong's remark basically eliminates any possibility of building an imposing palace. Indeed, Gyeongbok Palace seems to be built much more closely to human scale compared to the Forbidden City, which seems too gigantic for a small human being to live in.

Before we enter the palace to see how the members of the royal family lived, there is one more question to consider. Which spot would be the best place to appreciate the palace according to the intention of the architect? Because buildings in Joseon were always constructed in

Gyeongbok Palace seen with the mountains in the back

relation to its surroundings, the building looks best when it is viewed with the mountain in the background. Only when a building is viewed within nature does it reveal its true values. Then, which place offers the best view of the palace with the mountain in the backdrop? The answer to this question is an open secret that most Koreans are not aware of. When crossing the Gwanghwamun intersection from the east to west, you can have a decent view of the palace. However, the current reconstruction of Gwanghwamun obstructs this very view, and we will have to wait until construction is completed in 2009.

We will now turn to the streets in front of Gwanghwamun, where the major government offices used to stand during the Joseon Dynasty. This tradition from the Joseon Dynasty seems to have been inherited, as the district still serves as the administrative center of Korea. Some of the ministries are situated on both sides of Sejongno, which cuts through the Jongno district starting from Gwanghwamun. However, there is one building in this district that does not match its historically significant surroundings, and that is the U.S. embassy. The presence of the American Embassy seems a bit odd amidst Korean government buildings in the heart of Korea's administrative center. This clearly reflects the degree of American influence on Korean politics. How else could an embassy of a foreign country be sitting in the very heart of a capital city?

Entering the Palace

Let us now enter the palace. The palace served as both the residence and working quarters of the king. When a king died, his body was buried in a designated royal tomb on the outskirts of the capital, and his spirit would be enshrined in Jongmyo Royal Shrine, located on the lefthand side of the palace. Thus, the palace was the space in which the king spent his life. We will break down the palace into three categories—working space, sleeping quarters and resting space—and examine each

Forbidden brook with a funny stone animal

space in detail. These spaces appear in sequential order on our tour, and thus will be easier to understand.

Our first stop is the working space of the king. In order to reach this area, we must pass through several gates. Since Gwanghwamun is no longer used for entry and exit purposes as it directly faces the Gwanghwamun Intersection, we will use the second gate, Heungryemun, to enter the palace. It is this gate that probably suffered the most excruciating ordeal of all, since the Japanese authorities completely demolished this gate in order to build the colonial governor's building on this spot. There is a lot to say about Heungryemun and the surrounding area, but we will sidestep all of this for now to save it for later sections.

Stepping into the gate, you will notice a small creek called Geumcheon, meaning 'forbidden brook,' and a bridge. The creek was artificially created to prevent bad energies from entering the palace; whether this is actually an effective measure remains to be seen. Next to the bridge stand four imaginary animal figures, guarding the stream. The facial expression of one of them is full of mischief—it looks as if it is teasing someone with its tongue sticking out. It is extraordinary to find such a comical look in what is supposed to be a solemn and dignified place. This is a typical example of the humor and spontaneity found in Korean aestheticism.

In Front of the Best Architectural Masterpiece of Joseon

The third and the last gate to pass before we reach king's office chamber is called Geunjeongmun. Considering that one needs to pass nine gates in order to reach the main hall of the Forbidden City, the Hall of Supreme Harmony, Gyeongbok Palace is much more modest and simple—one of the realities of being a tributary country. Upon entering through Geunjeongmun, one can see a large and imposing wooden building. Geunjeongjeon, which served as the main office of the kings, is the largest and best example of Joseon architecture. Designated as National Treasure No. 223, the craftsmanship is flawless and it is impossible to find better Joseon architecture anywhere else in Korea. Korean architectural tradition was heavily influenced by the Tang and Song Dynasties in China. The Tang and Song methods of building palaces and Buddhist temples were adapted and modified over the years to fit Joseon style and taste. Although the architecture of China, Korea and Japan might look all the same to the untrained eyes of foreign tourists who are not familiar with Northeast Asian architecture, there is a distinctive style for each country. Koreans argue that their style is the

Geunjeongjeon(Geunjeong Hall) viewed from a 45-degree angle

most nature-friendly, and this is due to strict adherence to *Fengshui* principles.

Upon entering the Geunjeongjeon area, most people just proceed directly to the building. We will also view Geunjeongjeon carefully, but there is one more place to visit beforehand and that is the spot from which you can view Geunjeongjeon at its best. Northeast Asian architecture is the most beautiful when viewed from a 45-degree angle. This can be accomplished by standing at one end of the front courtyard; in the case of Korean architecture, as I have mentioned countless times, the most beautiful view always includes the mountain in the back. The building alone is magnificent, but it looks better with the mountain in the background and the roof of the corridor serving as a frame. The picture you see in this book was taken at that very spot. Taking pictures is a great way to preserve this beauty. However I notice whenever I visit here that few people view the building from this point. I wish the cultural authorities would take note of this fact and establish a photo point to promote this spot.

Let us now proceed to Jeongjeon. On the way to the building, you will notice that the courtyard was completed using stones with very rough surface. This is not a result of carelessness, but an intentional device intended to keep everyone's head down when walking around the king's quarter. Because of the rough surface, people must have had to face the ground in order to watch their steps. In the courtyard, there are two rows of twelve stone tablets indicating the rank of officials. Civil officials lined up on the right and military officers on the left. The courtyard was open only on special occasions: regular meetings of the officials that were held two to three times a month, the visits of foreign envoys, or for celebratory occasions of the royal family. Aside from these cases, this front courtyard was rarely used. Every time I look at the courtyard, I wonder how the kings' words were transferred to the officials standing far down the row in an era with no megaphones or amplifiers. I have yet to find a satisfactory answer.

We are now in front of the building. Although it looks like a two-storied building from the outside, it is in fact a large one-story building with an extraordinarily high ceiling. Let us now focus on the tall columns that support this height; they were made with the best lumber available in all of Joseon. The part of the interior that deserves the most attention is the seat of the king. The king's chair is called 'dragon's seat,' because the dragon, the highest animal, traditionally symbolizes the king. Although not clearly visible, there are also two sinewy yellow dragons carved into the middle of the ceiling. Yellow is one of the five cardinal colors of direction that represents the center. The remaining four colors are personified in animal figures that are carved into the balustrade outside Jeongjeon. Besides the four cardinal animals, there are also statues of the 12 animals that represent time. In this way, the seat of the king is positioned so that it is at the center of the universe.

Behind the king's chair, there is a simple painting that only the king can have in his possession. Called Il-wol-o-ak-do, the painting is laid out according to its name: underneath the sun and moon, the five major mountains in Korea (Baekdu, Geumgang, Samgak, Jiri, Myohyang) and a turbulent sea below the mountains are all depicted in a simple, abstract style. This painting symbolically states that the king is at the center of the entire universe, and because of this symbolism, this painting is placed wherever the king happens to be. The painting also boasts a unique feature that not many Koreans are aware of. When you look at the chair and the painting on the back, you will be able to spot a small door for

Il-wol-o-ak-do

the king's exclusive use through which he would enter and exit. Why did the kings need this small door on the back of their chair? Because kings are sacred and mystical beings, they cannot be easily exposed to the eyes of ordinary people easily; thus, entering the building through its front door would be unheard of. A back door was a useful tool for the king to make an unusual and sudden appearance without making others aware of his whereabouts. Kings used the door at the rear of this building and the back door on the chair to sit in the dragon's seat at their discretion.

The time has now come to leave Geunjeong Hall. Yet another way of savoring the beauty of traditional Korean architecture is to look up to the corner of the roof from directly below. You can see the roof tip in the picture, looking as if it could take flight at any moment. As is often the case with architecture of supreme quality such as a palace, its eaves are painted with a variety of colors called *dancheong*, which serves to drive away evil spirits and to symbolize the dignity and authority of the occupant. Since the cost of *dancheong* is similar to that of the entire construction, its very presence becomes a conspicuous demonstration of power and authority. A close look at the eaves reveals that they are covered with net-like material. What is this covering for? The answer lies in a very practical cause: to prevent birds' nests from ruining the *dancheong*. With the price of *dancheong* being what it is, this type of preventative measure seems only natural.

Dancheong of Geunjeong Hall

In the Birthplace of Joseon Documentary Culture

Geunjeong Hall was used only on special occasions, and the king usually administered the affairs of state with his officials in a far smaller building located behind the hall. Named Sajeongjeon, it is where the king presided over the equivalent of cabinet meetings. The building itself is not much to look at. It seems rather small for a place to carry out state affairs and there is not much to wonder about except how meetings could possibly be held on the wooden floor during the severe winter cold. Moreover, the sight of the king and his men sitting on the floor while discussing important matters would look utterly strange to Westerners who are accustomed to seating in chairs. This was probably inevitable because sitting on the floor back then was the custom due to *ondol*, the unique Korean floor panel heating system. At any rate, the modest size and appearance of the royal conference room can be attributed to Neo-Confucianism, which gives little

The first Annal of the Joseon Dynasty

consideration to outward appearance. It is not such appearances but the activities conducted within that deserve our attention. In the history of humankind, Joseon is renowned for its rich tradition of historiography. How many people would believe that two of the world's most famous documentary heritages were produced in this small room? Let us now look at the behind-the-scenes story.

Joseon paid a great deal of attention to the recording of history, and historiographers took especial interest in a balanced documentation of kings' words and deeds. Such interest in unbiased documentation is based in the Confucian dictum that correct disciplining of a king would bring comfort to all his people. As a result, Joseon statesmen gave lessons to their future king three times a day from his early princehood. Taught by the most renowned scholars of the day, the king continued to have these lessons even after he was crowned. In this sense, Joseon kings may have been the most educated royalty in history. In addition to their formal education, every aspect of their speech and behavior were put in writing to set a good example to posterity, and this practice of recording probably functioned as a good checks-and-balances system. What king would freely speak his mind and act however he wished if he knew that his every word would be bequeathed to posterity? The kings of Joseon were far from free. From morning to night, they could not meet anyone without being accompanied by the royal chroniclers; the private life of the king was public in its entirety.

Two chroniclers were required to be present to document and record cabinet meetings, held in this buliding where we now stand. The records that they leave behind later become UNESCO Memory of the World Heritages. The primary chronicler, called *sagwan*, served as the official government chronicler, while the secondary chronicler, called *juseo*, served as official recorder of Seungjeongwon, the personal (Secretariat) office of the king. The records of these two chroniclers are registered as documentary heritages on UNESCO Memory of the World, The *Annals of the Joseon Dynasty* (*Annals*) and the *Diaries of the Royal Secretariat* (*Diaries*), respectively. These two books deserve a great deal of explanation since they are part of the world heritage, but we will cover them only briefly for lack of space. In a single phrase, the *Annals* are defined as 'the world's greatest historiography of a single dynasty.' Containing the recordings of 472 years, there is no parallel in history; consequently, the sheer quantity of the *Annals* is immense beyond imagination. Consisting of over 50 million characters, they are all the more amazing because they were not handwritten but printed in movable type, even though only four copies needed to be produced.

However, the focal point of UNESCO's recognition of these historical documents lies somewhere else: the king was not allowed to read the records, despite the fact that Joseon was an absolute monarchy. Such preventative measures were legally enforced from the beginning of the dynasty. No amount of curiousity could justify the wish of a king to read the *Annals*. As a result, historiographers were able to make an objective compilation of the king's words and deeds. 'Objectivity' in this case was an evaluation from a Confucian standpoint of how true the king was to his subjects. The king thus had no choice but to be discreet in his speech and conduct. Few kings could have done everything in their own way, unruffled by the fact that all his words and deeds were being recorded.

The true greatness of the *Annals* lies in their upholding of the king's accountability even though they are historical records from a premodern age.

The records of Chinese dynasties differ sharply in this respect. In fact, such historiographical convention of compiling the entire speech and conduct of the king originated from the Chinese Confucian tradition. Thus, Chinese dynasties left behind such records and obviously the Ming and Qing dynasties have historical records as well. However, these records are not listed as UNESCO documentary heritages. There are several reasons for this failure, but above all, the Chinese records are far less objective than their Korean counterparts. In China, the emperor exerted such strong power that many of them often read these records. Parts not to his liking were summarily removed. Furthermore, there was an emperor who even abolished the office of historiographer when he became greatly displeased with the constant compilation of his words. As mentioned earlier, the *Annals* of Joseon were printed in beautiful movable types even though only four copies were needed, while Chinese records were merely handwritten. For this reason, some parts are said to be illegible. In light of these differences, one wonders whether which the truly civilized nation is. Would it be a stretch to construe Joseon, which made efforts in documenting historiography, as more civilized than China, which boasted the construction of massive palaces?

When compared to the *Annals*, the *Diaries* are even more remarkable. In describing the most salient feature of the *Diaries*, some would declare that they are 'the world's greatest historical documents.' They are the writings in which the Royal Secretariat, called Seungjeongwon, recorded the daily routines of the king. Their greatness can be found in the total number of characters, which exceeds 240 million, about six times that of the *Annals*. This immensity of volume reflects only the half of the writings that remain; factoring in the missing half would certainly inflate the total number of characters to twice that number. The other half of the *Diaries* was burned to ashes during the Hideyoshi Invasions in the late 15th century. Unlike the *Annals* that cover 472 years of the history of Joseon, the *Diaries* hold records that span only 288 years. Moreover, these records were not printed in movable types, but handwritten. This feature, therefore, caused the amount of records to expand.

There are various factors that enabled these records to make it to the World Heritage list, but the most important of these is probably the degree of meticulousness under which the compilation was done. Among other things, the minute recording of meteorological and astronomical phenomena, including weather, rainfall, or trajectory of stars, is highly acclaimed. A detailed daily record of the weather was kept using more than 100 ways of describing meteorological changes. The amount of rainfall and snowfall was also accurately recorded. Joseon's keen interest in astronomy is demonstrated in the daily observations of the night sky and meticulous recording of the falling of a shooting star. Similarly detailed records, kept for hundreds of years, cannot be found anywhere else in the world. The passion of the Joseon Dynasty for the humanities is probably among the greatest in the world. Joseon also produced far more documents in addition to these records. Their abundance is proven in a statement by a French naval officer whose regiment invaded a Joseon island in the late 19th century. He recalls that the presence of books in every house made him feel inferior, a telling testimony of the advanced state of Joseon's documentary culture.

A Day in the Life of the King

The king's private bedroom is located directly behind his royal office. Separated by only a wall, workplace and bedroom seem to be located too closely together. Such proximity may be the reason why the king suffered from a chronic lack of exercise; the life expectancy of a Joseon king was not long. Moreover, he had to endure the constant strain of overwork. He had too many daily tasks to complete in his many waking hours, beginning before sunrise at four or five o'clock in the morning and ending far past 11 at night. Befitting a Confucian nation that upholds respect for age, the king's first duty in the morning was paying a visit to the elders of the royal family. He then ate breakfast and engaged in morning studies, which was also deemed an important tradition in Confucianism. The political ideals of Confucianism are very simple. Because the king is the father of the people, the proper education of the king would ideally have the spillover effect of rendering the whole country peaceful and prosperous. To achieve this ideal, the king had three tutorials every day starting from his days as crown prince. He was taught to become a great king by the best scholars at the time. These private lessons continued even after he succeeded the throne, but changed from purely academic lessons to more of a conference format in which the king discussed pending political issues with his royal ministers.

Many interesting things can be found upon entering the king's bedroom, Gangnyeong Hall, which means 'a building for resting comfortably.' The bedroom is usually divided into nine sections, of which he slept in the middle one. In the surrounding eight sections, court ladies kept watch all through the night in the event that any mishap should fall on the king. The modest size of the bedroom reminds us once more of the frugal lifestyle of Joseon kings. A replica of the king's dining

Dining table of the king

table in this building is also striking for its simplicity. On the king's table are placed 12 kinds of side dishes in addition to a pot of stew, 12 being the maximum number of side dishes that could be placed on a table in the Joseon Dynasty. Notably, the table size is quite small for a ruler of a nation. To exemplify the virtue of plain living for all his people, the king was not permitted to indulge even in dietary extravagance. Austerity did not stop there; in case the country was ravaged by natural disaster such as drought or flooding, the king ordered a reduction in the number of side dishes. Ascribing the sufferings of his people to his lack of virtue, the king suppressed even this most basic necessity. This single detail reveals the king's discretion in even the smallest aspects of his life.

Of course, the king did not always sleep by himself in his bedroom. Court ladies, carefully selected on the grounds of producing a prince (or a princess), went to bed with him on occasions. These women bathed and then wrapped their naked body only with a single cloth before entering the bedroom. It is said that the complete nudity was to make sure there were no hidden weapons. Selected court ladies were given ample warning beforehand, and they were sternly warned particularly against harming the king's body under any circumstances. In one instance, a certain court lady ended up leaving a scar on the king's body as a result of excessive intensity during intercourse; she was later severely punished. Of course, it was preferable for the king to produce a prince with his queen. In this case, the king went to the queen's room located behind his own room, instead of the queen going to the king's bedroom. When a date was set in accordance with the principles of *yin* and *yang* and the five elements, the king went to the queen's quarters. At this time, only a few of the queen's court ladies remained while the rest were duly removed from the vicinity. This was probably a show of respectful consideration towards the royal couple so that they could engage in an exceedingly private and solemn activity in complete privacy.

We find that the queen's bedroom is small as well. Her bed is very low and small, and she may have slept in a room far less elaborate than that of average aristocrats in other countries. We are not sure whether this is due to the small dimensions of Joseon people or the traditional Confucian emphasis on modesty, but such dedication to restraint was most likely due to the latter; Confucian teachings state that one ought to suppress one's desire with superhuman patience. There is one more aspect of the queen's bedroom that deserves attention, and it is a garden located in the back courtyard of this building. In a typical Joseon house, there was always a garden in the back courtyard. The front courtyard was usually left empty as a space for work and play. For housewives who spent most of their time inside the home, it was necessary to create a garden behind *an-chae*, the womens' annex. Its design, however, is very different from the Western concept of a 'garden' in that it was very simple. As shown in the picture, the garden of an aristocrat's house in the Joseon Dynasty was made up of steps. These steps were called *hwagye* (flower steps) because flowers were planted on them. An oddly-shaped stone represents a mountain, while water was poured into a groove on this stone to represent a pond. This arrangement was probably intended to replicate all of nature within a limited space.

Although this garden could be far more beautiful than it is now, it does not seem to have been restored to its original condition. The flowers and trees seem to be inadequately chosen, and the iron fence gets in the way of a proper view of the garden. One comforting aspect amidst these glaring flaws is the presence of a chimney that is also a National Treasure; chimneys were elaborately decorated in the Joseon Dynasty and treated

Backyard garden as seen from the queen's bedroom

as objects of art. This particular chimney was built to pass underneath the backyard to be connected to the *ondol* (heated floor panel) in the queen' s bedroom. It was placed far from the queen's bedroom because a longer chimney tends to exhaust smoke more effectively. The surface of the chimney was engraved with flowers and species of flora and fauna believed to enjoy longevity. Among the various figures, a strange animal engraved at the bottom of the chimney captures our attention. It is an imaginary animal called Bulgasari that spends most of its time eating fire. It may sound superstitious, but perhaps the rationale behind it was to take a preventive measure in the event of fire. We need to find the best point of appreciation in order to fully appreciate this small garden, which in this case is the view that the queen had of the garden. This garden was specifically designed to look most beautiful when she viewed it from inside her room. Therefore, the best way to appreciate the garden is by sitting in the queen's bedroom. If we view it while sitting on the ground

Chimney in the backyard

Flower wall

of the garden, our perspective will be the same as that of a court lady working crouched on the ground and it will not be of much help to our overall appreciation of the garden.

Speaking of chimneys, there is another famous chimney in Gyeongbok Palace. Walking out of the queen's room and going behind it, you can see a beautiful wall decorated with flowers. In fact, the wall itself is also a well-known structure. The house built over this wall is the residence of the king's mother, the most respected elder in the palace. As part of the space reserved for women, the wall was ornately decorated in a delicate and feminine style with various flowers. At first glance, these flowers do not look special. These are actually not engraved but baked and designed clay patters placed like puzzle pieces on the wall. The wall is considered to have high value because of the unique decorative method. This sort of wall would have been impossible to pay for by

Chimney wall

anyone other than the king, and for this reason is designated as a National Treasure as well. However, many tourists often overlook this flower wall because they do not recognize its aesthetic value. This type of elaborate pattern composed of puzzle-like pieces can also be found on the chimney located in the back courtyard of the queen-mother's residence. This chimney looks more like a wall because of numerous exhausts on top that resemble bird nests. Were it not for the inscription plate, we might not know it is a chimney at all. Decorated with puzzle-like pictures like the flower wall, it is incomparably larger than the latter. It it likely that the largest budget was set aside to decorate the place occupied by the most senior member of the royal family. The designs on the chimney panels include creatures that represent longevity, good health, or many children, reflecting the wish for longevity of the elders of the royal family. One thing that baffles me about the back courtyard is the absence of a garden. The answer to the question of why there is no garden when such a large sum of money has gone into building the backyard has yet to be found.

The King's Entertainment

So far we have had a quick overview of the way the king engaged in his work and daily life. Next to this area where the king worked and slept is a large pond and a beautiful building called Gyeonghoeru Pavilion. What is this place for? There are Koreans who do not know the exact answer to this question, but Gyeonghoeru Pavilion was the official setting where the king held parties for VIP guests such as foreign envoys.

Gyeonghoeru Pavilion

Consequently, it was a very private place open only to those closest to the king. Now, however, you can hardly find even a remotely similar aura of intimacy as Gyeonghoeru stands fully exposed to the outdoors. It is easy to assume that this place was always open in this fashion, but in fact it was enclosed on all sides by walls. It was thus a secret space that was open exclusively to the king and his close associates only on special occasions. Even most high officials were not allowed to enter this place, and an anecdote of a minor official who was caught sneaking into the pavilion at night further testifies to its shroud of mystery.

If Gyeonghoeru Pavilion was used for official royal banquets, where could the king rest in private? This resting place is located toward the rear of the palace, and we will discuss it further when we arrive there shortly. The surrounding area of Gyeonghoeru Pavilion is known as a magnificent royal garden that has a beautiful landscape. Numerous records of visiting foreign envoys remain that all laud the splendor of the scenery at Gyeonghoeru. Because of its beauty, Gyeonghoeru Pavilion has been designated as a National Treasure, one level higher in the Korean heritage classification system than a Treasure. Influenced by Chinese custom, members of the Joseon elite thought it natural for a garden to include a pond and a pavilion on which to recline while viewing the pond. In practice, however, they came up with a style largely independent of Chinese influence. Joseon aristocrats preferred to dig a rectangular pond and create a miniature island in its center. The structure of this design produced an appearance that is markedly different from the Humble Administrator's Garden in Suzhou, a famous Chinese garden. There are a wide variety of garden styles in China, but it is hard to find among them a design favored by Joseon aristocrats while we can easily see that the typical Chinese garden style involves far more complex design. Why, then, is the Joseon garden characterized by such shapes as a circle and rectangle? According to conventional interpretation, the rectangle and circle represent earth and heaven, respectively. Here you can see how the people of Joseon tried to contain the universe in the garden by incorporating these shapes in the design.

How can we properly appreciate the view of the building and the pond? The most important aspect to consider in the evaluation of a building is to find out for whom it was built. You should never forget the fact that this building was constructed in a way that could provide its occupants with the most beautiful scenery possible when they looked outside from within. Of course, the owner of this building was the king. Foreign envoys were certainly important guests, but they are not for whom it was built. In that case, where did the king sit? The king sat in a specially designated space on the second floor (upper level). This space is divided into three layers with the center area the most elevated and the remaining areas lowered by one step. It is at this highest point in the center area that the king seated himself. Seen from this vantage point, Mt. Bukak and Mt. Inwang look like a beautifully framed piece of art. Natural scenery appears more beautiful when we stop seeing it as it is and imagine looking at it as a framed picture. The architects must have taken this view into account when designing Gyeonghoeru Pavilion. Formerly closed to the public, this elevated space has recently been opened only on set days and times at extra admission. Since I have hardly heard anyone who has been there complaining of the extra cost, I strongly recommend a view from the seat of the king.

As is often the case in a Chinese garden, the method of borrowing other scenery is often used in Korean garden landscaping as well. It is called *chagyeong* (borrowed landscape) method; the Korean technique is

© Kim Sung-cherl

On the second floor of Gyeonghoeru Pavilion

noticeably different from its Chinese counterpart. In a Chinese garden that is often arranged to block the view of the nature that exists outside its borders, it is almost impossible to view the external landscape. In contrast, the Korean garden tries to engage in a dialogue with the outside world and to incorporate the view of what lies beyond the garden. Then, how is it possible to bring in the natural environment such as the mountain and sky? Koreans came up with a clever way of achieving this effect. To sum up the method in one sentence, they decided to put all of nature into a pond. The pond itself is not large, but it is miraculously spacious enough to contain both a huge mountain and the sky. Seen from the second floor of Gyeonghoeru Pavilion, the pond contains a serene reflection of the mountains and the sky. In this manner, sky, mountain, and water—the major elements of nature—are replicated together in one place. You can appreciate this replicated version of nature while sitting inside the peace and quiet of your home. As for Gyeonghoeru Pavilion, it is probably best to view the scenery from the second floor. However, it is also quite nice to look at it from the outside as well. There are many angles of beautiful scenery to be enjoyed while walking around the pond. The building looks equally beautiful against either Mt. Bukak or Geunjeongjeon. I would like to end this section by adding that the pond was created not only for viewing but also to row a boat in. Judging from the steps underneath the pavilion that lead down to the water, you can see that people must have actually used boats here in the past.

Sujeongjeon (Sujeong Hall): The Birthplace of Hangeul

Many people just take off once they are done with their tour of Gyeonghoeru Pavilion, but there is a building facing the pavilion that is equally important; even Koreans are not well aware of its historical significance. This building is called Sujeong Hall and should not be overlooked since it is the birthplace of *Hunminjeongeum* (Correct Sounds to Instruct the People), a documentary heritage listed on UNESCO's Memory of the World. *Hunminjeongeum* is the book that explains the principles that formed Hangeul, the unique Korean alphabet that Koreans could not be more proud of. In this book, King Sejong the Great (reign 1418~1450), the creator of Hangeul, gave detailed explanations of this new alphabet. Hangeul is a unique alphabet that elicits a lot of attention in numerous aspects. It is the only script in the world of which the inventor, date of formal announcement and publication, and principles of creation are all known. Unlike other letters that have gradually developed over long periods of time, Hangeul is a mysterious script invented by the genius of King Sejong within a relatively short time period. A monarch marked by distinguished scholarly achievement, King Sejong established an academic research institute housed in Sujeong Hall that would serve as his think tank. King Sejong made a large investment in the institute, and the fact that the research building was installed with the best heating system available at the time reflects such efforts; an additional wooden floor was placed on top of *ondol*, the most prevalent heating system at the time. The addition of this floor aimed to make up for a weak point of *ondol*. *Ondol*, albeit favored by many people for its many advantages, made warm only the part of floor nearest to the fireplace. As a remedial measure, a wooden floor panel was added to help evenly spread this heat all over the floor. Although such work required a large sum of money, King Sejong gave unsparingly of support for the institute so that

Sujeong Hall

he could provide an environment conducive for his favored scholars to focus on their studies.

Thus born, Hangeul is regarded as more advanced than the Roman alphabet. Koreans often tout Hangeul as the most scientific alphabet in the world. The evidence offered for this claim is that any college-educated foreigner can write their name in Hangeul within one hour of learning; the scientific system of Hangeul makes it that easy to learn. In practice, Hangeul consonants are easy to memorize because they are modeled after human speech organs. The similar shape of consonants that belong to the same group forms a strong relationship between the shape and sound of each letter. For this reason, many scholars classify Hangeul as a feature-based writing system. Let us look at a simple example. The letters in the Roman alphabet that have similar sounds as the Korean letters 'ㄴ', 'ㄷ', and 'ㄹ' —all of which belong to the coronal sound group—are 'n,' 't,' and 'r' respectively. However, no connection can be found between the Roman alphabets and their sounds. In the case of Hangeul, adding a few strokes, for instance, to 'ㄴ', one of the basic consonants, forms other letters. Therefore, once you understand 'ㄴ', other letters can be quickly learned with little trouble. This operational principle makes it possible to quickly memorize consonants. Hangeul vowels are far easier to learn than consonants because they simply consist of one dot(•) and a couple of lines (—, ㅣ). The dot represents heaven, while the two lines resemble earth and

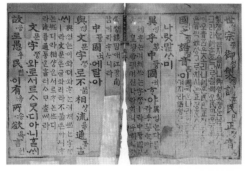

Hunminjeongeum

human being. In fact, the most important essence of the universe is embodied in these three elements. That is why Hangeul is considered to be both a scientific as well as philosophical alphabet. Through a proper combination of these elements, Hangeul enables us to write more vowels than any other alphabet.

We do not have enough space here to expound upon all the principles of Hangeul. In addition to what has already been discussed, countless diverse and complex linguistic principles are hidden in Hangeul. Let us keep in mind that UNESCO presents an award called the UNESCO King Sejong Literacy Prize to those who have contributed to the struggle against illiteracy. However, this does not mean that Hangeul is a perfect alphabet. Since it is a young alphabet at only 550 years old, Hangeul still has a lot of growth potential. Furthermore, Koreans have failed to devote their energies to further developing their own alphabet in the race to learn Chinese or English. Consequently, it appears to foreigners that Koreans these days heap only superficial praises on the excellence of Hangeul while using too much unnecessary English in their daily life. Considering the fact that nowhere in Sujeong Hall, the birthplace of the Korean alphabet, is there an explanatory placard that the Korean alphabet was born at this spot, it is not without cause that Koreans are accused of not being interested in Hangeul. Does Sujeongjoen Hall not deserve at least a guide plate providing background information on the creation of Hangeul?

At the Scene of Korea's Turbulent Modern History

Let us leave Gyeonghoeru Pavilion behind and move on to the back of the palace. Besides Sujeong Hall where we have just visited, there are some other places that I should have explained before leaving, but I

Hyangwonjeong Pavilion

boldly chose to forgo explanations for the sake of the flow of narrative. One example is Dong Palace, the residence of the crown prince, meaning 'eastern palace.' It earned its name for being located in the eastern part of Gyeongbok Palace, but I do not think people are likely to come here solely on account of its former occupant. One conspicuous feature of Dong Palace is the presence of a toilet restored to its original form. It is one of the numerous toilets that were built to accommodate the thousands of people living in the palace. Should anyone be curious about what toilets looked in the Joseon Dynasty, this is a good place to stop by. Now we are headed up to the north of the palace. In no time, a pond comes into view. This pond is also in the shape of a rectangle, but it is

Interior of Hyangwonjeong Pavilion

not as completely rectangular as the one in Gyeonghoeru Pavilion. Instead, it is formed with straight lines that create a more accomodating space. In the middle of this pond is a circular islet that symbolizes heaven. A lovely pavilion named Hyangwonjeong along with a bridge is built on this surprisingly large islet. This area is the private garden of the royal family. While Gyeonghoeru Pavilion was their official garden, this was the garden where the king and his close relations to come to rest. This explains why it is located in the far back of the palace grounds.

Since this pond garden is beautiful in itself, it requires no further explanation. The look of the garden varies according to the angle from which it is viewed, and looks particularly splendid against Mt. Bukak. As was the case with Gyeonghoeru Pavilion, the best spot to view the garden is the second floor of the pavilion on the islet, the private resting place reserved for the king. Much to our regret, we are not allowed a view from this point because the pavilion remains closed to the public. This pond is also historically significant in a different sense; it is the place where electricity was used for the first time in Korean history. King Gojong, the last king of the Joseon Dynasty, had asked Thomas Edison for help with the installation of electricity in Joseon since 1883; finally, in 1887 he had electric light bulbs lit over this area. The garden was chosen for this first experiment with electricity since it was close to the royal residence and water was needed to operate the generator. Joseon's adoption of the electric generator preceded that of China by two years. Why did King Gojong try to bring in a generator ahead of China? The answer lies in an unexpected source. Toward the end of Joseon, coup d' état outbreaks became frequent. They mostly occurred in the palace and under the cover of night. King Gojong was distraught by a series of nocturnal mishaps and resolved to import a generator upon first hearing of it. He may have thought that a brightly lit night would allay his fears.

At the back of this garden sits a restored house similar to a *yangban* residence called Geoncheong Palace, the residence of King Gojong and his wife, Queen Min. Due to various reasons, they did not live in Gangnyeong Hall and Gyotae Hall, the official quarters of the king and queen. Instead, they lived in Geoncheong Palace, later the site that witnessed the most tragic event in the history of the Joseon Dynasty (The royal couple actually resided for a longer period of time in Changdeok Palace than Gyeongbok Palace). Queen Min was murdered in 1895 by Japanese assassins in her residence. Amidst the rise of imperialism, the powers in the East and the West were frantically vying for hegemony over Joseon; Japan was the most aggressive of these. Aware of the ambitions of the Japanese, Queen Min tried to hold Japan in check by bringing in Russia. To eliminate perhaps the most formidable impediment in the solidification of Japanese influence in Joseon, Japan secretly sent in assassins and killed Queen Min. Invading Geoncheong Palace, they threatened King Gojong, knocked his son unconscious with the back of a sword, and then proceeded to locate Queen Min and kill her immediately with swords. Her body was then burned and discarded nearby. Few queens in world history have died such a gruesome death. In recent years a musical on the tragic life of Queen Min was made and also performed abroad. It is said that King Gojong became more afraid of the night because the Japanese ronins invaded the palace and killed his wife at night. The reason for illuminating the area with light bulbs can also be better understood within this historical context.

Leaving Gyeongbok Palace

Our general tour of Gyeongbok Palace ends with Geoncheong Palace. To go out, we can take either of the two exits. One is the north gate of Gyeongbok Palace. On the way out, we can briefly drop by Jipokjae — the king's library. We can tell at a glance that this building, recently restored, is different from other buildings that we have visited. It is hard to put a finger on the differences, but Koreans may find it a touch Chinese. I think the place is worthy of a visit for its exotic-looking interior. Right behind Jipokjae stands the north gate of Gyeongbok Palace. The gate leads to the Cheong Wa Dae (Blue House: the executive office and official residence of the President of South Korea) area. In fact, there is more to see in Cheong Wa Dae than just Cheong Wa Dae itself; many visitors take an additional tour of Chilgung (Seven Palace). Chilgung is a shrine built for mothers of kings in the Joseon Dynasty who were not queen. The garden built within the shrine receives a lot of attention as the only garden in Gyeongbok Palace that is designed in the unique palace style—gardens designed in the official technique are Gyeonghoeru Pavilion and Hyangwonjeong Pavilion. The street directly in front of Cheong Wa Dae is also laid out in a tasteful manner. In autumn, the street is laced with the foliage of ginkgos and comes to rank among the most beautiful streets in Seoul. A little further down the street is the Samcheong-dong area. A number of gift shops in the area offer a variety of cultural products, including accessories. Due to the presence of numerous art galleries, the area is also being spotlighted as a rising

National Folk Museum

cultural street in Seoul.

Instead of taking the north gate, we are going to go off to the side and exit through the National Folk Museum gate. This route will take us to the Changdeok Palace area by way of Bukchon Hanok Village. If you are not particularly pressed by time, the National Folk Museum is worth a visit. For our purposes, we will skip the Museum and directly head to Bukchon (North Village). But on our way to Bukchon, I would like to say a few things about the Museum. Among other things, the design of the buildings comprising the museum is problematic. Such large buildings do not lend themselves to the atmosphere of the palace. This is an inevitable consequence of prior mismanagement by those in charge who did not have a proper understanding of Korean culture. They were advocating a restoration of the palace while continuously destroying it at the same time. Put lightly, the museum buildings are quite a sight. Few Koreans can understand why these three large buildings take on such an appearance. By way of explanation, they were constructed after the model of Korean temple architecture. In their rightful place, they would have looked beautiful, but when ballooned in size in this way and placed on the wrong ground, an eyesore is the nearest thing they can come to. The construction of these buildings was carried out at a time when Koreans had little understanding of both design as well as their own cultural heritage. The trouble lies in the fact that such work is easy to do but difficult to remedy. Would it be possible to raze all three buildings and rebuild a reputable museum? Once destroyed, culture is exceedingly difficult to restore.

2. In Search of Bukchon: Where Joseon's High Officials Lived

'Bukchon' literally means 'north village.' Then, what is Bukchon north of? Bukchon is a reference to its location, which is north of Cheonggyecheon. To the east and west, Bukchon lies in the area between Gyeongbok Palace and Changdeok Palace. Namchon, its southern counterpart, encompasses the village south of Cheonggyecheon. It is said that its main inhabitants were *yangban* men who did not become government officials. In other words, Bukchon was a residential area for the class of people that controlled vested interests in both power and wealth. On the other hand, those out of power or a part of the opposing faction usually lived in Namchon. At any rate, Bukchon must have been the most affluent area in the Joseon Dynasty. It seems only natural that those in power at the time could afford to live in Buckon because they also owned great wealth.

Bukchon Yesterday and Today

Given the nature of its former residents, Bukchon had the largest number of fine *hanok* (traditional Korean houses) and still does today. A tour of this village gives us a glimpse of the centuries-old lifestyle of the upper class. A common misconception even among Seoulites is that most *hanok* in Bukchon are authentic. Currently there are about 900 units of *hanok* left here but there remain only a few houses where upper-class

Scenery of Bukchon

families of Joseon resided. The size of the houses of the nobility was usually huge, but the houses that can be seen in the village today are not that large. This is because these modestly sized houses that stand roof to roof were built not too long ago; constructed in the 1930s, they are barely 80 years old. Consequently, these *hanok* houses were built not by the aristocracy but by architects of the 1930s. In the course of Japanese colonial rule, the culture of the upper-class was cruelly suppressed and the succession of its cultural legacy almost came to a halt. In the process, the majority of *yangban* houses were torn down and smaller *hanok* houses built by house sellers came into its place. This practice is similar to the building and selling of apartment houses by real estate developers today.

Arriving at Bukchon from Gyeongbok Palace with this train of thought, we can find newly-built *hanok* houses scattered across the village. These houses are the ones most recently renovated, largely with the financial support of the Seoul metropolitan government. Had it not been for the city's help, house sellers of the late 20th century could not have been able to avoid the demolition of the *hanok* houses. As house sellers in the 1930s built multiple units of small houses on the sites that *yangban* houses used to occupy, they started to remove *hanok* houses and build low-rise apartment buildings. Both practices were driven only by the economic logic of profit-making. Citizens concerned with the future of *hanok* houses launched campaigns for better preservation, later financially supported by the city. These concerted efforts have now caused the price of land and houses in the area to soar. As an additional result, Bukchon has become an exclusive residential area for the wealthy, a stark contrast to the time when the village was mostly shunned. In addition, the heavy influx of people in the arts into Bukchon has brought about overcrowding.

What are characteristics of Korean Architecture?

Because we are in Bukchon, age-old Korean architecture should be properly savored. The finest *hanok* in the neighborhood would be the house of Yoon Bo-seon, the second President of South Korea. The house, currently inhabited by his descendents, remains off-limits except on special occasions. We will have to be satisfied with the pictures of the house shown here. Let us now go to a house that is far smaller yet open to the public. This house, sharing a fence with the Yoon's residence, is occupied by a civil organization that specializes in the preservation of

Residence of Yoon Bo-seon

Korean culture and traditional Korean houses in particular. Its occupants are an organization called 'Areumjigi,' and the house they use showcases the most successful restoration of *hanok* to the original form. Since the house is open to the public from 9 a.m. to 5 p.m., you can make a reservation any time and visit.

Upon entering the *Areumjigi* house, it is easy to see that its interior space is very small. Although the size of the courtyard is also tiny, somehow this is not felt to a large extent. The view of the sky through an opening in the roof makes the house look larger than it really is. Until the mid-20th century, three generations of a family lived together in such a small house. The most salient feature of a traditional Korean house is the co-existence of *ondol*, a kind of heating system originating from present-day North Korea, and (*daecheong*) *maru* (a wooden-floor style space

Interior space of *Areumjigi*

Maru

located between the private rooms) believed to have been brought from the southern region. This type of space composition is found in neither Chinese nor Japanese culture, even though they belong to the same Northeast Asian cultural sphere. In fact, these two architectural components are not compatible to each other. Fire is an essential element in the *ondol* structure, which simultaneously poses a serious threat to wooden-floor *maru*. In light of the contradictory nature of *ondol* and wood, it is unusual for these two elements to exist in the same space. Koreans sleep in *ondol*-heated rooms while having meals and conversations chiefly on the *maru*. In winter, however, all activities are withdrawn to *ondol*-heated rooms. In a *hanok* house, *maru* serves the same function of a modern-day living room and at the same time is a sacred space. The House Deity, protector of the head of the household, is believed to dwell in the *daedeulbo* (the main beam supporting the roof) of the *maru*, and it is on this floor that *jesa* (ancestral rites), the most important religious event of a family, takes place. On the other hand, activities of daily life are carried out chiefly in *anbang* (lady's room). *Anbang* is a place not only for basic domestic functions including eating, sleeping, and doing household chores, but also for childbirth and child rearing. Therefore, in contrast to *maru*, this room is regarded as a non-sacred space for mundane activities.

Ondol is a unique heating system in many respects. First of all, it is unusual in that it heats the floor; it is made warm by heating a stone called *gudeul*. Once heated, this stone remains warm for days. Since there is no need to heat the room every day, *ondol* is an economical heating method. One of the advantages of *ondol* lies in its ability to make warm an entire room just by heating the floor. It is common knowledge that cold air, heavier than hot air, comes down to the floor; *ondol* heats this cold air and thus allows it to rise. In contrast, other heating systems— for example, a fireplace—cannot warm the cold air that is near the floor. For this reason, people accustomed to a non-*ondol* heating system keep their shoes on inside of their house; the floor is too cold to take off one's shoes. In consideration of our feet, however, it would be far better to be free from shoes at least indoors. Furthermore, it is necessary, as *ondol* advocates argue, to keep hands and feet warm and head cool in order to stay healthy. In this sense, *ondol*, with a warm floor and cool room air, serves as an optimal heating system.

For the first time in their 2,000-year history, Koreans have completely abandoned their traditional building style in favor of that of the West. As a result, the majority of Koreans live in apartment buildings. Although the interior of a Korean apartment is chiefly designed after the Western style, *ondol* is the one traditional component that Koreans firmly adhere to. Whether they live in an apartment or a western-style house, there is no house that does not use *ondol*. In the past, Koreans had meals and slept on the floor. Now they eat at a Western-style dining table and sleep in beds. Despite such thorough adoption of elements of Western housing, Koreans do not go so far as to remove the *ondol* system and walk around indoors in their street shoes. This continuous use of *ondol* probably has to do with its numerous advantages. Otherwise, Koreans would not have insisted on using *ondol* while converting all else into the Western style. *Ondol* is an ideal heating system for Koreans who love to warm their bodies by stretching out on a heated floor, and thus have the most advanced *jjimjilbang* (large public family bathhouse) culture in the world.

Still, this does not mean *ondol* is free of faults; nothing in the world possesses only merits. Inadequately installed, *ondol* makes only the part of floor near the fireplace warm while the rest remains cold. In a room heated by flawed *ondol*, we would be able to see our breath while our feet feel too hot. It is difficult to sleep in such a room: some parts of the floor are too warm while other parts are too cold due to an uneven distribution of heat. The following morning, a glass of water that was left on the cold part of the floor overnight can be found frozen. All of these problems arose from improperly installed *gudeul*; because installing *gudeul* is not an easy task, there were quite a few homes in the past that experienced such problems. At present, electric coils installed under the floor are replacing traditional *ondol*. This modernized *ondol* heating system evenly heats the floor, allowing for a slight increase in room temperature. Koreans seem to continue to uphold their *ondol* tradition because such modern developments like heating coils are making up for its weaknesses. It is strange that they should stick to *ondol* while forgoing all of their other traditions, but then such an attitude is understandable when considering the excellence of *ondol* as a heating system.

Another unique feature of *hanok* is the presence of numerous windows and doors. The fact that there are many windows and doors indicates the priority placed on the communication between *hanok* and nature. Nature is believed to come more deeply into the house when doors and windows are opened. There are many windows and doors in the *Areumjigi* house. Koreans are proud of their ancestors' eco-friendly lifestyle. This tendency can be found in China and Japan as well, but each of the three Northeast Asian nations seem to have developed a way of perceiving nature that is unique from the others. Befitting its status as a great power, China brought nature into the home exactly the way it is found outdoors. The Chinese created an exact replication of nature in their gardens, far larger than those of Korea and Japan. On the other hand, the Japanese created a miniature universe in their gardens by dwarfing the size of everything. They seem endowed with the gift of making an artificial replication seem as real as its original. In contrast, Koreans seem to have thought that nature is at its most natural when left as free of human touch as possible.

This issue will be revisited later when we get to Changdeok Palace. In addition to generous use of windows and doors, a *hanok* house employs another device that allows people to come a little closer to nature. It is difficult to find in a small house like the *Areumjigi* house and is used instead mainly in larger *hanok*. All the windows and doors can be lifted and hung under the eaves by hangers. Open directly to the outdoors, the house eventually become so assimilated with nature that the boundary between home and nature becomes difficult to

Window hangers

Windows hung under the eaves

discern. Left only with the main supporting columns that block the sunlight, you feel as if you are a part of nature. This was the Korean interpretation of 'eco-friendly.' When all the windows and doors are hung, an open space is created as you have nothing else left but the floor, columns, and roof. It is into this open space that nature strides in. A *hanok* is built of natural materials such as wood and earth. In this sense human beings truly become part of nature, even though the house is man-made.

Now we move on to a discussion of *hanji*, which is traditional Korean paper. The interior of *hanok* is chiefly made of wood and earth, but all of this is covered with *hanji*. Bracing myself against criticism that Koreans always tout their products as the best in the world, I must say that *hanji* has the reputation of being the world's finest paper. Even the Chinese, the first inventors of paper, acknowledge the superior quality of traditional Korean paper. Of course *hanji* was undoubtedly of great quality in the past, but this is not necessarily the case nowadays. The place where *hanji* is most noticeable is on the windows and doors that you have just seen. Treated with *hanji*, these wood-framed windows and doors form a barrier against the outdoors.

Here *hanji* carries out multiple functions. First of all, it controls the brightness of light. Since *hanji* converts sunlight into indirect lighting by mitigating the initial dazzling shine of sunlight, there is no need for curtains. Light filtered through *hanji* is said to provide an optimal level of illumination. Secondly, *hanji* regulates humidity. When it is humid, *hanji* absorbs moisture in the air; when it gets dry, *hanji* evaporates previously absorbed moisture back into the room. A view through a microscope reveals that the surface of *hanji* is not smooth but has numerous empty spaces scattered here and there—pores that allow for ventilation. With *hanji*-treated doors, ventilation is done automatically. Thus, it is not necessary to open the doors to ventilate the room. *Hanji* also purifies the air by filtering dust. According to some accounts, *hanji* is said to prevent the formation of mold. If this claim is true, it is probably due to the ventilation function we have just mentioned. I recently watched a documentary on *hanji* that reported that a house wallpapered by *hanji* can even help cure patients of atopic dermatitis. If this is true, *hanji* is truly wonderful paper.

A closer look at this house will reveal that *hanji* is not just used for the windows and doors; the interior of the house is covered all over with *hanji*. In traditional Korean architecture, *hanji* is applied to the entire interior of a house. In Bukchon, however, we can rarely find a house that has properly followed this method. Let us first take a look at the floor. We also find it papered with specially-treated *hanji*. Since *hanji* has a low degree of water tolerance, it should be waterproofed at least to a small degree before use. Soybean oil is what is usually applied to make it water-resistant. Treated in this way, *hanji* becomes very durable floor paper, hard to tear and able to withstand water. Moreover, we cannot find any element that is harmful to the human body in this oiled paper because soybean oil is an entirely 'natural' product without preservatives. Standing on the oiled floor, I imagine that just lying on it could make a skin disease go away. Not more than a few decades ago, most people preferred varnish to soybean oil on the grounds of economy and convenience. Needless to say, however, varnish is not beneficial to our health.

Even the wall is entirely covered with *hanji*. In general, *hanji* takes on a milkish color, not so bright but with a subtle glow. No pattern is

Anbang (lady's room)

engrained on its surface. The entire wall is tinged with nothing but a soft milk color. To me, this is the color of Joseon. At the same time, it is the color of Joseon white porcelain. The most well-known white porcelain of the Joseon Dynasty is the moon-shaped porcelain shown in the picture. The color of this porcelain is exactly that of *hanji*. The people of Joseon savored such simplicity and moderation. This type of porcelain, bare of patterns, is not easy to find in other countries. Like Joseon porcelain, the wall of a *hanok* room is white and left undecorated. The *hanji* applied on the wall has the same

Moon-shaped porcelain

functions of humidity control and air purification as that on the windows and doors.

We may have spoken highly of *hanji*, but this does not mean *hanji* is all perfect. No matter how elevated it is, *hanji* cannot avoid the basic limitations of paper; it is weak against water and tears easily. For this reason, *hanji* applied on a door gets punctured easily. Children would playfully poke their finger through the *hanji*, so hardly a day went by that it was left undamaged. I still remember that only a few days after the doors in my childhood home were freshly papered, holes began to appear here and there. This was because we children punctured holes in it just for fun. I must say that the sight of patched-over doors was not exactly pleasing to the eye. As troublesome as it may have been, the doors thus needed re-treating every two to three years. In this regard, *hanji* is highly impractical, particularly when compared to the semi-permanence of glass.

Moreover, *hanji* may not provide as effective protection against severe cold. Memories of shivering in the room in winter are nothing new. That shivering was, in a sense, inevitable. There was not much that a single layer of *hanji* could do against the cold. Surprisingly, however, a study has reported that *hanji* is a far more effective insulant than glass; it seems to be a warning against underestimating a sheet of *hanji*. The insulating effect of *hanji* will improve further if multiple layers of paper are applied on both the interior and exterior of the door. Reportedly, the reason for treating only one side is to reveal the beauty of patterns on the wood. Then why is it that we felt so cold? In my opinion, this was probably because of cold drafts that came through a crack where the door did not completely fit into its frame and not because of *hanji*.

Alleyways: Symbol of Bukchon

I think we have had a sufficient view of *hanok*. Now we will be heading to the alleyways, considered the symbol of Bukchon. The finest alleyway is the Bukchon *hanok* Alleyway, located a ten minutes' walk from Areumjigi house. As seen in the picture, this alleyway functions as the main street of Bukchon. Nevertheless, it is not broad as is the case with most streets in the residential areas of Korea. In the case of the West,

Main street of Bukchon

a church and a square typically occupy the center of a village, although a direct comparison with the Western case may not be valid here. Villagers get together in the church or the square to discuss important matters. When I was studying in the U.S., I found it strange that many houses were located on the roadside. Sometimes houses sat right beside a vehicle road—cases mostly confined to urban areas in Korea. I suspected that this type of residential arrangement would be stressful to Westerners, but they never seemed to mind. I thought they might feel uncomfortable with a view of a busy street when they walked out of their house. Such thoughts at the time were based on the knowledge that Koreans in the past led a very different urban lifestyle.

A typical Korean village or city does not have a square or a central building like a church—although there is a pavilion at the entrance to a village. Influenced by Confucian teachings, Koreans above all valued their family and family clan. Although they did discuss matters concerning the welfare of the community with others, this does not seem very befitting of Koreans. They tried to solve problems within the boundary of the family as much as possible. All that was necessary was a meeting of the family elders. It seems that this is why a residential area in Korea was formed around numerous alleyways rather than a public square as its center. Because of the tendency to regard private space as more important than public space, Koreans seem to have prefered building their houses deep within the city, away from busy roadsides. In addition, they were more in favor of curving roads than straight ones. If you walk around Bukchon, you will find very few straight roads. Moreover, roads were not built in accordance with plans designed in advance, but were created in any place where it was deemed necessary. That is why these roads seem to lack order; another road starts its meandering course at a point where we think there will not be any more connecting road. This is the true picture of Bukchon alleyways.

In fact, alleyways go well with the introvertive disposition of Koreans. Westerners, who lead more public lifestyles, prefer building their houses beside a big street. In contrast, Koreans avoid building their house at the roadside as much as possible. It thus takes several turns of alleyways before the appearance of a major street. In a sense, such a winding route to the outside may provide psychological comfort. On their way to work, the first road to pass is a narrow alleyway. The closeness of this road would resemble the close privacy of the home that was just left. Passing through two or three more alleyways will lead to a main street. Now they are back in the outside world. In the meantime, they are getting themselves ready to go out to the world. The same applies for the return home. The street becomes tighter as they walk home from the main street. At the same time they gradually prepare themselves to enter home, the most private of spaces, leaving the public space behind. When they set foot in the small alleyway right in front of the home, they come to feel at ease.

Even so, this does not mean that Koreans do not communicate with their neighbors. The alleyway was their space for such communication. In the evening, people started coming out to the alleyway as if it was promised beforehand. There, children played and grown-ups talked about what had happened that day. It is in Bukchon alleyways that all of these occurred. The alleyways that we see now were probably far narrower in the past. As the neighborhood developed, the alleyways were inevitably broadened, losing much of their unrefined charm. These changes do not do the alleyways justice, making them like a plain farmer who is suddenly given a clean shave. Because of this, I always feel whenever I come to Bukchon that it would be so much nicer if the alleyways had remained intact. I just cannot shake off the idea that the Bukchon alleyways had plenty of potential to be able to resemble the back alleys of Kyoto.

Alleyways are easily found in Bukchon. Virtually all the streets are alleyways. A stroll through these alleyways will take you to places where you can experience traditional Korean culture. In a small museum where Korean folk paintings are exhibited, for instance, you can paint folk art and make talismans. There are places for making decorative knots or for making traditional wrapping cloth. You can also find places where *hanji*

A guesthouse in Bukchon

craftwork is sold and *hanji* craft can be experienced. In addition, there is a shop that specializes in crafting and selling furniture only made of bamboo. This shop is an example of a Bukchon house where the Seoul metropolitan government allows artisans, who are designated as human cultural assets, to use the traditional house as their workshop in order to preserve traditional Korean culture. The government established this shop to allow the general public to feel and experience Korean culture more easily. It should also be mentioned that some *hanok* houses serve as guesthouses; lodging charges vary from house to house. I think it a good experience to stay overnight in a guesthouse, but I strongly hope people will not compare these guesthouses to Japanese inns. Through long experience of running inns, the Japanese have been providing fine facilities and the very best of service for which they charge dearly. In comparison, traditional Korean guesthouses in Bukchon have not been able to develop their own management know-how. This lack can be explained by the fact that it has only been a few years since the traditional guesthouse business has started.

In addition, Bukchon has several traditional Korean restaurants. Among them is a restaurant run by a person knowledgeable in Korean royal court cuisine. From my experience, although the food itself may have its origins in the palace, the way it was served did not look authentic. (In fact, the food did not seem much like royal cousine, either. This is because cooking based strictly on the culinary method of the royal court would have cost too much.) One of my colleagues who is an expert on Japanese culture frankly told me that the food seemed too heavily influenced by Japanese cuisine. To be honest, when it comes to traditional Korean food, I have yet to see a traditional Korean restaurant that offers Korean food consistent with tradition in terms of content, serving manner, and interior design. This attests to the withering of Korean traditions. The state of Korean culinary tradition is in such dire straits that few contemporary Koreans have any idea of genuine Korean tradition. The preservation of traditions requires the existence of a class of people to enjoy it. It costs a lot of money to preserve high culture that is also old. Until just recently, hardly any Korean could afford to pay handsomely to enjoy their own traditional culture. Now that the nation's successful economic development has created many prospective consumers of culture, the trouble is that Koreans have largely forgotten what to enjoy and how to enjoy it because too much tradition has already been lost. This is the tragedy of Korean history.

Each time I visit a historic district like Bukchon, there is one thought that always occurs to me. While I enjoy fragments of old traditions, I find it lamentable to see Koreans who have failed not only to preserve tradition but also to understand what went wrong in the first place. The

Traditional house combined with western design in Bukchon

situation is gradually improving, but it is all the more frustrating because so much can be achieved with just a little effort but most people do not try to invest even this little bit. For this reason, I always regard the current situation with resignation. But let us leave Bukchon, putting such a state of mind behind for now. There are quite a few interesting things to see on the way to Changdeok Palace. As shown in the picture, you will see buildings with traditional design and Western architectural design harmoniously combined as well as a museum of Buddhist art. These are the buildings you can see while walking down along the outer wall of Changdeok Palace. Soon, we will arrive at Changdeok Palace, which is better preserved than Gyeongbok Palace. Now we have arrived at Changdeok Palace, a World Cultural Heritage designated by UNESCO for its excellent state of preservation and distinct features as a palace.

3. The Most Nature-Friendly Palace in Northeast Asia—Changdeok Palace and Huwon (Secret Garden)

Standing in front of Changdeok Palace

Most people enter Changdeok Palace right away upon arrival. But they miss an opportunity to fully appreciate Changdeok Palace—to be more precise, Donhwamun Gate (Donhwamun), which is the main entrance (gate) of the palace. Korean architecture—palaces in particular, which were built on the basis of *Fengshui* theory—should be viewed against the background of a mountain. This has already been pointed out in discussing Gyeongbok Palace. Then, what is the best way of viewing the facade of Changdeok Palace, which in this case is Donhwamun? For the best view, you have to walk about 100 meters away from it. The problem with this, however, is that you will find yourself in the middle of traffic. Thus, there is no choice but to take a glance of it while crossing the road at a green light. As seen in this picture that was taken during such a crossing, the view of the gate is partially blocked by a building and a tree on either side of the road. However, just a view of what is visible is enough. Mt. Maebong, which backs Changdeok Palace, is on the outskirts of Mt. Bukak, the guardian mountain of Gyeongbok Palace. Over Mt. Maebong, you can also see part of Mt. Bukhan, which is also visible from Mt. Bukak. With the gate, Mt. Maebong, and Mt. Bukhan all aligned within view, you can come to full appreciation of Donhwamun.

Main gate of Changdeok Palace with Mt. Maebong in background

The gate was built in the early 15th century, but was burned down during the Imjin War and later rebuilt in the early 17th century. Donhwamun is the oldest among the main gates of the royal palaces in Seoul and has long since been designated as a National Treasure.

On approaching Changdeok Palace, you will find a roadway on its right side as can be seen in the picture. Originally this road did not exist, but was grafted by the Japanese colonial government—another example of a Japanese atrocity during the colonial years. Initially, Changdeok Palace was incorporated with Jongmyo, the royal shrine of the Joseon Dynasty, as we will discuss later. Changgyeong Palace, located nearby, was also connected to Changdeok Palace. The area that encompasses Jongmyo, Changdeok Palace, and Changgyeong Palace covers a wide stretch of land. All combined, the area would be far larger than the Forbidden City of China. However, imperial Japan decided that they would debase the authority of the Joseon royalty by creating a zoo and a botanical garden inside Changgyeong Palace, and altered the original form of Changdeok Palace by making a street (Yulgokno) between Jongmyo and the palace. Although Korea should maintain a good relationship with Japan when considering the future, it is heartbreaking to encounter in our daily life the irreparably deep scars left by Japanese imperialism. Right in front of the gate, there is a cornerstone similar to those found in front of all other palaces. Until just recently, these cornerstones remained covered with earth. Now we have recovered their original form after removing the earth that was placed there by the Japanese. They must have hidden this cornerstone underneath layers of earth when they built the street (Yulgokno) that I have just mentioned. Its recovery notwithstanding, the cornerstone now sits too close to the street. In general, the front of a palace should occupy a large space; the Japanese eliminated much of such space by creating Yulgokno. Lighting that lights up the gate at night does not seem to sufficiently bring out the stately appearance of the gate, even though it is quite an exquisite piece of architecture. We have seen enough of the entrance of Changdeok Palace. Now let us begin our tour of the palace itself.

Changdeok Palace, Different from Gyeongbok Palace from the Entrance

Upon entering the palace through Donhwamun, you soon realize that it is very different from Gyeongbok Palace. In Gyeongbok Palace, everything including Geunjeong Hall (the royal audience chamber) all the way to the residential quarters of the king and queen can be seen stretching out in a straight line at a 90-degree angle to the entrance. Such a spatial arrangement cannot be detected at all in Changdeok Palace.

Bridge of the Forbidden Stream

When passing through the entrance, there is only an open space with neither a gate nor a Jeongjeon (Main Hall) in sight. A look into Gyeongbok Palace from Gwanghwamun, its main entrance, offers a view of the other two gates of the palace as well as part of Geunjeong Hall. However, the only thing visible upon entering Changdeok Palace is Geumcheon (Forbidden Stream) and a stone bridge that spans it. As pictures show, this stone bridge (Geumcheongyo Bridge) is bent to the right. You have to make a sharp right angle turn before entering Injeong Hall, the formal audience reception chamber of Changdeok Palace.

Around the Forbidden Stream

Let us move on past the bridge. Straight ahead of the bridge are two gates that appear to be overlapping. Strangely, the central axis of the bridge is not aligned with that of the gates. I will explain this further shortly, but it is unlikely that a large degree of freedom was given in the construction of Changdeok Palace, even though it was admittedly built in a style that heavily

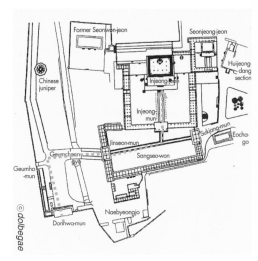

From Donhwamun Gate to Injeong Hall

deviated from the design norms at the time of the construction of Gyeongbok Palace. This particular misalignment of the bridge and the gates was probably the error of contemporary Koreans in the process of renovation. Presumably, people at the time would have moved along the straight line of flow after making a right angle turn upon entering Donhwamun, and making another right angle turn in front of Injeong Hall gate before entering the courtyard of Injeong Hall as seen in the picture. In the above scenario, the bridge and the axis of the gate would have been exactly aligned. It may be that the bridge was not restored in its original position. This discussion may sound a bit technical, but I bring it up in advance, because we will soon see quite a few errors in the way other architecture in Changdeok Palace was restored. The yard lying outside of Injeong Hall also attracts our attention. Its shape is not rectangular but trapezoidal. There are several explanations for the shape of this yard, the most convincing one being that it was an outcome of design aimed at harmony with nature.

Changdeok Palace also has other unusual features in addition to its off-center alignment. Originally, you had to pass through three gates to go to Injeong Hall as is the case of Gyeongbok Palace. In Changdeok Palace, there are only two gates that lead to Injeong Hall. Of course, there is one more gate in the middle, but it is not a formal gate. Changdeok Palace was built without the restraints of the architectural norms of its time, probably because it was not the official palace. Changdeok Palace, a secondary palace, was elevated to a more official status after Gyeongbok Palace was completely burned to the ground by the Japanese army in the late 16th century. Thus it had always been a secondary palace compared to Gyeongbok Palace. Unlike Gyeongbok Palace, built in accordance with the rules stipulated by China, Changdeok Palace was perhaps built in a manner that satisfied Korean aesthetic sensibility. Traditionally, Koreans are known to dislike anything symmetrical. I can well imagine why the term 'asymmetrical' always emerges in discussions on the beauty of Korea. From my past studies, I can conclude that Koreans do not seem to greatly favor symmetry or perfect balance and sometimes they experiment with designs that radically depart from the norm. A work of art that epitomizes this tendency is a pot, affectionately known as moon-shaped porcelain. Its color has already been discussed, but the most important characteristic of this pot lies in its shape, which is not symmetrical. Instead, one side of it is slightly lopsided. This lack of symmetry is ascribed not to the inadequacy of craftsmanship or lack of budget, but to Joseon's traditional perception of beauty. The people of Joseon did not think highly of perfection or extreme symmetry. They usually upset the balance of perfection by adding a few touches of imperfection to any part that was deemed too flawless. They seem to have thought it more natural in this way. In the physical world of nature, it is hard to find perfectly symmetrical structures. Mountain, river, and sea—do they not all lack symmetry? For Joseon people, art was an act of realizing the natural state of all things.

I have used an example from pottery, but now let us ponder the aesthetical tendency of Koreans in the realm of architecture. For Changdeok Palace, two turns were created at the axis on the path leading to Injeong Hall from the main gate. A similar approach, if not as drastic as that of Changdeok Palace, can be noticed in a traditional Buddhist temple in Korea. Let us take a look at the blueprint below. This is a blueprint of Buseoksa Temple (Buseoksa), acknowledged within Korean Buddhist architecture as a temple created in complete harmony with the topography of nature. According to the blueprint, we have to pass numerous gates before entering Dharma Hall. This element of design reflects the doctrines of Pure Land Buddhism, but we will not delve into a

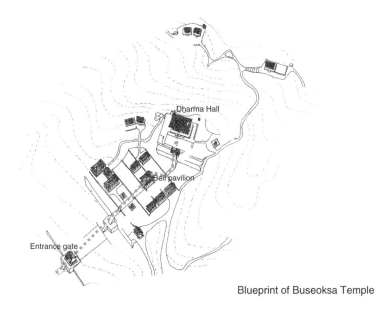

Blueprint of Buseoksa Temple

discussion of this design because it would become too technical. What I would like to focus on is the fact that the central axis of Buseoksa turns to the left at a spot approximately $\frac{4}{5}$ of the way into the temple. This axis is not a straight line to begin with, and yet it turns again toward the rear as if it needs further bending. Constructed in Chinese style, the axis would have been made straight and spared such a turn. One aspect of Korean architecture that comes into view here is that the most important building should not be located where it can be readily seen. This is understandable because the sanctity of an important building may be undermined if it can be seen from anywhere. Because the axis of Buseoksa is not a straight line, this makes it hard to see Dharma Hall, which is located far in the back. An added twist to the axis makes it even harder to see. The graceful figure of Dharma Hall looms up suddenly as we pass the final gate. The presentation of Dharma Hall is tantalizingly

Dharma Hall (hidden in the back) of Buseoksa Temple

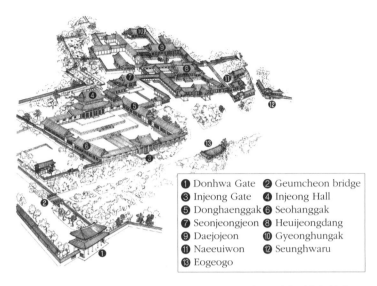

1 Donhwa Gate 2 Geumcheon bridge
3 Injeong Gate 4 Injeong Hall
5 Donghaenggak 6 Seohanggak
7 Seonjeongjeon 8 Heuijeongdang
9 Daejojeon   10 Gyeonghungak
11 Naeeuiwon   12 Seunghwaru
13 Eogeogo

Around the Main Hall

delayed all the longer for its rarefied status. A dramatic reversal in design
thus makes a more enduring impression on people visiting the temple.

Changdeok Palace can be understood in the same manner. Upon
entering Donhwa Gate, the main entrance of Changdeok Palace, there is
nothing to be seen as we have mentioned before. All that we see is the
wall at the spot where we turn to the right before crossing Geumcheon
bridge. Not until we pass its entrance can we see Injeong Hall. Most
people like the fact that this route to the center of the palace seems less
boring, and it seems more human. Such an idiosyncracy makes
Changdeok Palace more easily approachable than Gyeongbok Palace. As
for Gyeongbok Palace, the alignment of the main gate, Geunjeong Hall,
and the king's residence on a straight line is uninteresting because it is
too simple and lacks congeniality. That is why most kings of Joseon
preferred Changdeok Palace to the more official Gyeongbok Palace. It
seems only natural that human beings should like to live in this sort of

space. People dislike living in a space where everything is exposed and placed in straight lines. There are times when they wish to hide a part of themselves, while at other times they want to expose everything. In this regard, Changdeok Palace is considered a good place to live. As we will discover shortly, there are many other such human-friendly elements in the palace.

Korea now has seven properties that are registered as UNESCO World Cultural Heritage. As we have mentioned when discussing Gyeongbok Palace, the *Annals of the Joseon Dynasty* and the *Diaries of the Royal Secretariat* belong to the list of documentary heritages, not to that of cultural heritages. To be designated as World Cultural Heritages, historic remains must have exceptional value. A historic relic, once celebrated as a World Heritage, ceases to belong only to its country of origin and becomes a property of all people. Only a cultural heritage considered to be extremely rare, the best, or the first of its kind can be part of the World Heritage List. Gyeongbok Palace is not included in the list as it does not meet such criteria. Changdeok Palace became a UNESCO World Heritage in 1997. Other World Heritage properties in Korea include Jongmyo Shrine, Hwaseong Fortress in Suwon, Dolmen Sites, Bulguksa Temple and Seokguram Grotto, and Gyeongju Historic Areas.

In Seoul there are five remaining palaces of the Joseon Dynasty; of these, Changdeok Palace is the only one to be on the World Heritage List. The other four were destroyed so severely during the Japanese colonial period and the Korean War that their application to be on the list could not even be submitted. By contrast, Changdeok Palace received a high score from the UNESCO committee because it has a well-preserved original form and the royal garden also retains much of its appearance. We already had a discussion on the royal garden when we reviewed

Gyeongbok Palace, but the royal garden in Changdeok Palace is considered a one-of-a-kind and the finest in the entire Korean peninsula. Despite being a palace, it is highly venerated because it incorporates buildings into the natural topography of the site without disrupting its surroundings and thus accomplishes harmony between the man-made building and nature. Probably because much Korean sensibility is preserved in Changdeok Palace, a world-famous French architect said that he always stops by when visiting Korea. For him, it was a way of feeling the essence of Korea. He further emphasized his point by adding that Koreans should visit the palace three or four times a year to remind themselves of their Korean identity.

In the Front Courtyard of Injeong Hall—thinking of the beauty of Korean architecture

That will be enough for background knowledge of Changdeok Palace. With this information in mind, let us walk into the front courtyard of Injeong Hall. There is not much to say about Injeong Gate, its main entrance, except that it is where the kings—at least eight kings, including King Yeongjo and King Gojong—held their coronation ceremonies. Contrary to popular belief that the coronation would be held in Injeong Hall, the king received the royal seal at the gate and proceeded through the east wing of the front courtyard into Pyeonjeon Hall, where Cabinet meetings were held.

If you have visited Gyeongbok Palace, you will soon realize that Injeong Hall is very different from Geunjeong Hall. Injeong Hall is rather small in size—its front courtyard occupies a far smaller space than that of Gyeongbok Palace. The front courtyard looks even further diminished due to the non-axial arrangement of Changdeok Palace. Injeong Hall here

Injeong Hall

stands alone with neither supporting buildings at its sides nor a mountain in the back. In view of the entire palace, it is pushed aside to the left corner away from the center. Its location at the corner does not help its appearance.

Unlike Geunjeong Hall, its rear is not an open space. As in the picture, the space does not appear free flowing, enclosed by a fence and the woods. There is hardly room (or reason) to establish a photo point. Geunjeong Hall looks stately by contrast, especially when seen against Mt. Bukak. Injeong Hall does not give us such an aura of grandeur, but is nevertheless designated as a National Treasure along with Geunjeong Hall. In view of the entire layout of Changdeok Palace, I do not think the Hall is an integral part of the palace. Otherwise, there is no way to explain the lack of thought put into the background view of Injeong Hall. Its relatively small area in proportion to the entire palace also leads us to the same conjecture. Indeed, the buildings are not what first come to mind when we think of the palace. Instead, first thought goes to the most exquisite royal garden in the Joseon Dynasty. When there is an occasion to introduce Changdeok Palace with pictures, mostly images of Buyongji Pond—one of the ponds in the garden—are used while buildings such as Injeong Hall are rarely shown. For this reason, the discussion of this chapter will also focus on the garden, Huwon (Rear Garden) rather than on the buildings. We will discuss the beauty of Korean architecture, since much of the explanation on traditional Korean architecture has been covered in the section of this book on Gyeongbok Palace.

It is not my intention to suggest that Injeong Hall is not beautiful because it is modest in size and not as stately as Geunjeong Hall. Its beauty certainly is worthy of designation as a National Treasure. In this case, what is the essence of Korean beauty manifested in such a building? At first glance, there is not much difference between ancient Korean and Chinese buildings. Therefore, it is not easy for people with little understanding of Northeastern Asian culture to distinguish Korean, Chinese and Japanese architecture. But Koreans with only rudimentary knowledge of Korean culture can point out their traditional architecture without much difficulty among examples of architecture from all three countries. It is important to distinguish architectural similarities and distinctiveness among Korea and China (Japan), yet there is a paucity of in-depth studies that deal with this matter. Therefore, we will have to settle for now on sketching out of the general features.

Generally, Koreans consider their architecture to be the most nature-friendly as well as characterized by a uniquely Korean form of beauty. But we should not forget that Korean architecture basically inherited the Chinese style. Few Koreans are aware that traditional Korean architecture

Typical Chinese architecture with high eaves

has absorbed much from its Chinese counterpart. Which period of Chinese culture did it embrace? We have to specify the exact period when studying Chinese influence on our architecture because Chinese architectural style varies for each dynasty and each region, given its long history and vastness of territory. The first image that comes to mind in traditional Chinese architecture is that of the eaves with a dramatically raised tip, as shown in the picture. Of course this is not the only style of architecture found in China. For example, the main hall of the Forbidden City lies in stark contrast to the buildings with their flamboyantly raised eaves; those of Taihe Hall are not raised at all. Skimming through the history of Chinese architecture, we learn that the eaves of buildings were originally made straight like those in the Forbidden City. Then during the Tang and Northern Song Dynasties, the tip of the eaves is gradually raised in a rather exaggerated manner. This tendency becomes more pronounced in the southern regions of China and this later on is imprinted in people's minds as the prototype of Chinese architecture.

It is during the Tang and Northern Song Dynasties that Korea (and Japan) actively adopted Chinese architecture. While Korea has preserved the Chinese style relatively well, China itself took a different direction.

Taoist temple in Shanxi Province, China (Tang-style building)

Palaces and temples of the two Chinese dynasties had a direct influence on Korean architecture. The Chinese style, first imported by Silla and Goryeo, constitutes the architectural style of palaces and Buddhist temples in the Korean peninsula at that time. This style then proceeded to exert great influence on the way houses of the nobility and common people were designed. Ancient Korean architecture thus came into being under the absolute influence of the Chinese style. However, such a process is not odd because it is no different from the current situation in which most Koreans live in Western-style housing. In the way that Western culture universally dominates *modus vivendi* nowadays, Chinese culture was the dominant force in the lives of the people of Shilla and Goryeo. However, the interior of Korean architecture is completely

Residence of Chinese aristocrat

different from that of Chinese architecture. This aspect has been briefly discussed in the section on Bukchon. The outer architecture may be similar but the inner content is diametrically different. The most striking difference is that Koreans, unlike Chinese, have *ondol* (heating system) and *maru* (wooden flooring) installed in their house where they reside without shoes. To a certain degree, palaces and temples of Korea look similar to Chinese architecture. However, the situation is quite different in the case of the houses of the nobility and common people. Above all, the arrangement of each building within a house compound takes on a different form. In the house of a Chinese aristocrat, buildings are arranged to form a rectangle, with a courtyard in the middle and each unit of the house aligned. On the other hand, building units in a Korean house are rarely arranged in a straight line. The *sarangbang* (husband's room) and *anbang* (lady's room), both of which carry out the most important domestic functions, are each freely positioned in separate spaces and are rarely aligned together.

We can find many more differences between the two traditions. For example, the walls in a Chinese house are very high, thereby shutting out most of the outside. The low height of walls and buildings in a Korean house, by contrast, reflects a strong will to communicate with the outside. Our interest does not only lie in such structural details. We are want to find the reason why we can distinguish between traditional Korean and Chinese architecture that have such similar appearances. To probe into this question would go beyond the scope of our discussion, but we can say for now that traditional Korean architecture is structurally identical to that of Chinese architecture. It is not an exaggeration to say that the method of connecting roofs and columns is the same in both traditions. When comparing these two buildings, they resemble each other to such an extent that one can be mistaken for the other. The Korean architecture that we see here is the famous Dharma Hall in Buseoksa Temple and its Chinese counterpart Guanyinsi Temple in Shanxi Province, a Tang period structure. The next two pictures are the main halls of Gyeongbok Palace

and the Forbidden City, both built at a similar period. Their basic structure is similar, but there is something that strikes a different chord. We do not need to compare just these two structures, but their comparison can be justified in that each is representative of its architectural tradition.

Dharma Hall of Buseoksa Temple

And there seems to be no need to consider southern Chinese architecture for a comparison, for it has a distinct look from that of Korea as can easily be seen in the picture. In these buildings, the most distinct difference is in the eave lines

Guanyinsi Temple in Shanxi Province

Geunjeong Hall

of the roofs. The Chinese eaves are extended upward as if to fly away, while Korean eaves have their tip raised at a smaller angle. This difference is so obvious even to the untrained eye that we will refrain from dwelling on it further.

Such simple one-to-one comparison will doubtlessly be prone to intense criticism from architecture specialists. This is because although not untrue in Korea, the structure of Chinese architecture varies particularly widely with each period and each region. Whenever a question arises on which architecture epitomizes Chinese tradition, we only look at the general trend. While there are differences in details, we should identify the more defining characteristics of Chinese buildings and use these in a comparison with Korean buildings. In order to do so, we need to look at the most representative Chinese and Korean buildings, particularly those that were built within a similar period. This type of approach aims to see

Taihe Hall at the Forbidden City

the forest rather than the trees. While attention to individual parts should not be neglected, it is also extremely important to try to see the whole in trying to understand the world around us. In our following discussion, we will take the latter approach.

Generally speaking, Northern Chinese architecture looks rather heavy compared to that of Korea. By contrast, Southern Chinese architecture is characterized by lightness and brings to mind a swallow that kicks off the ground and swiftly soars into the air. In this regard, Korean architecture lies somewhere on the continuum between Northern and Southern Chinese architecture. Why does Korean architecture look light? This is probably due to the method of construction favored by Korean architects. They seemed to like using the *'gwisoseum'* technique (ear-raising technique), in which the corner columns are extended slightly higher than the columns in the middle. They even used a technique that tilts the

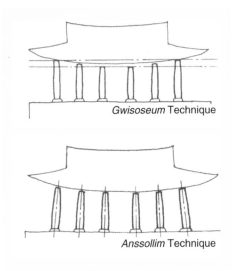

Gwisoseum Technique

Anssollim Technique

corner columns slightly inward. This is called '*anssollim*' *technique* (inward-tilting technique), which makes a building take on a trapezoidal shape at the exclusion of the roofs. This trapezoidal shape is not easily discernible to the naked eye other than to an expert.

Why are such techniques used? They seem to have been devised to correct potential optical illusions. In the case of a tall building, a problem would arise if columns of the same height were erected at a right angle to the ground. While it is not a problem when seen up close, the columns would look tilted outward when viewed from a distance, thereby causing the building to look disorderly. The *gwisoseum* and *anssollim* techniques are intended to correct this optical illusion. When columns are built with a slight inward tilt, a building will appear to stand straight. Another technique with a similar effect is called the '*baebeullim*' technique (belly-enlarging technique). Known as entasis in the West, it is a technique that slightly enlarges the lower one-third of the column. Given slight convexity, columns look well-ordered; otherwise, their middle would appear to sag inward. This technique was not applied to Geunjeong Hall, but the Dharma Hall of Buseoksa is a building well-known for the application of entasis.

With the corner columns slightly extended, eave lines are accordingly bent slightly upward. Koreans take great pride in these delicate eave lines. They think Chinese eave lines are excessively curved—although those of the Forbidden City are rather close to a straight line—while those of Japan are too linear. Each country thinks its own eave lines the most natural and beautiful. It is in the visual elegance of eave lines that they find the salient feature of their traditional architecture. As we have seen, eave lines in architecture from the Tang and Song Dynasties are built at an angle very similar to those of Korea. Chinese architecture continued to undergo changes in subsequent dynasties, while the style of

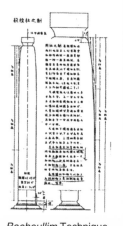

Baeheullim Technique

Korean architecture remained much the same. As a result, regardless of architectural type—whether it be a palace, a temple or a house of the nobility—Korean architecture adopted this style, which later came to be regarded as the embodiment of Korean architecture.

Even so, Koreans did not always preserve the Chinese style in their architecture in unaltered form. In addition to eave lines, a slightly bent ridge located on the top of a roof is another example. This effect in shape is a result of *anssolim* Because columns supporting a roof are tilted slightly inward, it is better to have the ridge slightly bent in order to connect these columns. This style, albeit originated in China and partially employed there, can be found in most Korean architecture. Thanks to this technique, Korean architecture looks light in its own unique way—almost as if walking with light footsteps. Such minute analysis of architecture may sound rather technical, but we would also like to point out the difference in proportion of a roof to a column between Korean and Chinese architecture. Generally, the proportion in Korean architecture is

Bottom view of columns
with "*Greng-i*" Technique

1:1. In relation to the column, the roof is a little longer in Chinese architecture.

There are some additional miscellaneous differences. The part connecting a column and the foundation stone is very rough in Korean architecture except that of the palace. This tendency is particularly pronounced in Buddhist temples. In Korean temples foundation stones were never honed to a smooth surface as shown in the pictures; the stones were simply used as they were. The bottom of the columns was crafted and molded to fit the contours of the foundation stones and afterwards just placed on top of the stones. This process was done with what is called '*greng-i*' technique, and only carpenters with at least 20 to 30 years of experience were allowed to use this method because it is very difficult to implement. The *greng-i* technique is not found in China or Japan. It seems that the rough-hewn nature of the technique did not match well with their cultural sensibilities. By contrast, we can find a lot of things that are rough and unhoned in traditional Korean art. This

Columns made with crooked trees

respect for the natural state of things can be detected in places other than foundation stones. Koreans often use gnarled trees for columns exactly as they are found in nature. We find ample cases of this tendency in

Korean Buddhist architecture, which has relatively free reign in its artistic capacity. As seen in the picture, some columns look as if they have been altered by computer graphics. Although I have not traveled extensively in Japan and China, I must say I have never seen columns with such style. Koreans often use crooked trees even for the crossbeam of a building. These cases all reflect Koreans' dedication to curvilinear freedom, a phenomenon rarely found in other countries. Let us stop our discussion on traditional Korean architecture and go inside Changdeok Palace.

Buildings in Changdeok Palace

It is true that the buildings in Changdeok Palace, including Injeong Hall, do not offer many viewable features. As is the case for Gyeongbok Palace, there are not many buildings that remain today. Paintings of the palace produced in the late 19th century indicate that many more buildings existed back then, as seen in the pictures. With Changgyeong Palace (a palace which served as residential quarters of queens and concubines) located right next-door, the Changdeok Palace area abounded in palatial buildings as if it suffered from 'palace complex.' The degree to which Changgyeong Palace was destroyed is no less than other palaces, but let us avoid discussing that subject.

We can tell that Injeong Hall was built more modestly than Geunjeong Hall in Gyeongbok Palace. Geunjeong Hall looks majestic with a stone-made balustrade on the platform and stone statues of animals placed on important spots, but the platform of Injeon Hall is bare of any decorative elements. But unlike Gyeongbok Palace, its interior is splendidly arranged. Features deemed as unbecoming of an old palace include glass windows with curtains and even lightbulbs—the outcome of repairs that were done in the early 20th century when the Joseon royalty introduced

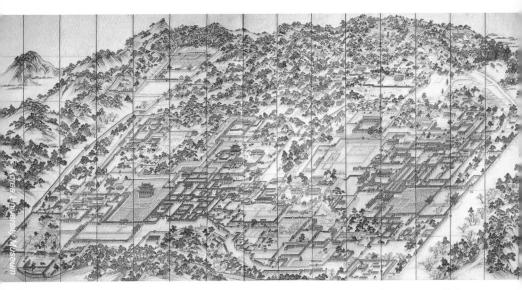

Picture of Changdeok Palace and Changgyeong Palace

Western culture into the country. The floor was stripped of bricks and installed with wooden flooring. Injeong Hall achieves a kind of unique quality by achieving harmony between a Korean-style exterior and a Western-style interior. As we have seen in Gyeongbok Palace, this building was mainly used as a ceremonial space and was not utilized for ordinary occasions. It was a sacred place used solely for the reception of important guests such as foreign envoys, coronation of kings, and celebrations given by royal ministers. In Injeong Hall, a ramp, which was a route for the king's passage, is located on the left of the building. The king entered Geunjeong Hall from the rear in Gyeongbok Palace Hall. Here in Injeong Hall the king entered from the east, because his residential quarters were also located in the east.

We are now about to go to the king's residence. At this point in our tour, we need to pull out a map for an overview of Changdeok Palace. This will help us understand how free-spirited and nature-friendly the construction of the palace really was. As in Gyeongbok Palace, Chinese and Korean palaces had important buildings arranged on an axis. Changdeok Palace, however, deviated from this rule of axial arrangement. Generally, the buildings of Changdeok Palace are built around three axes. Donhwa Gate, the main gate, assumes the role of one axis. On this axis lies only this gate and nothing else. It is still important because it is the main gate of the palace. The next axis is none other than the one formed by Injeong Hall and Injeong Gate. Then where is the third axis? This is the line that connects Hwijeong Hall and Daejo Hall, the king and queen' s quarters. These axes as seen in the picture are neither parallel to each other nor are they bent at a regular angle. They just stand there 'randomly.' Is this another example of free-spirited Korean style? According to experts, the buildings in the palace were arranged in a way that fitted the natural contour of the site. When we visit the palace in person, we realize that the palace could have been built in a more orderly manner. For example, there was no large hill in the site at the time of construction. Even if there had been one, they could have conformed the area to convention after leveling the ground. But they never did. This tells us that the architects of the palace intended to plan the site as we see it today from the beginning, rather than take a more passive approach and try to arrange the buildings

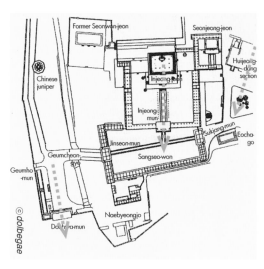

Three axes of Changdeok Palace

along the topography of the site.

On that note, let us leave Injeong Hall. The next building we find on our path is Seonjeong Hall, the place where the king had cabinet meetings with his ministers. For unknown reasons, it is closed to the public. The salient feature of this building is the roof hung over the king's passageway to secure his safety. Moreover, Seonjeong Hall is roofed with blue-glazed tiles, befitting the status of the king's office. Blue-glazed tiles are probably the most expensive, made in the same manner as celadon porcelain. The current South Korean President's official residence is called Cheong Wa Dae (Blue House), the roof of which is also covered with blue-glazed tiles. We will have to bypass Seonjeong Hall, since we are not allowed to enter it.

The building right next to it is called Huijeong Hall. It was originally the king's quarters, but converted to the royal office later on. Furnished in Western style, the inside of the building has a carpeted floor, conference tables, and even glass windows. What is distinctive about this building is its porch that was made to help the king get on and off a car as we see in the picture. We will get back to this car later. Huijeong Hall itself does not offer much to talk about. As visitors are not allowed to enter inside, we will move further into the inner side of the palace. Daejo Hall, as mentioned before, is the building where the queen resided. To its left lies a large open space, its wall terraced with steps. In a palace, such large open space rarely exists. The building that took up this space is all gone. One thing to note about this building area is that soy jars were arranged in a row on these steps. They served as a soy jar stand for the royal kitchen that was located right next to it.

Daejo Hall was originally the queen's quarters, but later used jointly by the king. Nevertheless, they did not sleep in the same room; the king

The entrance of Huijeong Hall

slept in the room on the left while the queen occupied the one on the right. Of course there is an open intermediary *maru* (wooden floor) between the two rooms. The king used to sleep in Huijeong Hall located in front of this building, and probably moved to the queen's quarters when Huijeong Hall was converted to an office. Unlike in Gyeongbok Palace, we cannot get inside of the building. From the outside, only the wide chairs on the floor can be seen. According to literature on Changdeok Palace, there was a western style bed in the queen's room, but we have no way of knowing what it looked like. Both Huijeong Hall and Daejo Hall have huge paintings by the finest

Inside of Huijeong Hall

Daejo Hall

artists of the day hung on both sides of their living rooms. It is not easy to have a close look at these paintings because of poor lighting and inadequate viewing angles. In front of Daejo Hall there is a structure that looks like a stage. This place is called *woldae* (Flight of Stone Steps), where the queen hosted numerous royal events in what would today be the capacity of the First Lady. *Woldae* used to be surrounded by a low fence. It was only natural that the fence existed, because the sanctimonious presence of the queen could not be exposed to everyone. In accordance with the doctrine that stipulates a rigid distinction between men and women, the fence was a kind of blockage that was created to prevent the queen from being exposed to males in the palace.

Adjacent to Daejo Hall, the royal kitchen interestingly also had Western features. It has columns lined with white tiles and a cast-iron stove—features that are hardly found in a traditional Korean house. These elements of Western design were incorporated into the building,

The royal kitchen

probably because King Sunjong, the last emperor of the Joseon Dynasty (the son of Emperor Gojong), continued to live in Changdeok Palace even after the start of Japanese colonial rule. A little further inside the palace, we see a building called Gyeonghungak. It used to keep the garments given by the emperor of the Ming Dynasty, but frankly I do not wish to talk about the buildings here. The reason is that of Huijeong Hall, Daejo Hall, and Gyeonghungak Pavilion, there is no original building left. The huge fire of 1917 burned down all the original buildings and the buildings that we see today are ones that the Japanese colonial government relocated from Gyeongbok Palace and remodeled in Changdeok Palace. Perhaps this is why they appear somewhat strange and out of place. What we must pay close attention to in the area behind Daejo Hall is *hwagye*, the flower steps. We will not talk about *hwagye* here since we have already covered it in our tour on Gyeongbok Palace. I must add, though, that the sight of the *hwagye* left unattended is troubling. The flower steps, which otherwise would look far more beautiful, only seem to make the landscape more bleak. It is difficult to believe that the queen's garden in a superb palace like Changdeok Palace is left in such a depressing state. All we can see are a few pine trees and some oddly shaped stones, and thus the scenery looks uninspiring to say the least. If only we could see *hwagye* as they were in the past. At the top of *hwagye*, we see the gates that lead to the outside. In fact, we have to go through one of the gates before directly reaching the pond located in the most beautiful garden in this palace, famously known as Rear Garden. We cannot use the gate today because it remains shut. Instead, we have to leave the palace and go through a large street to get to the pond area. This route, which we will talk about shortly, is not a very good one for appreciating Changdeok Palace. For now, let us leave the royal living quarters with this thought in mind.

As we walk out, we can see a few isolated trees standing amidst a

Hwagye behind Daejo Hall

S e o u l

lawn. As I have said before, it is very unusual to have such an empty space in a palace. Of course the area here is replete with buildings, one of them being the place where the *Diaries of the Royal Secretariat* were written. Seungjeongwon, the Royal Secretariat of the Joseon Dynasty, had to be located just a stone's throw away from the king. A building right in front of it suddenly comes into our line of vision. Originally this place was not a garage, but a conference hall of the royal functionaries. It was converted to a garage during the reign of Emperor Sunjong, who technically had no subjects under Japanese colonial rule. Now this place displays not only the automobiles of Emperor Gojong and Emperor Sunjong, but also the royal sedan chair for Emperor Gojong and his mobile lounge in which he could rest during trips.

There is an amusing anecdote told of the emperors' automobiles. Emperor Gojong will be remembered as the first Korean person to ride in an automobile in Korea. It was in 1903 that he first rode in a Ford-made automobile. As the story goes, the automobile made so much noise that his ministers implored him not to ride in it. They thought the noise too disgraceful. This automobile, however, vanished without trace after the Russo-Japanese War that broke out in 1904, and no one knew what had become of it. Later in 1911, Emperor Gojong purchased another automobile from the Daimler Limousine Company in England. This is the automobile that we see today housed in the royal garage. About ten years ago, the South Korean government decided to restore the automobile that had been left idle until then. Specialists who were sent from the Daimler Company for the consultation were astounded to find the auto parts preserved in their original state even 80 years after the automobile was made, adding that the automobile should be a National Treasure. Rumor has it that it is the only remaining automobile among the ten identical

Royal garage   Royal automobile

automobiles made at the time. We learned, however, that the automobile, which was restored perfectly by Korean technicians with the aid of the Daimler Company, cannot run. In light of this anecdote, it seems the Joseon royal family was the most modernized group of people in Korea at the time. The first use of electricity in 1887 in Gyeongbok Palace and the first ride in an automobile in 1903 testify to their pioneering modernity.

When we look to the left, away from the royal garage, we find a cluster of buildings. For convenience's sake we call it the Nakseonjae Pavilion area. This is where the king or his family resided, but there are some other reasons why it is given attention—this is the area of Changdeok Palace that was used until most recently. Amidst the interwoven histories of Korea and Japan, this is where the last crown prince of Joseon resided. His name was Yi(Lee) Eun, also known as King Yeongchin, and he was forced into marrying Yi(Lee) Bang-ja (whose Japanese name was Masako), a member of Japanese royalty. King Yeongchin was the second son of Emperor Sunjong. Upon becoming Crown Prince, he was taken hostage to Japan and became forcibly Japanized. This was all part of the Japanese scheme to perpetually

King Yeongchin and Madam Yi

Main gate of Nakseonjae

deprive Joseon of its independence. The marriage between the two was part of such calculation. Although the couple tried to return to Korea after the end of World War II in 1945, they were denied entry to the country by the new South Korean government that strongly disliked the Yi family. Moreover, they were not even allowed to have their Korean nationality reinstated. Not until 1963 were they allowed to return and settle in this Nakseonjae Pavilion area. King Yeongchin passed away in 1973, and Madam Yi Bang-ja also passed away here in 1989. Other royal family members led far more complicated and miserable lives, but this is not a discussion for this book. Madam Yi dedicated her life to welfare work for the disabled until her death, and she received occasional media coverage. Reportedly, Japanese tourists thought it a great honor to meet Madam Yi in person when visiting Korea; this is probably because it is almost impossible for them to meet or seem members of the royal family in

Japan. King Yeongchin and Madam Yi had one son between them, and his fortune was as checkered as that of his parents. While studying in America, he met and married a white woman. When she failed to bear a son, the family forced him to divorce her. All things considered, the royal family of Joseon ended in tragedy.

Huwon(Rear Garden)—The Most Beautiful Garden in Korea

Leaving all such gloomy tales behind, let us now go over to Huwon, more commonly known as Biwon (Secret Garden). A tour of the Nakseonjae Pavilion area, which is designated as a special tour area, requires an extra admission fee and is permitted only on set days. Still, it is worth visiting at least once for its buildings with alluring beauty. This time we just have to satisfy ourselves with the pictures of the area, and move on to Huwon.

On the way to Huwon, there is a gate at the mouth of the street leading up to Huwon—the entrance to Changyeong Palace. From here, we can see that the street is very broad, but it is not portrayed in this way in paintings of the past. As I walk along the wall enclosing Huwon, I begin to feel that the sight of the street is deplorable. Streets of such width could not have existed in the past. This street is detrimental to the intricate harmony of nature and the work of human hands orchestrated by Huwon, harmony so subtle as to defy distinction between the two. Morever, it did not even exist here originally. Old paintings show that there were several gates to Huwon as well as walls to surround it. We are not sure which way was taken by the king and his suite to enter the garden. However, one thing we can say for certain is that they approached the garden unnoticed and very quietly. In other words, they would not have moved along the side of such a wide street. They would not have wanted the king's procession revealed with fanfare while he was on the way to the most private space in Changdeok Palace.

The only way to make sense of this dilemma is to assume that those in charge of the maintenance of this place may have thought such a wide street could better accommodate a huge influx of visitors. If so, should sightseers not be informed of such a fact? Those unaware of the truth behind this road would firmly believe that the king and the queen trod on this wide path. Furthermore, they might presume that the gardens of the Joseon Dynasty would be as shabby as the street. We come across the same situation in Huwon, but we will discuss it later. At any rate, let us pass over a little hill leading down to Huwon. Coming down the hill, we can gradually make out the sight of a beautiful pond. This is Buyongji Pond (Buyongji), regarded as the most beautiful feature of all royal gardens in Korea. Buyongji Pond is translated as Floating Lotus Pond, 'buyong' meaning 'floating lotus' and 'ji' meaning 'pond.'

Buyongji Pond 1

The overall shape of the pond is rectangular. We have already offered the standard academic explanation of the meanings embedded in the geometric shapes: that the overall rectangular shape represents the shape of the earth and the round islet in the middle represents heaven. Once we arrive here, no further explanation is needed. Just the sight of it can allow us to fully savor its ethereal beauty. Many tales have been told of this garden. One story goes that a Korean brought a Westerner here— probably a French person—wanting to show this foreigner the most beautiful garden in Korea. After letting his friend get a good look of the garden without saying a word, the Korean suggested leaving. The Westerner reminded the Korean he had yet to see 'the most beautiful garden,' to which the Korean replied that it was what they had seen thus far. The surprised foreigner is said to have asked, "How could this possibly be a garden? It is nature." This tale is often cited when Koreans make a case for their traditional gardens as being the most nature-friendly

Buyongji Pond 2

gardens in the world. However, it remains an open question whether the Chinese and Japanese who share the same culture sphere with us will agree with this position.

Come to think of it, objections to this argument are not likely to be easily dismissed. Let us consider one conceivable counterargument. If the shape of a pond is rectangular, is this not itself an ample sign of human touch? In nature, it is difficult to find a shape so sleekly rectangular as that of a Korean garden. Another question may naturally arise concerning why those who planned this garden went out of their way to dig a pond in the ground instead of creating a natural one by trapping flowing water. In addition, the argument continues, the idea that the shape symbolizes earth is equally contrived. It is possible to argue that people who see this pond for the first time are not likely to regard it as embodying heaven and earth, since thinking of earth as a rectangle and heaven as a circle is a forced method of conceptualization. *Hwagye* (the Flower Steps) next to the pond is not free from such criticism either. Some people may question the purpose of such formal steps when planting flowers on the hill and placing rocks instead would make the garden look genuinely natural. All these arguments may well make sense. Nevertheless, it is true that despite such an artificial arrangement, this garden does look natural. Apart from digging a pond and building the flower steps, few man-made devices were incorporated into the garden. We see, of course, a few houses and pavilions, but they do not look terribly artificial as they give an impression of being part of nature and not against it.

How do we go about properly appreciating this garden? First of all, we should find out for whom it was built and where in the garden this person's seat is located. This garden, of course, was made for the king. As shown in the picture, his seat is located inside the pavilion that is in the

Side view of BuyongPavilion

middle of the pond. Thus, the most beautiful view of this garden was intended for the king and can be enjoyed from this pavilion. The pavilion is in the shape of a cross, and the most highly raised part in it must have been the seat of the king. Koreans say they are proud to be the only people in the world to make one side of a pavilion projected out over water, but we have yet to vet the claim by looking into the cases of other countries one by one. At any rate, it would be quite an experience to sit on the front section of the pavilion because of the sensation of floating on the water. A seat deeper inside of the pavilion would reveal the breathtaking scenery captured in the doorframe. Tourists usually do not go toward the pavilion, and this is the same as saying that they do not wish to relish the garden. But let us come over to this side and view the landscape through the door. We see a round islet in the very front, and not only the sky but also trees, clouds, and buildings on the steps mirrored in the water. As we have discussed earlier, borrowed landscape is a technique that borrows the view beyond the garden and places it before us in a different form. In this way, we are able to have the entire sky come into the garden. This pond garden is said to be beautiful all year round, but it is

Buyong Pavilion and its interior

particularly beautiful in autumn, they say, when the trees bursting with brilliant autumn colors show off their beauty twice over—in the fallen leaves on the ground and reflected on the surface of the pond. Indeed, the beauty of the pond, captured in the pictures taken around this time of the year, is simply beyond words.

However, a closer look at the pavilion reveals some problems. First, it is not properly cleaned. Even if it is closed to the public, I still think it should be kept clean. In addition, the doors do not appear tightly attached to their hinges. The pavilion looks fairly good from a distance. Closer up, however, we find it riddled with problems. There is a ubiquitous presence of filth and the *hanji* is coming loose from the doorframe. The litany of complaints can go on indefinitely. It seems that Koreans still need to learn to pay attention to such minute details. Unfortunately, we see another much more serious problem. As indicated by the garden's other name—Biwon (Secret Garden), it is a very private and secretive area. Neither tour guides nor guide plates ever mention that there used to be walls around the garden. They do not point out this extremely important aspect of the garden, the value of which is reduced

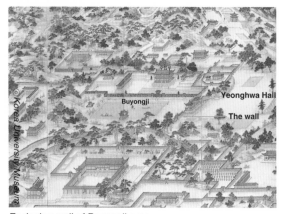

Buyongji

Yeonghwa Hall

The wall

Enclosing wall of Buyongji area

by half without the enclosing walls. In their presentation of the garden, tour guides fail to mention this point and instead give only peripheral facts such as the holding of state examinations in front of Yeonghwa Hall. Let us take a close look at the garden while imagining it surrounded by walls. The inside space, then, will feel much more like a snug and comfortable place to rest.

Another problem catches our eye—we keep digging up problems because they can help us have a better understanding of this area. There is an islet in the middle of the pond, on which stands a large pine tree. The tree itself is a wonderful addition to the overall view. The problem, however, is that it would be a severe impediment to the king's view from his seat in the pavilion. As a result, he would not be able to enjoy the beautiful flower steps, the buildings and the scenery mirrored in the pond. To verify our hypothesis, we will examine some old paintings. On this painting, only small trees are planted on the islet; I think this is the way the arrangement should have been. Only with such short trees could the king have been able to relish the surrounding landscape, his view clear of any obstacles. And the painting also portrays two boats. It is recorded that the king and his ministers fished in this pond and still present are the very boats they may have used for this purpose at the time.

Across from the pavilion lie the flower steps, in the middle of which there are three gates. There is also a large building at the top of the steps. This building was used for various purposes, but one of its important functions was to serve as what would today be a research institute, the think-tank of King Jeongjo (reign 1777-1800), one of the most astute kings of the Joseon Dynasty. This academic research institute is called Gyujanggak Archives, and its namesake archives currently exist as a part of Seoul National University. But why does *hwagye* have three entrances? The middle entrance was for the king's exclusive use and the other two on the side for his ministers. Let us think for a moment about the inscription on the king's entrance. It reads 'Eosumun,' meaning 'the Gate of Fish and Water.' The name was intended to remind the monarch that he is a fish while his subjects are the ocean; in other words, his

Gyujanggak Archives

subjects are as indispensable to him in the way that fish cannot live without water. From this we can learn that the rights of the Joseon people were theoretically no less powerful than the kingship even under an absolute monarchy like that of the Confucian Joseon Dynasty—at least powerful enough to be able to admonish the king. But people who see this place are likely to wonder about these three gates that each stand alone without being connected to anything. I myself wondered about this when I first saw these gates, but my curiosity was quenched when I looked at an old painting of this spot. The painting shows that from either side of Eosumun Gate ran a low wall. In short, it was a boundary demarcation. This would then explain why the gates are at their current location.

The landscape including the pavilion, seen from Gyujanggak, is equally beautiful. Much to our dismay, however, the absence of walls around Yeonghwha Hall prevents the concentration of energy. I cannot seem to remove the wish for walls from my mind. The name of this pond means 'lotus,' so it is natural that lotus flowers should be planted in the pond. Lotus blossoms in full bloom would be a sight to see, as well as

Bullomun Gate

the view of the sky and the buildings reflected in the openings between the lotus blossoms. At any rate, let us have a full view of this garden from various angles while walking around the pond. Afterwards we will move on to Aeryeonji Pond which is right next to it. In order to go to Aereyonji Pond, we have

Aeryeongji Pond

to pass through Bullomun Gate (the Gate of Eternal Youth), which literally means that one would stay forever young on passing through it. What is more noteworthy than the name itself is the fact that this gate was made out of a single stone. Such was the ancient people's wish for longevity that they gouged out almost all of the stone into a huge opening. Upon walking through Bullomun, we see another pond with a pavilion immediately to the right. The pond is Aeryeonji Pond. I expected to find a great deal of lotus flowers in the pond in accordance with its name, but not many can be seen. Overall, this pond garden is too simplistic in various repects. Views from the outside of the pavilion are not particularly inspiring. The correct way of seeing this part of Huwon is to capture an accurate viewpoint—that is, to look out of the pavilion as we did in Buyongji Pond. Beautiful scenery comes into view especially when brightly-colored trees are framed in the pavilion columns in autumn. Since the surroundings of the pond look too simple, we take a look at the old painting to detect any change, but we can hardly find anything in the appearance that is drastically different from that of the past.

Just a little distance from Aeryeonji Pond stands a house named Yeongyeongdang. The king, whose confinement to the palace always made him curious about the lifestyle of nobles, allegedly had this house built to copy the style of an upper-class villa. However there are some scholars who argue against such an explanation; to them, the house is too large to be used by the upper-class. We still do not know for sure which argument is more historically accurate. In front of the house there is a

Interior of Yeongyeongdang

bridge. Next to it is an oddly-shaped stone with four toads engraved on it, symbolizing the moon. It is as if we passed the moon, crossed over the Milky Way—symbolized by the stream— and finally entered the world of a Taoist hermit. This is because the

Reception Hall

entrance of the house is thought to lead to the palace where these hermits live. Since we have already discussed this type of *hanok* in some detail, I do not feel it necessary to explain it further. One noteworthy attribute of this house is the arrangement of *sarangchae* (men's annex) and *anchae* (women's annex). In the Joseon Dynasty, the upper class had the *sarangchae* and the *anchae* placed far apart in the front and in the back, following the tenet of Confucianism that stipulated rigid gender segregation. Therefore, the *sarangchae* was built near the gate for the master of the house to receive his guests. The women's annex, *anchae*, was placed in the inner area of the house and men who were not family members were absolutely forbidden to enter it. Strangely, however, the two annexes in this house are located side by side. We can tell the house is very well-built and kept clean. Right next to the main building of the house, there is a unit used both as a reception room and a study. The sides of the house are lined with bricks—probably in imitation of the Chinese style—an act of extravagance in terms of Joseon architecture. It should also be pointed out that the pent roof makes the house look odd. It was designed to prevent the light of the setting sun from deeply making its reach into the house that, interestingly, faces the west;

however, to my eyes, they seem to do a disservice to the otherwise beautiful appearance of the house.

This house is said to be the place where Emperor Gojong and Emperor Sunjong received foreign dignitaries. Such a regal usage may explain the elegance of the house. The pavilions at which we will stop by in Huwon all belong to Yeongyeongdang. This display of extravagance has provided fodder for the opinion that the house may not have been meant for an upper-class family. Let us take a quick look and move on to a more serene area of Huwon. With the presence of lush woods, numerous ponds and pavilions, this is probably the most graceful place in Changdeok Palace. Since this area is open to the public only one day of the week (Thursday) from April to November, we have to make sure we do not miss this day. We are allowed to come all the way up here since this is a day on which unlimited access is permitted. Such a tour costs five

Fan-shaped pavilion in 2000's

times the regular admission fee, but we are not likely to regret spending the extra money upon seeing Huwon. In a sense, this part of Huwon Garden is more beautiful than the Buyongji area that we have just seen. The path on the hill is peaceful and elegant, with beautiful pavilions and ponds scattered around it. In the thickly forested interior of the garden, we feel as if we are in a village nestled in the mountain even though Changdeok Palace is located in downtown Seoul. The well-maintained paths have a calming quality.

The first things we see when walking down the forest path are a fan-shaped pavilion and a pond that takes a unique shape. The pavilion is called Gwallamjoeng Pavilion. The pond is named Bandoji Pond for the similarity of its shape to that of the Korean peninsula. We cannot say this area is not beautiful, but at the same time there is something different about it. The shape of the pond is particularly so. Most of the ponds we

Bandoji Pond in 1910's (Source: Cultural Heritage Administration of Korea, *Changdeokgung Sajincheop* (Pictures of Changdeokgung), p. 41)

have seen are rectangular, but this pond breaks rank to take on the rabbit-shape of the Korean peninsula. Another unusual feature is the presence of stones that line the pond; this decorative technique does not seem Korean at all. We also find the pavilion equally unusual, because it has a fan-shaped plan unlike typical Korean pavilions that are rectangular. To find out more about this exceptional design, I think we need to go back to the old paintings. Our examination reveals that such an arrangement did not originally exist in Huwon. In other words, it cannot have been here. In the painting are only three ponds with no sign of a pavilion. In addition, a pavilion called Seungjaejeong Pavilion, which is now located across from Bandoji Pond, is not present in the painting. However, when we look at a picture taken during the Japanese colonial period, we find Gwallamjeong Pavilion roofed with tin and a pond

Jondeokjeong Pavilion in 2000's

shaped like a peninsula with even a bridge built over it; the garden on this picture looks unmistakably Japanese. We cannot tell exactly when this change was made, but it is clearly another attestation to the extent of the damage done by Japanese colonialism. Fortunately, the presence of a slightly exotic building and pond in this area does not look so bad.

Looming right over Gwallamjeong Pavilion, a pavilion named Jondeokjeong Pavilion occupies the space in the center of the garden. We can see that it is elaborately built with a two-story roof and a hexagonal column structure. The ceiling adorned with drawings of blue and yellow dragons indicates that Jondeokjeong Pavilion is a building of exalted status associated with the king. Probably he would usually take a rest in this pavilion when visiting Huwon. What I am curious to know is the mode of transportation the king used to get here and the specific ways in

Jondeokjeong Pavilion in 1910's (Source: Cultural Heritage Administration of Korea, *Changdeokgung Sajincheop* (Pictures of Changdeokgung), p. 30)

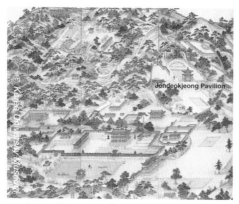

Jondeokjeong Pavilion

Jondeokjeong Pavilion area

which he took a rest. When he came to rest, whether he walked or was carried in the royal sedan chair, where he sat and what he did once he got here—I would like to know these things, but few books offer detailed explanations on such matters. Perhaps I should look this up in the *Annals* or the Royal *Diaries*, as these sources are sure to have such details. What is available for now regarding those questions is nothing more than a guess that the king would read or take a nap in a pavilion called Pyeomusa Pavilion.

I hardly think it necessary to explain this pavilion area in details either. They simply dug a pond and built a pavilion for rest in nature. Even here, we can get a glimpse of Korean people's tendency to minimize human intervention in forming a space. The only thing to point out is the pond's rather strange shape. As seen in the picture, it takes on an atypical shape. Like Gwallamjeong Pavilion that we have just seen, this pavilion does not have a spatial design that is frequently adopted in Korean gardens. When we see an old painting of this area, we also find what we see now is different from what it was in the past. They made the two separate ponds—one rectangular and the other semi-circular-into one by digging up the ground between them. As a result, the pond came to look rather unusual, but it is beautiful nonetheless. Like other pavilions in the garden, it is at its most splendid in autumn.

We are now on the last leg of our tour in the garden. We cannot help but feel as if we are going deeper and deeper into the heart of a mountain, for we have to pass through the hill before reaching the Ongnyucheon Stream area. This place is considered to be the culminating point of the beauty of Huwon. Located in the north valley, it takes up the innermost part of the garden. Now we realize we cannot go any further, as we can see the wall of Changdeok Palace running behind it. One rock that sits here in a stately manner is called Soyoam. The pavilion built next to it is named Soyojeong Pavilion after the rock. 'Soyo' literally means 'strolling' and the first chapter of *Zhuang-zi*, the most famous of Chinese Taoist texts, is entitled 'Soyo.(*Xiaoyao* in Chinese)' Zhuang-zi used the term to describe the feeling of leisurely contemplating the universe, but it is unlikely that the Confucian garden builders had in mind a Taoist

Ongnyucheon Stream area in 1910's (Source: Cultural Heritage Administration of Korea, *Changdeokgung Sajincheop* (Pictures of Changdeokgung), p. 26)

Rock stream at Poseokjeong Pavilion

philosopher when they decided on the garden's name. Five pavilions are built surrounding this rock; however, I do not feel the need to observe them one by one. Needless to say, the highlight of this area is none other than this rock.

A u-shaped channel is carved in the rock to let water flow in a circular shape and then form a small waterfall. As the story of the rock goes, the king and his ministers entertained themselves, letting cups of wine float on the meandering water and composing poems. A similar rock to this one can be found in Poseokjeong Pavilion, located at the bottom of Mt. Nam (with the same name but different from its namesake in Seoul) in the city of Gyeongju. The Poseokjeong Pavilion water channel is artificially made—well enough for cups to float smoothly, but it is not easy to imagine how well wine cups fared on this rock. The water channel does not appear to have been carved deep and nor is it particularly long. In addition, we can hardly imagine how people could drink and write poetry while sitting on top of this rather uncomfortable-looking rock. It simply looks too small for a place that engaged in such activities. More than anything, we wonder why the treatment of the rock looks so obviously touched by human hands. The right-angled corners that were formed in carving out a small waterfall give an excessively artificial impression. I have thus far expounded upon the greatest possible reduction of contrivance as the hallmark of Korean garden-making technique, but we notice a great deal of human intervention in this rock

Ongnyucheon Stream

—so much that it almost nullifies my definition. Resorting to an old painting of this area, we find little in the look of the rock that is different in either the past or the present. The same question always comes up regarding the rock everytime I visit this place, but no one has yet offered a satisfactory answer. Nevertheless, it is still true that the Ongnyuchoen Stream area is relatively much less artificial than traditional Chinese or Japanese gardens.

On the surface of this rock, we find a poem etched in Chinese characters as well as an engraving of the name of this area, Ongnyucheon Stream. It is said that King Sukjong composed the poem and King Injo himself provided the calligraphy that reads 'Ongnyucheon.' However, I do not greatly favor the tendency of Joseon people to carve letters into stones. This is because exhibiting something on such a visible place as

Changeuijeong Pavilion

the surface of this stone simply because it was composed or calligraphed by the king could undermine the overall look of the garden. It would be nicer to have the work carved on the side or, if need be, on a less visible spot. The act of carving calligraphy—which is a highly artificial act—into stone, an object in nature, do not seem to go well together. This act of stone carving is probably an old custom of Joseon scholars who so loved the written word.

Right behind Ongnyucheon Stream, there is a rather unusual-looking pavilion and a pond-like place. This is where rice was grown. Similar to the philosophy behind the dairy farm that was built near Marie Antoinette's quarters so that she could experience the life of a milkmaid, the king of Joseon would try to feel sympathy for the plight of the peasants and grow rice here as a way of acting this out. There was also the belief that if the king, the center of the world, worked on this field, all of Joseon would have a good harvest as a result of the auspicious energy created by the king's labor. It may be for these reasons that a pavilion (named Changeuijeong Pavilion) built in the ricefield is roofed with thatches rather than tiles. It is the only pavilion in the entire palace that has a thatched roof. A closer look at the roof will reveal that the interior of the pavilion is not simple but rather complex, despite having been built to resemble a typical peasant's thatch-roofed house. Also, there are three more pavilions in addition to this one that are mostly used as a place for rest or reading. We might ask whether the king of Joseon read during his leisure hours. We professors who always have to read usually wish to stay away from books while resting, but the king must have been a much more studious individual.

Leaving Changdeok Palace

This pretty much wraps up our tour of Changdeok Palace. Of course, there are some parts of the inner area of the palace that we have not seen, but this is not a significant loss because they are closed to the public to begin with. The most famous among those places that we have yet to see is called Daebodan Altar. Literally translated as "the Altar that remembers Past Kindness," it was an altar built to perform religious rites in commemoration of Emperor Shenzong of the Ming Dynasty that sent reinforcements to Joseon during the Hideyoshi invasions of the late 16th century. This alter was made in 1704, 60 years after Ming had perished, as a statement of Joseon pride in being the spiritual heir of Ming even when Joseon was a formally a tributary of the Qing Dynasty at that time. Two more emperors were honored in this fashion later on, including the founder of the Ming dynasty. This area is located in the far back of the northwest boundary of Changdeok Palace, and most people are not aware that such a place even exists. The altar was built in such a remote place because Joseon did not want to raise a diplomatic dilemma that

Man-made stream in the back of the Palace

would upset Qing. They did not want the envoys of Qing to discover the altar. This is because continuing to pay homage to Ming even after its demise was technically a betrayal of Qing. Such concerns may sound amusing to us today, but they must have been issues of supreme importance at the time. The literati class of Joseon, who believed that genuine Chinese culture was brought to Joseon from China with or without the collapse of Ming, may have been followers of Ming but also had strong pride in the traditional culture of Joseon.

The path that leads us out of Changdeok Palace is very simple. All you have to do is follow a quiet, picturesque trail. Come down from the hill, and there is a man-made stream. The water flowing down from the mountain is gathered in this stream and then directed to Geumcheon Stream in the front of the palace. As shown in the picture, the stream is considerably wide. We wonder whether such a large volume of water really flowed through this opening, but because old paintings indeed confirm that the stream was as wide as it is now, we can safely assume that quite a lot of water found its way into Geumcheon. Walking further along the stream, we see a gnarled Chinese juniper that is hundreds of years old. The tree was used to make incense for the building next-door, in which the portraits of past kings were placed and ancestral rites were regularly conducted. Once we pass this area, we will arrive at the exit. There is a store right beside the gate that sells souvenirs and books on the palace. If we have rightly felt many things about Changdeok Palace, it might be nice to purchase some related materials from this store.

Religious Relics that Have
Shaped the Korean Mind

Chapter **3**

A variety of relics can be found in Seoul, not a few of which are related to religion. Now we will search Seoul for religious relics that have helped form the Korean mentality. Korea today is strewn with churches as if it has became a Christian country, but Shamanism, Confucianism, and Buddhism comprised the mainstay of religious tradition in Korea long before Christianity began to flourish. Such tradition is directly reflected in the relics of Seoul, and we are first going to take a look at those of Shamanism—the eternal religion of Koreans.

1. Shamanism, the Eternal Melody that Moves Koreans to Dance: Going Up to Guksadang Shrine

It is interesting to note from a religious perspective that Koreans never acknowledge their dependence on Shamanism, even though it is the religion most closely intertwined with their lives. We will not further elaborate upon this aspect of Shamanism as it has already been explained ad nauseum in my other writings. When defining the nature of the relationship between Koreans and Shamanism, it is important to note that Shamanism has existed alongside the Korean people since the beginning of their history and thus far functioned as a continuous undercurrent flowing through the center of Korean culture. We should also remember that Shamanism is the root of Korean culture, with folk culture in particular.

This means that many elements of traditional Korean culture are closely related to Shamanism. A close investigation of the basis of Shamanism reveals strong ties of convergence between shamanist tradition and aspects of contemporary Korean culture, let alone traditional Korean culture. Let us look at one such example. Few people would object to listing *pansori*, *sanjo* music (virtuosic solo music), *salpuri* (exorcist dance), and *samulnori* (percussion quartet ensemble) as representative art forms of Korean folk culture and that are also popular worldwide. Yet all of these invariably originated from *gutpan* (shamanic ritual stage). *Pansori, sanjo* music, and *salpuri* have their origins in the *gutpan* of Jeolla province, while *samulnori* is an offshoot of peasant music. Peasant music is related to *gut* (shamanic ritual) in that it is performed during village *gut* or festivals. The Korean fusion cultural performance group *Nanta*, the focus of immense international popularity, is also a variation of *samulnori*. Under these circumstances, the roots of Korean folk culture can safely be said to lie in Shamanism. Even world-renown video artist Baek Nam-jun once performed his own unique version of *gut* for a colleague who passed away, and had shamans appear in one of his other works. The famed Korean composer Yun Yi-sang once recalled that one of his earliest musical inspirations was the music that he had often heard at neighborhood *gutpan*.

Koreans are more dependent on Shamanism, which is classified as a primitive religion, than any other people in the world. Although an exact figure is unavailable, the number of shamans in Korea is estimated to exceed 100,000. These shamans scattered all over the country perform *gut* everyday. A reading of the daily sports newspapers alone is enough to bring home the sheer size of the shaman population. As shown in the picture, we can find fortune teller advertisements featured in at least two bottom columns in each of these papers. This advertising space is bought by dozens of shamans to advertise their services and it is reportedly a

Fortune-teller advertisements

good source of profit. Fortune teller advertisements capture our attention even in the subway. Moreover, diverse forms of fortune telling thrive in the vicinity of university campuses; shaman houses can often be found not only all over Seoul but also throughout the entire country. Few countries in the world have as many shamans as Korea. This unique social condition can also be felt in the nature of Korean TV shows. Mureupak Dosa (Knee

TV show set resembling fortune-teller house

Master), an immensely popular TV show currently in 2008, is an alternative-version talkshow that is set in a fortune teller house with the host playing the part of a fortune teller. In the show, the host finds a solution for the problem presented by the guest and in doing so talks about various matters both discreet and indiscreet concerning the guest, which is exactly what the main task of a shaman is all about. The age-hold custom of turning to a shaman for the solution to a difficult issue is still widely practiced by Koreans.

In Search of Guksadang Shrine

Where should we go to meet Korean Shamanism? A shaman house is without a doubt the best place to gain hands-on experience of Shamanism. Nevertheless, Guksadang Shrine, the center of Korean Shamanism, is worthy of at least one visit. We already briefly mentioned Guksadang Shrine when discussing Mt. Nam. Originally located on the peak of Mt. Nam, it was forcibly relocated to Mt. Inwang in 1925 when the Japanese built Joseon Jingu (Joseon Shinto Shrine) halfway up the mountain. Guksadang Shrine was a national shrine built under the reign of Yi Seong-gye to worship the mountain deities of Mt. Nams. Later on, it was loved by shamans to the point of becoming the most reputable *gutdang* (shamanic ritual shrine) in the Seoul area. They may have liked this place all the more because it was established for them by the state.

To go to Guksadang Shrine, we get off at Dongnimmun Station on subway line 3 and climb Mt. Inwang. The route to the shrine frequently changes because of construction work on apartment houses at the foot of Mt. Inwang. When we are not sure of which route to take, we can follow directions in the guide plate placed near the subway station—a guide plate is provided because it is a historic site protected by the state. A *gut* shrine is a place to perform *gut*. Seoul alone has scores of *gut* shrines, but not many people are aware of their presence. This is because like Guksadang Shrine, most *gut* shrines are located in remote mountain areas. Koreans do not like to have *gut* shrines in residential areas because they shun Shamanism as superstition. In addition, considerable noise is made during *gut* from the use of percussion instruments such as *jegeum*

Guksadang Shrine

(the equivalent of cymbals) and *janggu* (hour-glass shaped drum). Few neighbors would be able to tolerate the level of noise produced from *gut*. The opposition to the presence of *gut* shrines has become even fiercer as the number of Christians increases. However, things were different in the past. The minute a *gutpan* started, the entire village joined in as if it were a festival. There they were able to dance as well as have free rice cake and drink. It was also a space of women's liberation—a place where women, who were suppressed most of time, could dance to their heart's content. Hence the old saying "You do not hold a *gut* lest you should see your daughter-in-law dance." Such a communal event has now degenerated into to a superstitious one that is only held under the cover of secrecy. At a time when 25 percent of Korean people are Christian, *gutpan* is being pushed farther away to the periphery of society.

Anyhow, let us climb the mountain toward Guksadang Shrine. As we come closer, the landscape, sound, and smell of the surrounding area start to change. First of all, we see a lot of buildings that look like Guksadang Shrine in the neighborhood. These buildings that appear to be Buddhist temples carry out tasks that are not unlike those carried out at a *gut* shrine. They perform Buddhist rites, but these often appear very much Korean while also mixed with strong shamanic tendencies. On a day when *gut* is held, we can hear the instruments even from here. *Jegeum* (cymbals) in particular can be heard from a distance because they are made of metal. The condition of the environment here is problematic, almost akin to that of what is commonly known as 'moon village' (hillside slums). Walking up such a path, we will arrive at a small *hanok* house. This is Guksadang Shrine (National Shrine), the head shrine of Korean Shamanism. One small building is all there is. I first visited here in the late 1980s, and was duly astounded to see the dismal state of Korean folk religion. It was simply too plain-looking to be the center of Shamanism, the mainstay religion of Korean culture. Virtually nothing has changed between then and now. But let us look at the case of Japan. Are not Shinto shrines, the center of Japanese Shamanism, supremely beautiful? They are easily accessible since many of them are located downtown in cities. Moverever, no one condemns them as being representative of superstition. By contrast, Koreans have remained consistently indifferent to the religion that constitutes their innermost disposition.

Since *gut* takes place whenever one is called for without *a prior* set date, we may be lucky enough to see one when we arrive at the shrine. *Gut* is usually held inside the building, where approximately fifteen paintings of shamanic gods are displayed. On these paintings are portrayed divinities served by shamans—gods that Koreans have worshipped in their collective unconsciousness since antiquity. Among them are gods that excel in song and dance and a goddess of prosperity. It is thought that Koreans unconsciously deified these beings as gods that would provide assistance. Of their many notable attributes, gods must first and foremost be powerful. In addition, if a great person dies harboring *han*(resentment), he or she becomes an immediate favorite in Korean Shamanism. For example, Guanyu, one of the most famous generals in Chinese history, was beheaded by his foes. Since then he has been elevated to deity status by the Chinese. Korean shamans adopted Guanyu as a god upon learning of his tragic death. They presumed that the general must have been full of pent-up *han* for being beheaded, and accepted him into the realm of the gods. Guanyu, a general who is famous among the Chinese for his intrepid character, was the incarnation of prowess to the Koreans. They thought he might need their help in

Painting of Shamanic gods

resolving his *han* and were consoled by hopes that Gwanwu would then reciprocate their kindness.

These paintings fill the walls of the shrine. The example shown here is considered a representative Korean folk painting. Generally, folk paintings are not known for sophisticated artistic technique, but the paintings in Guksadang Shrine are considered to be of high quality. Furthermore, all of them are distinctly Korean paintings that feature characters that look like the *ajeossi* and *ajumma* (middle-aged adults endearingly called by the Korean terms for 'uncle' and 'aunt') in our neighborhood. The sight of these images that mirror our own faces is comforting. For this reason, I always look at these paintings whenever I visit the shrine. I feel the unconscious spirit of the Korean people moving inside of me.

Gut and *Mudang* (Shamanic Ritual and Shaman)

Gut does not take place randomly. Clients seek the counsel of a shaman in the event of a grave happening. For instance, when a family member dies without an apparent cause or when a husband has a run of bad luck in business, a visit to the village shaman is duly made for the initial fortune-telling. If the divination tells that the event of such gravity can only be resolved with the aid of the divine spirit, *gut* will take place. We learn from this example that a shaman is a human being capable of communicating with a divine spirit. Therefore, not everybody can become a shaman. First, a person is chosen by the spirit to become a shaman. Then, he or she suffers a severe disease uncurable by Western medicine known as 'shamanic disease (sinbyeong),' possibly for years to come if the prospective shaman is unaware that the illness is a sign from the gods or is aware of this but attempts to shirk the calling to become a shaman. Lastly, the process of becoming a professional shaman is concluded when the spirit of *momju* (Lord Spirit) is transplanted in the body of the neophyte by an experienced shaman during *naerimgut* (initiation *gut*). From then on, the new shaman is endowed with the ability to perform *gut* and to solve the problems of clients by communicating with the spirit. In this regard, a shaman is a folk priest.

As we can see at a *gutpan*, *gut* consists mostly of singing and dancing. Approximately 12 acts are performed in the course of one *gut*, each made up of singing and dancing. A different god appears in each act and the shaman receives each god by performing songs and dances and delivering messages from these gods to clients. He or she offers a send-off performance when the spirit departs. Because *gut* is made up entirely of song and dance, performing *gut* is more frequently expressed as 'playing *gut*' than 'doing *gut*.' Interestingly, the religious rituals of *gut* appear more playful than solemn. In this sense, we do not feel much piety in *gut*. However, the idea of pious religious ritual actually only applies to certain religions. More often than not, religious rituals in the past were characterized by festivity. During a bout of play, participants of *gut* experience ecstasy and the knots of worry and tribulation in their heart are then undone. *Gut*, however, is not all about playing. When the spirit of someone who died harboring pent-up *han* possesses the shaman, a *gutpan* is suddenly filled with wailing. In this manner, the shaman controls clients at his or her will, freely alternating between crying and laughing. Apparently, *gut* is more of an ordinary daily event than a religious ritual. It may be for this reason that the shaman often engages in private conversation with a musician during the *gut* performance, usually the drummer. They exchange a lot of jokes as well. While the shaman never answers the phone, the drummer often does. Can you imagine a member of a choir answering the phone during a performance?

Dancing shaman at *Gutpan*

Anyhow, we can watch *gut* at ease. Since *gut* runs all day long, a meal is provided. Shamans never eat alone; instead, they always like to have company. They also offer rice and fruit before the meal. This scene of communal eating that overflows with affection strikes us as being distinctively Korean. *Gut* is not a solitary event intended only for a few.

Rather, *gut* turns into a village festival as its participants attend to other people. In some cases, shamans will tell fortunes for those who come to see *gut*. They usually offer brief divination services to all who are present. As a token of gratitude, people sometimes pay the shaman a small sum of money. In other cases, shamans let clients wear their costumes and dance. In this way, the client becomes the shaman and is allowed to play to the fullest as the master of ceremones, alternately playing out and resolving their unresolved sorrows and grudges. In *gut*, therefore, the boundaries that divide the shaman, believers, and spectators are not strongly enforced. Although there is a theoretical division of roles in *gut*, the distinction is usually entirely blurred at various points. The idea is that everyone deserves to be embraced in this spiritual journey as children of the spirits.

The tendency to care for and accomodate can also be found in the ritual content of *gut* itself. *Gut* always begins with a ritual that makes a *gut* site sacred, called '*bujeonggeori*.' *Gutpan*, where the divine spirits descend, should be expunged of evil spirits. In *bujeonggeori*, shamans scatter alcohol all over the area while singing. Clients do not have to be present at this act of *gut* because the divine spirits have not yet come down at this point. Once *gutpan* is purified, *gut* begins in earnest and lasts all day long. There is one last thing that shamans have to do after sending clients home when *gut* is concluded—to bring in and treat those evil spirits who were alienated from *gutpan*. They spend some time invoking the evil spirits that they drove away. This is an example of the generosity of Korean Shamanism, as shown in its caring of all spirits whether they are divine or evil. Korean shamans were originally practitioners of such a lofty ideal, although many of them have since become very secularized.

Koreans and Shamanism

Koreans never acknowledge Shamanism as their religion, but foreigners have long argued that Shamanism is the true religion of Korea. One common example that proves this point is the common observation concerning Korean religion of American missionaries who worked in Korea at the end of the 19th century. In a nutshell, they write that "Koreans think like a Buddhist, live like a Confucianist, but run to a shaman when something comes up." That is to say, they turn to shamans for help as a last resort in solving problems. We often hear this sort of story from shamans even today. I recently had a chance to see *gut*, which had surprisingly been requested by a Christian. The client, a merchant, asked a shaman to hold *gut* because he was not making much money. However, he did not show up for the *gut* because he felt that showing up would not be appropriate as someone who had been raised Christian. The *gut* was forced to proceed—much subdued—without the client. When I hear from shamans that quite a few Christians request *gut*, I once again realize the relevance of the American missionaries' observations.

The reason why Koreans cannot do without shamans is probably because shamans have become indispensable. Shamans help Koreans resolve problems that are difficult to discuss with anyone else. For example, let us assume that a husband has another woman. His wife is extremely upset but she cannot share what is on her mind fully with anyone else. She can turn to neither the minister of her church nor a Buddhist monk. When she goes to see a shaman, he or she not only provides her moral support through comforting words but also suggests various solutions to solve the aforementioned problem. Let us consider another example. The business run by a husband is on the verge of bankruptcy. The matter is pressing, but this also is a delicate problem that his wife cannot discuss with priests of established religions. On the contrary, she can always count on a shaman for an uninhibited discussion as well as practical assistance.

Shamans are the most distinctly Korean priests; they offer solutions that are both comforting and satisfying because they are perfectly compatible with the Korean disposition. For example, a person works hard only to reap a mediocre outcome. Asked the reason for such a turn of events, the shaman answers, "You are walking at night dressed in silk." The implication here is that people will not notice the elaborate attire of a person who walks around at night when it is too dark to see. People tend to find such an answer comforting. They think that their efforts fail to see the light because the timing is not opportune. Therefore, the problem is not within, but without. People find consolation in the idea that whatever is wrong is not their fault. They do not need to blame themselves. Solutions suggested by shamans are in many cases closely connected to religious incantations, but believers are nonetheless greatly comforted.

In this sense, I would like to call shamans psychic counselors. Just as psychiatrists help patients with problems that they cannot solve themselves, shamans try to help their clients with their difficulties. Most people who go to shamans bring along serious and difficult problems. While clients unload their problems, shamans hear them out and enthusiastically express their agreement with what is being said. A shaman is always on the side of the client. How relieved clients are when shamans not only listen to them but also offer specific support as they narrate problems that they cannot share with anyone else? In principle, counselors should never criticize their clients. What a relief it must be for the client when the shaman, instead of placing blame, takes their side. In counseling, much is resolved simply by giving vent to matters that were kept deep inside. Shamans carry out such a function at their own discretion. Of course, this does not mean that I agree to all solutions that are offered by shamans. One of the most common of these is the relocating of ancestral graves or holding of *gut*. They argue that such measures should be taken to placate ancestors harboring *han*. Clients, however, should carefully reconsider such advice before carrying it out, because they are usually not the result of a logical thought process but of the application of incantations. In any case, shamans are psychic counselors who solve the most private and fundamental problems of Koreans.

We find traces of Shamanism not only within the religious realm but also in the daily lives of Koreans, who have a reputation the world over as heavy drinkers and lovers of singing and dancing. Korean per capita consumption of alcohol is ranked second in the world right behind Russia, a fairly good indicator of how heavily Koreans drink. Moreover, it is very rare for Koreans to simply consume alcohol. Their drinking never ends with the first round. They usually go for a second round, where they usually sing while drinking. Koreans' love for singing and dancing seems to be boundless, and there is plenty of evidence to corroborate this tendency. One example is popular Korean TV programs. TV programs aired on Saturday and Sunday nights are cluttered with entertainment programs that are mostly made up of singing and dancing. In addition, a walk through downtown Seoul close to midnight on Sunday will reveal that most *karaoke* rooms are still open. Even though the next day is Monday, Koreans still drink and sing. This unusual passion for drinking, singing and dancing is so widespread among Koreans that even professors who are relatively far-removed from these activities are no exception. If a university has an overnight meeting of its entire faculty, for

Most favorite place of Koreans'-*karaoke* room

example, it always holds a talent show after dinner in which each college sings to the accompaniment of a one-man band that is invited especially for this purpose. The singing does not end here. Afterwards, faculty members of each college entertain themselves by singing all night at *karaoke* rooms. It seems that singing and dancing are engrained in the Korean gene.

There are tens of thousands of *karaoke* rooms in Korea that are intended to accommodate such zeal, and there are hardly any places overseas where Koreans are that do not have *karaoke* rooms. It is as if Koreans have only been waiting for *karaoke* machines to be invented, although the Japanese were the first to invent them; they have spread swiftly all over the country since their first import. However, whereas their love for singing is such that the whole country is plagued with *karaoke* rooms, Koreans have been slow to open libraries—places diametrically different from *karaoke* rooms. It may be that Koreans are not inherently compatible with libraries—places where we think while sitting quietly, rather than relieve our emotions or get worked up. Considering that there are only 500 libraries in all of Korea (half of which are university libraries), we can see how far removed Koreans are from books. Koreans, on the average, do not enjoy having calm discussions or holding logical debates in which issues are systematically analyzed. Instead, they like to become emotional and engage passionately with other people rather than interact in a reasonable and disinterested manner. Koreans thus flare up easily and get involved in fights often.

What, then, is the source of the Korean love of singing and dancing? Does it not have anything to do with Shamanism, if not having originated from it? As we have mentioned earlier, *gut* is filled with singing and dancing. Koreans are said to be closer to Shamanism than any other religion. If that is the case, perhaps Koreans are incorporating into their daily lives the practices of Shamanism, the religion to which they are closest. In the same way that shamans enter ecstasy, Koreans generally approach ecstasy by drinking in addition to singing and dancing. Shamans can get into ecstasy at will, but ordinary people approach the state of bliss with the aid of alcohol. Koreans are obliged to maintain formal relationships dictated by Confucian rules of propriety by day; at night, they enter a world characterized by Shamanism-style freedom—this necessitates drinking, singing and dancing. In this context, I have often argued that it is impossible to discuss Korean culture without having visited a *gutpan*. It is because the innermost aspect of Koreans is revealed not during a Confucian-style ritual but in the midst of *gutpan* that have been held from time immemorial.

Passing over Guksadang Shrine

The space around Guksadang Shrine is actually too small to be having thoughts like this. When we come up to the Shrine, there is one more thing to see. When we go up the steps to the left of Guksadang Shrine, we see an oddly-shaped rock as seen in the picture. It looks like hardened lava rock because it is covered with holes. This rock is named Seonbawi (Zen Rock) after its similarity in appearance to the robe of a Buddhist monk. Come to think of it, it does look like a robed Buddhist monk. This rock stands out the most among several other similar ones that surround it. It seems to give off energy in its unique way. When

Seonbawi (Zen Rock)

people feel energy from such an odd-looking object, they begin to pray to it. In the field of religion, this practice is called 'animism worship,' the prototype of all religion. Directly in front of the rock is a space provided for praying and bowing. A lot of prayers come to this rock, but the great majority of these are those of housewives who wish more than anything to give birth to a son. I can never understand praying to the rock in such a fashion, but I think the number of people who come to pray for a son will begin to drop as Korean society continues to undergo change. This is inevitable because the long-held Korean notion of son preference is rapidly weakening. At a time when the nation's birthrate is little over 1.3 children, I wonder who would take the trouble to come here to pray for a son.

We will leave out of our discourse a tale about this rock involving Muhak Daesa (Great Monk Muhak), the teacher of Joseon's first king Yi

Hiking trail of Mt. Inwang

Seonggye, for we think it was made up much later on. Coming up to the back of the rock, we find candle holders everywhere. No sooner had people found a slightly odd-looking rock that they started to pray. It is truly difficult to understand why human beings, the lords of all creation, pray to a non-living entity such as this stone. In other words, we cannot easily understand why a stone which has been sitting in the same place for tens of thousands of years is thought to be capable of solving problems even though the driving force of this ever-changing world comes only from thought and action. The view of downtown Seoul from the rock is better than that of the rock itself. As we go up, we find a lot of rocks similar to Seonbawi and the views from these are equally beautiful. We can see Seoul Seonggwak (Seoul Fortress Walls) a little further on up. Seonggwak is the fortress walls that used to surround Hanyang, the capital city of Joseon. We have already seen it while climbing Mt. Nam.

Walking up a little further along the Fortress Walls, we find the way to the peak of Mt. Inwang. As we have said earlier, the view of downtown Seoul on our way to the mountaintop is supremely beautiful. There is no better place than here to have a panoramic view of all of Gyeongbok Palace. This is the only place at which such a view is possible. We have also already mentioned that the view of Mt. Bukak, the mountain at the back of the Blue House that overlaps with Mt. Bukhan, the one directly behind it, is excellent. Guksadang Shrine itself does not offer much to see and is not a huge source of exercise, but when we manage to come up to the mountaintop, it becomes a good half-day excursion course. Moreover, it is the most suitable way to understand Korean folk religion.

The problem with Guksadang Shrine, however, is that it is not always open. Originally it was open all the time, but this has since changed after larger numbers of people started to visit and also because it has paintings that are designated as important folk materials. Now it is open only on days when *gut* takes place, but it is hard to visit here on those exact days without prior knowledge. However, the maintenance office sometimes lets us in when we get in touch with them in advance. Since a visit to Guksadang Shrine involves this type of rather troublesome processing, I would like to instead recommend more lively places to go in search of Shamanism: the shaman houses strewn all over Seoul in which we can see shaman shrines and visit at any time. The altar in the shrine, as seen in the picture, is particularly colorful. There we find all sorts of paintings of shaman gods hanging on the wall and statues placed on top of the altar. Among the statues are those of the Jade Emperor, considered by Koreans as their heavenly god, and the mountain gods who are unique to Korea. Placed in front of the statues are items that the gods may like according to their individual dispositions and tastes, serving as offerings.

For example, toys or candies are placed before Dongjasin (Boy god). Before a statue of, say, the General god, we find cigarettes, meat, and even whiskey because believers think that a general, a male, would like such items. However, we do not find such secular objects in front of the gods of Buddhism. Instead, we find only vegetables and grains.

Every morning, shamans offer fresh water along with a prayer at this shrine. As priests, they perform a religious ritual according to their own style. What is wonderful about visiting shaman houses is that it allows us to talk with shamans. They know a lot of mysterious and trans-mundane tales because they are endowed with an extraordinary gift that allows them to communicate with the spirits. It is thus always interesting to talk with them. We can freely ask them about certain things about which we are curious in the course of the conversation. A formal counseling session costs money but a miscellaneous question can be answered free of charge. Of all the shaman shrines that I have ever visited, the most

Altar at shaman's house

Gutpan

memorable one is in Jangheung on the outskirts of Seoul. Worshipping General Choi Yeong, a Goryeo Dynasty loyalist, as its Lord Spirit, this shrine occupies quite a spacious area that exceeds 3200㎡. The clean and well-maintained appearance of the shrine is pleasing to the eye. Nestled in the mountainside, it has a nice surrounding environment that is kept clean, whereas most of its neighboring areas are not as tidy. If the outer appearance of shaman shrines measure up the way this one did, we will surely be able to introduce our folk religion to foreigners with pride rather than hesitation.

As we conclude our discussion of Shamanism, one final thing I would like to add is that Koreans should no longer try to hide Shamanism. It is neither beneficial nor desirable to cast aside Shamanism, one of the religions that exert great influence on the lives of Koreans. Instead, we need to take a more open approach toward Shamanism. If we can polish it up, its elements in our culture can become excellent resources of the tourism industry. It is only natural that we should want to see indigenous culture when visiting a foreign country. Among things indigenous to Korea, Shamanism is at the top of the must-see list. Yet most foreigners are not aware of the existence of shamans in Korea. A place in Seoul where *gut* is performed everyday would be a tremendous tourist attraction, and it is something that foreigners who are genuinely interested in Korean culture would definitely be able to enjoy. In addition, Shamanism has many unearthed gems that remain to be developed. Still, they are left largely buried because Koreans neglect their own tradition. I would like to finish our discussion of Shamanism, very much hoping that Koreans will change the way they think about Shamanism, the basis of our folk culture.

2. Where the Spirits of Kings Rest — Jongmyo

A Joseon king lives in the royal palace while alive, but is enshrined in two different places upon his death. In Confucianism, a human being is composed of *hon* and *baek*—spirit and body. When a king dies, his body (*baek*) is buried in a royal tomb (*neung*). There are many royal tombs in Seoul and its vicinity. The most accessible of these is Seonjeongneung—there is a station on Subway Line 2 near this royal tomb with the same name. This royal tomb is located in Seoul's Gangnam ('south of Han River') area, right in the center of what is known as 'Teheran Valley,' the nucleus of the Gangnam area. Today this area is a bustling urban center, but in the 1970s it was almost entirely farmland. To get here from Hanyang, the capital of Joseon, you had to cross the Han River—not a short trip in those days. This royal tomb provides a wonderful place for Seoul citizens to relax and allows

Jeongneung

the city to provide greenery without having to build separate parks. When you visit a royal tomb like this, it is so serene that it is hard to believe that you are in the urban center of Seoul. The structure of the tomb is simple. On a hill lies a large grave, in front of which stand stone figures of civil and military officials and various animals. At the bottom of the hill is a house for performing ancestral rites. The body of a king is buried in a royal tomb like Seonjeongneung, but his soul is enshrined in the national shrine Jongmyo. Let us now go to Jongmyo, which is in the center of the Gangbuk ('north of Han River') area.

In Front of Jongmyo

It is easy to go to Jongmyo, because it is right in the center of the downtown area at Jongno 3-ga. Jongno was the main street of the capital during the Joseon era. It is then only natural that a building of supreme importance such as the shrine for royal ancestral rites was built on this street. The construction of complexes like Jongmyo was based on the system imported from China. According to the Chinese system, the shrine for performing ancestral rites of past kings was built after constructing the royal palace on the left side of the palace and on its right was built the altar or *dan* for performing rites for the gods of land and grain (Sajikdan). This system makes sense from the perspective of the *yin* and *yang* doctrine. The ancestors of the king represent the principle of patriarchy and symbolize *yang*, while the land or the grains produced from it symbolize *yin*. Is not our existence in the world made possible by *yin* and *yang*? According to Confucianism, we receive our life energy from the father and then live on the grains from the land. Therefore, Jongmyo symbolizes the principle of ascending into the sky and Sajikdan the principle of descending into the land.

Sajikdan

Joseon, in adherence to this Chinese system, constructed Jongmyo to the left of Gyeongbok Palace and Sajikdan to its right. Sajikdan, which is within walking distance from Gyeongbok Palace, is now being used as a park. Since it is at the base of Mt. Inwang, you can visit it on your way down from a hike. There is much to be said about Sajikdan, but since our subject is Jongmyo, let us move on. Before seeing Jongmyo, we should know that all of Jongmyo has been designated by UNESCO as a World Heritage Site. In Seoul there are two UNESCO World Heritage Sites, Changdeok Palace and Jongmyo. This implies the importance of Jongmyo's status among heritage sites in Seoul. But it does not stop here. The royal ancestral rites music performed at Jongmyo is also registered as a UNESCO Masterpiece of Oral and Intangible Heritage of Humanity. At Jongmyo, on the first Sunday of May each year, ancestral rites are performed for the spirits of the kings and queens enshrined here, and this ceremony is also on the UNESCO World Heritage list. We will return to this point later. Because the function of Jongmyo was so important, the Joseon Dynasty began its construction immediately after the founding of the kingdom. The building of the shrine began together with the construction of Gyeongbok Palace, but Jongmyo was completed earlier than the palace. This demonstrates the importance placed upon Jongmyo during that time. In Confucianism, ancestral rites for forefathers are the most important of the precepts, and this probably why the shrine was constructed relatively quickly.

Having received such a good impression of Jongmyo, you may find the site very different from your expectations when you arrive in front of the shrine. If you expected it to be very clean and neat because it is a world heritage site and a place where royal ancestral ceremonies are held, you are climbing up the wrong tree. In the front of the shrine is a small park that is always full of elderly people, most likely because admission to Jongmyo is free for the elderly. All kinds of activities take place here. If you take time to observe what these old people do, you will find many of them playing *go* (Chinese chess), some preaching to the crowd with a megaphone, and others holding drinking parties here and there. Some write calligraphy and display their work while others play the guitar and sing. One time I saw a group of Falun Gong practitioners practicing here in unison to protest the oppression of their movement by the Chinese government. The place has become a space for the elderly, and although old people do need such a place to gather, it does not befit the atmosphere of Jongmyo well. I wonder what foreign visitors will think of people drinking and frolicking in droves in front of the solemn royal shrine. But there are no alternative places for these old people and so it is a rather difficult situation. The front of Jongmyo is problematic as such, but the area next to the side wall is no better. Next to this wall is a parking lot while in front of that are cheap bars and people drinking in the street. I do not know what thought led to putting a parking lot adjacent to a world-renown heritage site, but it is definitely not a nice sight to see. Koreans are quick to boast of their 5,000-year history, but that pride does not seem to carry over to the preservation of great cultural relics inherited from their forefathers.

I am distressed by these things each time I visit Jongmyo. Before entering the royal shrine, there is another place to see. Across from Jongmyo is an awkward-looking building. Known as Seun Shopping Complex, it stretches a few blocks from across Jongmyo to Mt. Nam; when it was first built in the 1960s, it was the most cutting-edge building in Korea. It was the first residential-commercial building complex at the time with shops on the first five floors and apartments on the above floors. At the time, living in this complex was an enormous status symbol. Apartments were rare in those days, especially those with indoor plumbing, toilet and bathroom. Living in this building was seen as enjoying the most advanced possible lifestyle. Now it has become an outdated and underdeveloped place in which no one wants to live, a clear indicator of how much Korean living standards have improved. This is quite understandable in light of the miraculous growth of the Korean economy. There is another more serious problem about this

Seun Shopping Complex

building. It breaks the green belt that runs from Changdeok Palace and Jongmyo through Mt. Nam all the way to Yongsan. It is accused of breaking the ecologic flow that crosses Seoul. For that reason, Seun Shopping Complex will soon be demolished and an eco-friendly structure will take its place. The ambition of the Seoul Metropolitan Government is to create a green belt that will allow a raccoon playing in Maebong, the hill behind Changdeok Palace, to go back and forth between its home and Mt. Nam. As Korean economic conditions improve, more efforts are made toward recovery of the traditional Korean attitude toward environment preservation. Having touched on its surroundings, let us now go inside Jongmyo.

Entering Jongmyo

To enter Jongmyo, you need to pass through the main gate. Each time I visit, I am always perplexed as to why the main gate is so small. For a place that enshrines the spirits of kings, should the entrance not be somewhat larger? This feature does not cease to puzzle me. The statesmen of Joseon must have exercised extreme caution and been very modest. They seem to have thought that it was enough for a shrine serving the royal spirits to be a place of devotion and that all other external features including size was irrelevant to the purpose of the shrine. The buildings in Jongmyo were carefully constructed and none of them have colored patterns inside the eaves of the roof (*dancheong*). It was deemed improper to use bright colors in such a sacred place. Moreover, no hanging board was placed above the main entrance. All entrances and buildings in Joseon had boards hung outside them with edifying phrases engraved in calligraphic font for people to read and reflect upon, but such a common feature is noticeably missing here. This

Main gate of Jongmyo with mountain in the back

is thought to be due to the Confucian practice of not placing a hanging board on a shrine. This does not mean, however, that nothing was done on this gate. Originally there were steps in front of the gate that heightened its prestige. By installing these steps, the architects of Jongmyo tried to give a majestic appearance to not only the main gate but the whole of Jongmyo as well. But the steps were covered over when the front street was paved during the Japanese colonial period. Therefore, the original dignity of the gate has been greatly diminished. If the original steps were still in place, it would look much more majestic than it does now.

This gate, in keeping with conventional building techniques of the main gates of shrines, has a latticed opening that is meant to allow the spirits to enter and exit. Such a device is understandable but there is something odd about it nonetheless. If a spirit can fly freely around, there is no need for it to enter by this gate. Even if it uses the gate, it should not have any trouble going in and out since it is not a material being. Then why have a latticed opening? This is an unresolved puzzle, but there is a more perplexing question concerning Confucian doctrine that continues to be problematic even after entering Jongmyo. Fundamentally, Confucianism does not recognize the existence of spirits after death. So is it not contradictory for Confucianism to make a door for spirits to enter and then to perform ancestral rites for these very spirits? This issue has been pointed out within the academic commmunity but there has not been any satisfactory answer given by Confucians other than that there is a difference between Confucianism in theory and Confucianism in practice. That is, the existence of spirits is not recognized in theory, but it is recognized in our everyday custom and that is why ancestral rites are performed. When performing the rites, you pretend there are spirits, but in daily life you should not believe that spirits exist. I can not help but feel that this answer is inadequate.

Pathway(*eodo*) for spirits and kings

The first thing we notice

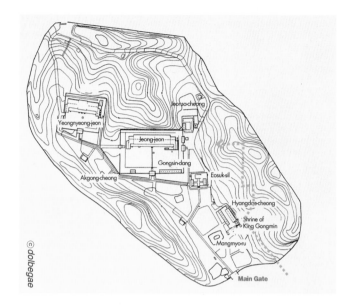

Layout of Jongmyo

inside Jongmyo is the stone pathway. It is called *eodo*, which means 'the road on which the king walks,' and if you look carefully, you will notice that it consists of three lanes. Although it is called the king's road, the path was also made for the spirits of past kings. The spirits travelled on the center lane, and it was raised a little higher than the two outer lanes because it was used by a higher entity than the king. The king and the crown prince used the outer two lanes, and the path leads all the way to the main hall, *Jeongjeon*, where the spirits are served. There are a few things to note about this pathway and the first is that it is made of rough stone. It is a reminder to be careful when walking on the pathway. That is, it is a reminder that you are on your way to pay respects to the spirits of your ancestors and to keep a pious attitude and watch your steps as you walk. Since the stones are so rough, you cannot walk very fast. And in some parts there are intentional elevations that require even more care.

In front of Eosuksil (royal bath chamber)

Such intention is well-taken, but the stones are still very rough. This may be a stretch, but in my personal opinion this may also reflect the aesthetic sensibility of Koreans. Korean people tend to like rough things. An example of this is *pansori*. It is difficult to find people in the world who favor such rough sound.

In addition to this, there is another Korean aesthetic sensibility shown in this pathway in that it turns right after only a short distance. Most people will not think much of this, but I think the aesthetic sensibility of Koreans is applied in this detail as well. If the Chinese had built this shrine, they would never have made the pathway turn in the middle in this fashion. According to Chinese sensibilities, a royal shrine like Jongmyo has to look majestic and therefore the pathway from the main gate to the main hall has to be a straight line. When you enter the main gate, the main hall has to immediately come into your sight in full glory.

East Gate of *Jeongjeon*

Near East Gate

But Koreans by nature do not like such straight, direct lines. As mentioned previously, Changdeok Palace is a typical example. Rather than showing an important building all at once, Koreans like to conceal first and then reveal it gradually in stages. It is similar to Korean Buddhist temples where the most important building, Dharma Hall, is always hidden from initial view upon entering and you need to go around a while to see it. This pathway turns at least twice before it goes straight to *Jeongjeon*. In this you can again see the Korean aversion to the straight line.

When you follow this pathway, you will see a pond and a shallow mound nearby. These were made based on *Fengshui* to harmonize *yin* and *yang*, but I am not sure why *Fengshui* theory has been applied here. In any case, after making a turn and going a bit further, we are led to the Eosuksil, the royal bath chamber where a king cleans his body and clears his mind before the ancestral rites. It is the facility for the king and the crown prince to bathe. What is interesting here is that the pathway divides in front of the bath chamber. The lanes on which humans walk turn into the bath chamber while the central lane for the spirits continues onward to *Jeongjeon*. We take a look at the bath chamber and continue on our way to *Jeongjeon*. On the way there is a wide and flat stone, which is a place for the king and the crown to have a brief rest on their way to perform the ancestral rites and put their minds in the proper state. We are now in the front of the east gate, the entrance to *Jeongjeon*. There is another wide stone here and it is also a resting place to set your mind right before entering the sacred hall. Here you compose your mind and announce to the spirits that you are entering. When you stand on this stone, to the right you will see a house. It is where the sacrificial offerings for the ancestral rites are prepared. And right next to the house is a large stone where the sacrificial offerings are placed and examined before use. On the right side of the entrance is a room where the administrators in charge of the ancestral rites slept. Now that we have had a sufficient look at these, let us go inside *Jeongjeon*.

Inside *Jeongjeon* (Main Hall)

Jeongjeon has three entrances, and if this building had been built for the living, the king would certainly have entered through the center gate.

Back wall of the Main Hall   Side view of *Jeongjeon*

However, since it had been built for the spirits of deceased kings, the center gate was reserved for the spirits and the king had to enter through the right gate. Entering from the right you see only the side view of the main hall. In order to see the front, you have to turn to the left. But before going that way, there is something here that we need to see. Let us first go up the steps of *Jeongjeon* and go to the back. This is to see the back wall of the main hall. This back wall has something not found in other buildings. As shown in the photo, the wall is made of bricks. The most expensive building material of the time, bricks were not popular in Joseon until the 19th century. Because of its elevated status, *Jeongjeon* was made of such expensive material. What is even more impressive is that this brick wall continues for 110 meters. This building is not only long but also made deep to establish the dignity of the shrine. You can see this by comparing *Jeongjeon* with the building on its right called Yeongnyeongjeon. We will talk about it more later on, but Yeongnyeongjeon is a shrine for the kings not enshrined within the main hall. Because it is less important than *Jeongjeon*, it is not as long and as wide, and thus lacks the gravitas of the main hall. Just by looking at the back wall, we can see how important *Jeongjeon* was during the Joseon period. In order to see exactly how long and majestic of a building *Jeongjeon* is, go up the steps again and look at the corridors. As shown in the photo, the repetition of columns drives home the tremendous length of this building. These two places—the back wall and the side wall—allow you to see Jongmyo from a completely different perspective, but average tourists rarely look at Jongmyo from these two vantage points.

To take a good look at the main hall, let us go right in front of it. *Jeongjeon* was not this long. That simply could not have been the case at the beginning of the dynasty because there were not as many deceased

Scenery of Jongmyo

kings. Yi Seonggye, the founder of the Joseon Dynasty, began by enshrining the Yi family patriarchs within four generations of himself beginning with his great-great grandfather. However, as a tributary kingdom, Joseon was limited to enshrining only the five nearest ancestral kings (China had a limit of seven emperors). As a result, *Jeongjeon* was quickly filled to the limit and additional shrines had to be built in which to transfer preceding generations of kings. However, after these separate shrines also eventually filled up, a permanent solution was sought upon considering the impossibility of building separate shrines forever. The aforementioned solution was to keep the memorial tablets of deceased kings in a single building partitioned into multiple chambers. When a room was filled to the limit, an additional room was created by partitioning. *Jeongjeon* and Yeongnyeongjeon today are the results of this method of partitioning and adding rooms. These two buildings are quite large, but each is a single structure.

Jeongjeon is perhaps the longest wooden building in Northeast Asia. This building began from the west (the right side) and continued being expanded to the east, totaling three extensions in all. You can see the

Front view of *Jeongjeon*

traces of such expansion at the base of the building, where there are marks left from steps that were moved. There are 19 rooms in *Jeongjeon*, and each hold one king and his wives. Since a king could have more than one wife, 19 kings and 30 queens are housed in *Jeongjeon*. In comparison, Yeongnyeongjeon has 16 rooms holding 34 royal memorial tablets. But what is the difference between the kings served in these two halls? It was not originally intended as such, but kings deemed to have noteworthy legacies are enshrined in *Jeongjeon*, while those with shorter reign and a less noteworthy legacy were placed in Yeongnyeongjeon. For example, King Gyeongjong, the son of the notorious Lady Jang, ruled for only three years. Having been very young and with no significant achievements to his name, he was automatically placed in Yeongnyeongjeon. But in the royal courts of Joseon, debate never ceased over where to enshrine deceased kings. Although in the case of Gyeongjong it is clear that he accomplished little of merit, dispute over

Yeongnyeongjeon

more distinguished kings is understandable.

It is now time to get a good look at *Jeongjeon*, but to do so we need to pay close attention to the function of this building. This is a shrine for worshipping the dead and not a space for the living. It is no ordinary shrine but one that serves generations of past kings, and therefore must be as dignified and solemn as possible. The building needs to overwhelm people. To do so, this building cannot be built to human scale. A building like this is usually built magnificently on a monumental scale. One of the most commonly used methods in building a structure on a monumental scale is to incorporate repetition. When this is applied well, it is difficult to recognize its scope. When people look at a building and are unable to get a grasp of it, they become easily overwhelmed. For example, how many stories of a building can a person take in with just one look? On average, people have difficulty in instantly grasping how tall a building is when it exceeds five stories. This is why human scale usually refers to

Interior of each room of *Jeongjeon*

buildings up to five stories high. But *Jeongjeon* does not rise up but stretches out sideways. It is stretched out by 19 partitioned rooms. People usually start to get overwhelmed after five partitions, and *Jeongjeon* is almost four times that threshold value.

To understand how overwhelmingly immense *Jeongjeon* looks from repeating the same elements, compare it with Yeongnyeongjeon standing next to it. *Jeongjeon* goes on in a single line without variation, but Yeongnyeongjeon has four rooms in the middle which are raised, as seen in the photo. Perhaps this is the reason, its overall look does not overwhelm. This building is divided into three sections with each section consisting of five rooms; therefore, it is of human scale. Since this building can be grasped in one look, it is not at all overwhelming. But the actual difference in length with *Jeongjeon* is only three partitions. *Jeongjeon* has 19 rooms and Yeongnyeongjeon has 16, which makes the difference three partitions. But how come the former overwhelms people while the latter does not? The answer lies in the use of repetition. *Jeongjeon* repeats the same pattern 19 times without interruption while Yeongnyeongjeon is interrupted every five partitions, which allows the viewer to rest

Space in front of ancestral tablet

twice in between. This is why Yeongnyeongjeon can be grasped with just one look and therefore does not overwhelm the viewer. I experience this each time I visit Jongmyo, and I am always amazed to see how one architectural device can make a building look so different.

On each wing side of *Jeongjeon* stands a building that protrudes to the front. They are interesting buildings, called *weolyang*. In adherence to the *yin* and *yang* doctrine, one building is built in the open style while the other is enclosed with screen doors. Put simply, one is closed and the other is opened. Sometimes a tent was put up here, and the king could step inside to get out of the sun or rain and get some rest. Next, when we look inside the building, we can see that the domain of the shrine extends deep inside the building. As shown in the picture, there is a rather large area in front of the place where the ancestral tablets are held. This is where the ceremonial water is placed during the ancestral rites. Aside from such practical function, this is symbolically the space between death and life, or *yin* and *yang*. The deeper part of the shrine is the space for the dead. Therefore it is a dark and full of *yin*. In contrast, the outer part where the ancestral rites take place is the space for the living. Naturally it is a bright space for *yang*. This large area is the space that

Haweoldae and Gongsindang

connects these two spaces. Therefore it has a neutral image, neither bright nor dark.

It is good to look at *Jeongjeon* up close from the front side, but to see the entire building you need to see it from its main gate. Only then can you feel its magnificence. Although this is a royal building, *dancheong* are not painted, making it look more solemn. As a place of devotion, it was probably deemed unfit to paint in bright multi-colored hues. Let us walk around in front of *Jeongjeon* and take it all in slowly. The place we are standing on now is *haweoldae*. This lower level is the base of the altar and the tablets of kings are placed one level higher in the weoldae. If you look carefully you will notice that the lower part of *haweoldae* is slightly tilted. This allows the water to flow down when it rains.

There are other buildings on the grounds of *Jeongjeon*, the most notable of which is right next to the front entrance and is called Gongsindang. This is where royal ministers who were instrumental in helping the kings achieve great legacies are memorialized. With 16 sections, Gongsindang is not a small building, but it

Mangryowi

does not look large because *Jeongjeon* is so immense and magnificent in comparison. But is it not natural for this building to look this way? The true masters of *Jeongjeon* are the kings, not the kings' ministers.

Waiting room for muscians

This building is not so noticeable because it is located right next to the walls of *Jeongjeon* and built in a similar style to the main building. However, this does not mean that the building was constructed without care. As a shrine built to serve the best of the kings' ministers, it is extremely well-constructed.

The last item that needs to be explained is called *mangryowi* and stands in the rear of *Jeongjeon*. This was built as a place to burn the incense and the memorial address papers that had been used in the ancestral rites. There are numerous theories on the reason for burning these materials. First, burning something means sending it to the sky, and therefore the act of burning symbolizes the return of the spirits memorialized by the ancestral rites to heaven. The burning of the items offered to the dead may also indicate departure. That is, it may symbolize the dead, who have reunited with the living through the ancestral rites, departing and returning to their world. It is similar to burning the possessions of the deceased after a funeral, a custom prevalent in Korea in the past. After seeing this, we can exit *Jeongjeon* from the west gate. As soon as we go out, we can see to the left a building which is open on all sides. It is interesting to note that this structure is of the lowest rank

Yeongnyeongjeon

among the buildings of Jongmyo. It is because this was the waiting area for musicians who performed music during the ancestral rites ceremony, Jongmyo *jeryeak*, which will be discussed shortly. Musicians belong to the lowest class in the Joseon social hierarchy, and therefore the building for their use was also of low quality. This building had pillars of different shapes, reflecting the fact that it was made from materials left over from construction of other buildings. Also, the building is located in a secluded corner in a wooded area. But such implications are all of the past, and now it is used as a space for showing a video on the Jongmyo royal ancestral rites. A full tour of *Jeongjeon* is tiring for the legs, so this is a good place to rest and watch the royal ancestral rites on video, 'killing two birds with one stone' as the Korean saying goes.

If you have seen *Jeongjeon*, you may choose to bypass Yeongnyeongjeon because the former has everything that you will find at the latter. But to understand *Jeongjeon* in greater depth, you need to compare it with Yeongnyeongjeon, so let us go check it out. When you enter Yeongnyeongjeon, you will feel a let-down after having seen the main hall. It is like going from a magnificent mansion of a millionaire to the smaller house of a low-level bureacrat. The grandeur of *Jeongjeon* cannot be found here, as explained previously. Because Yeongnyongjeon was built on a human scale, it fails to overwhelm. The middle four

Jongmyo *Jerye*

chambers serve four generations of the ancestors of Yi Seonggye; because this section is raised a little higher than the rest, the overall grandeur of the building is greatly diminished. In a way, Yeongnyeongjeon looks like a cauldron with two gates stretched out on each side. This effect fosters a feel of familiarity. The fact that Yeongnyeongjeon has been built of lower quality than *Jeongjeon* is shown in its *weoldae*. In the case of the main hall, its *haweoldae* was set quite high and thus displayed a sense of grandeur. In contrast, the *weoldae* of Yeongnyeongjeon is placed lower and thus makes the building feel more human and familiar.

Jongmyo Jerye and *jeryeak*

Jerye, the ancestral rites of Jongmyo, is as important as its buildings. Jongmyo Jerye, along with its *jeryeak* (ancestral rites music), was registered as a UNESCO World Heritage in recognition of such importance. But this royal ancestral rites ceremony is held only once a

Offerings devoted to kings and their wives

year and is therefore quite difficult to witness. We will not go into the details of the ceremonial procedures here, but will discuss the spirit of and the stories related to this royal ancestral worship. Jongmyo Jerye was the biggest ancestral rites ceremony of the Joseon Dynasty. In Joseon, the ancestral rites ceremony did not end with simply memorializing one's forefathers, but bestowed supernatural authority to the ruler and therefore was a political statement. Simply put, the ancestral rites ceremony was not merely a religious performance but a political act. In other words, the people in charge of the ancestral rites ceremony were those who wielded real power in Joseon society. Within the family, the father holds this position, while the king had the same role for the country. Although rare, if someone denied the legitimacy of the ancestral rites ceremony, he would be charged with the crime of challenging the state system and given the harshest possible punishment. A familiar example of this is the case of Catholic followers at the end of the Joseon Dynasty who were executed for not recognizing the ancestral rites ceremony.

In Joseon, which placed paramount importance on ancestral rites, the ancestral rites ceremony of the royalty was without a doubt the most important of all ceremonies. The scope of Jongmyo Jerye was immense. In a single day, ancestral rites ceremonies were performed for not only each of the enshrined kings but for all the loyal ministers as well. More than 5,000 ceremonial vessels were used. Food was set on the ceremonial altars as offerings—just imagine the amount of food placed in all those vessels. At the time, Jongmyo Jerye was performed each season and this was predictably a considerable burden on the royal coffers. The food served to the spirits is interesting. Since it was served to the spirits of kings, it had to be the best. Since royal food could not be same as that consumed by the common people, there was a great deal of raw food. This contrasts greatly with the fact that raw food is rarely used in the ancestral rites ceremonies held by the nobility and the common people.

The ceremonial procedure of the ancestral rites is not overly complicated. It is similar to that performed in a private household. First you greet the spirit and then offer ritual food. Then you pour liquor into a small cup and offer it three times to the spirit. Tea, rather than liquor, was used in the traditional ancestral rites during the Goryeo Dynasty when the state religion was Buddhism. But in the Joseon Dynasty, all used liquor for the ancestral rites except Buddhist temples. You may wonder why liquor was used and there are many possible answers to this question. It may be that drinking induces a low level of transcending the conscious state, similar to a religious experience. When we drink alcohol we reach a low level of ecstasy and we use liquor in religious rituals, thinking that it is the closest we can get to the state of ecstasy. After offering liquor three times, the person performing the rites must drink what is in the cup. This is the so-called *eumbok*. There are several

Officiators of Jongmyo Jerye

explanations for this partaking of sacrificial drink, but the most common is that by drinking the liquor given to us by our ancestors, we receive their blessing. Another interpretation is that by drinking the liquor that our ancestors drank, we symbolically become one with our ancestors, the source of our life. When the drinking is finished, there is a brief farewell to the ancestral spirits to see them off, and lastly, the paper on which the memorial address was written is burned to ashes to end the ceremony.

Although procedurally very similar to common ancestral rites, Jongmyo Jerye is unique in that is incorporates music and dance with the ceremony. At the *jerye* there are as many musicians and dancers as the people participating in the royal ancestral rites. The music and dance they perform, as mentioned earlier, are registered in the UNESCO Masterpieces of Oral and Intangible Heritage of Humanity. This ritual, performed for over 500 years, is the only royal ancestral rites ceremony in Northeast Asia that has been handed down for that many hundreds of years, and as such it has received worldwide recognition. Why was it not possible in either China or Japan to have such ancestral rites maintained and transmitted generation after generation? This is because neither had a royal dynasty that lasted as long as Joseon. Jongmyo Jerye was born based on the influences of Chinese Confucian doctrines, but after China fell under socialism and the Cultural Revolution in particular, the high culture of the past was cut off and did not survive in a form intact

parilmu

enough to be able to pass down.

Jongmyo jeryeak (ancestral rites music) was created based on the Confucian doctrine of ritual music. Confucius was the first to put forth the doctrine of *yeak* (ritual music), and here *ye* refers to social order, etiquette, ancestral rites and other proprieties, while *ak* means music. As is well-known, Confucius was a thinker who greatly emphasized *ye*. But together with this he also emphasized *jungyong*, or the mean. Emphasis of only 'proprieties' makes life too rigid and dry. It becomes too regimented. This needs to be balanced by softness, which is done by music by purifying our sensibilities. Music softens the temperament that has become rigid by 'proprieties.' Confucius considered a person with *yeak* in balanced proportions as one who possesses ideal personality. The great master himself is known to have often played a string instrument when happy or sad. It is been said that his musical ability was quite superb. In any case, supported by this doctrine, Jongmyo Jerye puts music together with the ancestral rites.

But when you observe Jongmyo Jerye, in addition to the music there is always an awkward-looking dance. This dance is called *parilmu* and is performed by 64 dancers forming a square with eight dancers in each line. In Northeast Asia, music and dance always go together; if there is music, it is always accompanied by dance. But the movements of this dance seem more like calisthenics than dancing. It is very slow. Not only the dance but the music is also slow and strange, sounding almost like modern Western avant-garde music. The story behind this music is that is was composed in the mid-15th century by King Sejong the Great, the greatest ruler of Joseon, from his imagination. I will not go into too much detail regarding the origins of this music, but it is said that this music had become extinct in its original home, China, and was restored in Joseon with painstaking efforts. Because this music is used for ancestral rites, it had to adhere to the principles of the universe such as *eumyang-ohaeng* (*yin* and *yang* and five elements) and also be very concise. In other words, this music is based on abstract principles rather than human emotions. That is why it sounds so unfamiliar. In the beginning it was even stranger than now, but as time passed it was gradually modified by musicians to incorporate many Korean elements. Thus, dancing to such music makes it difficult to use natural movements. Because the music is extremely restrained, the dance does not flow smoothly but is broken up into separate units of motion.

There are many technical explanations of this music and dance, and while an in-depth exploration of these goes beyond the scope of this book, there is a need to know what is generally going on in each phase of the dance. As mentioned before, there is accompanying dance and music each time an ancestral rites ceremony is held in each chamber. This music is called *botaepyeong* and *jeongdaeeop*. When the music begins, it is joined by singing as well. The content of the song is praise of the ancestral legacy. The singing is followed by dancing which expresses symbolic movements that praise the learning and military prowess of ancestral kings. This roughly covers music and dancing. There is an interesting anecdote that the king at times conveniently fell ill when the time for Jongmyo Jerye came around and had to send the crown prince in his stead to administer the ceremony. This is quite understandable because the whole procedure is extremely burdensome. If the ancestral rites are repeated in each chamber, consider how exhausting it must have been for the king. In cold weather, it would have been even more difficult to endure. Although ancestral rites are important for the king, he too is human and it is understandable how he may have not liked doing this.

This basically wraps up our visit to Jongmyo. There is another *jeryeak* that I would like to mention. Called Munmyo jeryeak, this music was played as part of the ancestral rites ceremony for Confucius. This ritual ceremony took place in Joseon's national university, Seonggyungwan, which is not too far from here. As mentioned earlier, Jongmyo is inside a complex like Changdeok Palace and Changgyeong Palace. Located right next to Changgyeong Palace, Seonggyungwan was a Confucian shrine and at the same time the foremost institute of learning in Joseon. Let us now go to Seonggyungwan and take a look at the education system of Joseon.

3. Seonggyungwan—The Top Think Tank of Joseon

The administrative system of the Joseon Dynasty was very much ahead of its time due to the existence of the state examination system. This examination system was a revolutionary political feature particularly within the fabric of premodern society. In premodern times, sons of nobility were ordinarily automatically allotted a high-ranking government position by benefit of birth and thus guaranteed all the comforts of a bureaucrat's lifestyle. This enabled the concentration of power in the hands of a few privileged members of the nobility. Under such circumstances, the political system is bound to lose its ability to function and fall prey to corruption. Moreover, talented brains from a more humble background have little chance of realizing their potential. When allowed to function properly, the biggest advantage of the state examination system lies in its meritocracy-based principles: it allows for people of ability to be chosen for government posts regardless of class. As we all know, the state examination system was originally imported from China.

Becoming a Government Official in the Joseon Dynasty

Seonggyungwan was the final checkpoint of the state examination system for the most talented brains in Korea. After a rigorous selection process involving a series of smaller exams, the final 200 were accepted to Seonggyungwan in order to prepare for the final and most important remaining examination. Before we move on, let us briefly review the exam-centered education system of the Joseon Dynasty. *Yangban* (noble) boys between seven and eight years old were sent to a small private school(*hyanggyo*) in the village to learn basic Confucian principles and calligraphy. At 15 or 16, they went to a government-run school to study Confucian classics in greater depth. Those who lived in the capital studied in *sahak*, a private school, and those who lived in provincial areas studied in *hyanggyo*, a local school annexed to the village Confucian shrine. These schools are the equivalent to secondary schools or a university preparatory course in today's education system. There are not many *sahak* that remain today, but plenty of *hyanggyo* still stand. The first round of examinations is called *sogwa*, meaning 'small examination.' One must pass this round in order to be admitted to Seonggyungwan and become eligible to take the real final examination, which is called *gwageo*. *Sogwa*, therefore, is like a college entrance examination. After passing the second round of examinations, one finally becomes a state official. The most convenient way to achieve this ultimate lifetime goal of a nobleman during the Joseon Dynasty—becoming a state official and making one's name known—was to enter Seonggyungwan.

During the Joseon Dynasty, which was dominated by Confucian ideology, fulfilling one's filial duty was the most important principle to obey and follow. There were many ways to be filially pious to one's parents, but the best that a man of noble birth could do was to become a state official. Once he became a government official, his achievement would be permanently recorded in the official family register and his title would be inscribed onto his gravestone and thus be remembered forever long after his death. Thus, gaining fame and bringing honor to one's family was considered the best way to fulfill filial duty during the Joseon Dynasty. Also, this was the best way to gain both personal wealth and honor at the same time. Because the entire social structure was built for the well-being of the upper class, becoming a statesman was the key to a happy life. In order to accomplish this, one not only had to be born into a noble family but also had to enter Seonggyungwan and successfully pass the state examination. The path to the highest education institute of the country was a tough one, as the quota was set at 200 and only 33 among these could pass the state examination that was held only once every three years.

Some Thoughts on the Nature of True Education

A visit to Seonggyungwan only has meaning if you have a prior understanding of what is meant to be a bureaucrat during the Joseon Dynasty. If you visit without any background information, Seonggyungwan is merely a small group of buildings. At first sight, it looks fairly modest in scale considering that it is a national university. The campus consists only of a shrine that worships Confucius, an auditorium that also functions as a classroom, dormitories, cafeteria, and a few school-affiliated buildings here and there. Seonggyungwan is situated inside Seonggyungwan University, but most Koreans only know of the university and not the identity of Seonggyungwan. There are even students of the university who are unaware that Seonggyungwan is a part of their campus and was the best state-sponsored university of the Joseon Dynasty. Seonggyungwan University got its name from Seonggyungwan, and for this was originally founded by a Confucianist foundation. However, the university has no affiliation with this foundation as of today.

As previously mentioned, we must go to Seonggyungwan University

文廟案内圖

Auditorium

Confucius Shrine

Dormitory

Map of Seonggyungwan

to see Seonggyungwan. As soon as we enter the front entrance of the university, it is on the right. Seonggyungwan is largely divided into two parts: as can be seen in the photo map, the front is the area of the shrine where ancestral rites for Confucius are performed, and the rear part is the education area where studying takes place. On normal days, the shrine area is locked up and cannot be seen. It is officially opened to the public only biannually when the aforementioned ancestral rites are performed. However, the maintenance staff will open it and even give a tour of the facilities if a written request is made in advance. In contrast, the rear section is always open to the public. We will first enter the Confucian shrine, the most important section of Seonggyungwan.

Before we look around the shrine in earnest, we may wonder why there is a shrine for ancestral rites on the grounds of a national university, an institution of modern Western-style education. If we apply this to the present-day, it is like having a shrine for deceased scholars on the campus of Seoul National University, currently the top national university in Korea. This would be rather strange from a modern-day standpoint. The shrine of Seonggyungwan is not merely ornamental; students perform ritual ceremonies here twice a month. The current Seoul National University students performing ancestral rites, even in abridged form, twice a month is unimaginable. Seonggyungwan was not the only place where ancestral rites for Confucius and studying were done at the same time. Both the ancestral rites ceremony and education were also simultaneously undertaken at the previously mentioned *hyanggyo* (provincial state-sponsored schools) and *seoweon* (private schools). To be more precise, a *hyanggyo* or a *seoweon* was different in structure from that of Seonggyungwan. While Seonggyungwan places the Confucian shrine in the front to emphasize its supreme importance, a *hyanggyo* or *seoweon* locates the shrine in the back.

There is a question that we can ask at this point. Why did students in Joseon (and China), while engaged in their studies, also perform ancestral rites worshipping the spirits of ancient sages? The answer is directly related to the Confucian view on education. In Confucianism, education involves more than just reading many books. An authentic book consists of the words and deeds of the ancient sages. They offer a model of living on various aspects of life for students to imitate, and students only need to do exactly that—imitate and act out the advice of the sages. In other words, rather than advocating something new, students needed only to imitate the ancient sages to achieve 99% completion of their scholarly goal. Any problem would lie in the failure to do so perfectly, not in the failure to develop new doctrines as is taught in universities today. In some respects, such a view can seem very conservative, but perhaps education is not all that difficult as long as one has a great teacher. There may be various goals for education, but few will disagree that the most important of these is to become a true human being. The best way to become a true human being is to follow the greatest teacher. Because the teacher is a true human being, you will also become a true human being just by imitating him. This is the basic philosophy on which the Confucian view on education is fundamentally grounded. True education for Confucius was first and foremost doing one's moral duty as a human being. Scholarship came second. This is well-expressed in the maxims of Confucius. Confucius said, "A human being must first show filial piety toward one's parents at home, and next show respect towards others, and pursue learning if there is time left." Studying is done after fulfilling the duties of a human being (from the Confucian standpoint), and it is not something on pursues ahead of the work of 'becoming' a true human.

Such precept is the justification behind why Confucian learning institutions regularly perform ancestral rites to the sages. The sages are the eternal mentors of the students as well as the final destination toward which their lives should be headed. However, the sages are deceased and not here with us. Therefore, the only way to remember them is to regularly perform ancestral rites. The students perform ancestral rites for the sages at least twice a month and vow to learn and live like them. This is certainly an outstanding educational method. In front of the sages, the student reflects upon them and in doing so examines himself, and these renewed vows are immediately put into practice in the studying area just behind the shrine. Simultaneous imitation and study is perhaps the most desirable educational method. Modern education appears to be weak on the imitation element. A lack of people who can serve as mentors may be a critical weakness of modern education. There are not many educators who think about this these days, but I am moved to think about the meaning of true education each time I visit Seonggyungwan.

Seonggyungwan 1 – At Daeseongjeon (Grand Hall)

The best way to see Seonggyungwan thoroughly would seem to be by entering through the main gate, but unfortunately this is impossible. A *sinmun* (divine gate), the main gate is the entrance through which only the spirits of the enshrined sages may enter and exit. This entrance, therefore, is opened only twice a year for the ancestral rites ceremonies. Even the king is not permitted to enter through this gate and must use the Eastern gate. In the picture, we can see that from this divine gate there is a *sindo* (divine path) that leads to the shrine of Confucius. It is forbidden for a human to walk on this path, but if it is necessary to do so, you have to announce your intention to the spirits before walking on it. Since we cannot enter through the main gate, let us take the side entrance. From the side gate, we enter into the studying area, but let us take a look at this area a little later. Upon entering the shrine area, we will notice that it is quite small. The main buildings in this section are the shrine of Confucius and the corridor surrounding the area. Marked by solemn features, the shrine is a very simple building without the ornamentations and multicolor patterns found in Jongmyo, the royal ancestral shrine. The name of this building is Daeseongjeon or Grand Hall, the name used for all shrines of Confucius in both China and Korea.

The birthplace of Confucius, as is well-known, is Qufu in China's Shandong Province. In Qufu there is a Confucian shrine of the same name, but in scale it cannot be compared to Daeseongjeon of Seonggyungwan. Built like a palace, its compound is so huge that there

Daeseongjeon and divine path

are dozens of buildings and gates. Of course it was built on such a large scale because Qufu is the hometown of Confucius, but we can also see that the people of Joseon had relatively modest taste. But what is interesting is the Chinese came here several decades ago to learn how to perform the ancestral rites ceremonies and in doing so videotaped all the ceremonies performed at Seonggyungwan. Of course they had their own form of ancestral rites, but it was all lost as China endured the ravages of socialism and the Cultural Revolution. In contrast, Korea had maintained the rituals first developed in the early Joseon era in their original forms and the Chinese wanted to learn this from the Koreans. Although I am not an expert on this issue, I am not sure to what extent the Chinese could have referred to the Korean materials, since the ancestral rites ceremonies performed for Confucius are bound to be very different in both countries.

Daeseongjeon is a great building. First built 600 years ago, it was reconstructed after being burned down during the Hideyoshi Invasion of 1592 and is therefore actually about 400 years old. It is quite old and thus designated as a National Treasure. Because it is locked up most of the time, many people do not know what is inside Daeseongjeon. The interior is quite plain. With Confucius at the head, the only objects present are the memorial tablets (*sinwi*) of great scholars of China and Korea. A *sinwi* is simply a block of wood on which the name and pen name of a person is written. Normally it is covered by a wooden box and the cover of the box is only removed in time for the ancestral rites ceremony. From this, we can see that Confucianism has no interest in beautifying the building that enshrines the sages. Confucius is the founder of Confucianism, and yet the shrine that upholds him is extremely austere. The situation is completely different for Buddhism and Christianity, which is easily seen in how splendidly the Buddhists and Christians decorate the buildings that enshrine their founders. By contrast, Confucianism eschews any outward appearance of splendor. It instead focuses on searching one's mind to find and stomp out any bit of selfishness. According to Confucianism, our heart is inherently good, but selfishness takes root when we seek self-interest that is at odds with this goodness. There is a famous story where a student once asked Confucius about the philosophy behind *The Book of Poetry*, one of the great books of Confucianism. To this the master replied, "It is having no wickedness in one's thoughts." If we put our individual goals before the interest of the whole community, this becomes selfishness. When we come to Seonggyungwan, we need to meditate deeply on the ideals of Confucianism. Merely looking at the buildings is not meaningful, and is the same as declaring that you do not want to learn anything from them.

However, this does not mean we should limit ourselves to just understanding the ideals. Inside Daeseongjeon are the memorial tablets for 39 great Confucian scholars. Along with the *sinwi* for Confucius, there are memorial tablets for 15 of his disciples and six giants (including Zhu Xi) of Neo-Confucianism from the Song Dynasty. In addition to these sages from China, there are memorial tablets for 18 preeminent Korean Neo-Confucian scholars. The *sinwi* for Confucius is placed at the deepest inner position in the center. Next to this are placed the tablets for the four great disciples of Confucius. In such order the memorial tablets for other sages are placed on both sides of the center. As mentioned before, the shrine door is normally locked. When we look at the closed door, we notice that the two wings of the door do not meet at the edges, creating a slight gap in the center. Initially it was thought that the wood, being old, lost its shape but it turned out that this was not the case. The gap was said to be created intentionally at the time of the door's construction to allow the spirits of the sages to enter and exit the shrine. On the one hand, we can see the thoughtfulness in caring for the ancestral spirits. But on the other, it is interesting to note that, although Confucianism does not acknowledge the existence of spirits after death, its followers engage in acts that appear to contradict Confucian doctrine at its very sanctuary.

Officiators of Munmyo *Jerye*

I have mentioned that students here perform an ancestral rites ceremony for the sages twice a month. They probably light incense and perform the rituals in a simple manner. But twice a year (in

February and August of the lunar calendar) a grand ancestral rites ceremony is performed and this is known as Seokjeonje. Much food is prepared and offered at this event, and as with the royal ancestral rites ceremony, the court music orchestra from the National Center for Korean Traditional Performing Arts is mobilized. Along with the musicians, a troupe of 64 dancers is also put into service. Because Confucius is almost equal in status to an emperor, the ceremonial protocol is equal to that performed for an emperor. This ceremonial protocol is called Munmyo Jerye. It is called this name because Confucius was referred to as Munseongwang, (literally 'the king who completed learning') since he was considered to be the one who brought learning to its completion. Hence, Munmyo Jerye can be deciphered as 'ceremony for the esteemed person who has completed learning.' We will forego a description of the details of this ceremony because it is almost the same as that of Jongmyo Jerye discussed earlier. There is no difference in the greeting the spirits, offering liquor three times and then reading the memorial address. Like the Jongmyo ceremony, it has music and dancing while the ritual food and liquor are offered. If there is a difference, it is in the music. But if you are not familiar with this type of music, it is difficult to know how it differs from the music of Jongmyo Jerye.

Then, who is the host of this ancestral rites ceremony? The head of Seonggyungwan may come to mind, but this is not the case. Who is Confucius? Is he not the most important and highest figure of a Confucian country? Since Confucius is at the level of an emperor, he occupies a higher position than a king. Accordingly, during the ancestral rites the king has to offer a cup of liquor. Thus, there is a space here that is designated for the king's palanquin. It is like a VIP parking space. Because Munmyo Jerye is attended by the king, everything is of the highest quality. The best ceremonial vessels, food, clothing, musical instruments, etc.—all the finest goods in Joseon at the time were supplied. In addition, because this ceremony was well-preserved in its original form and the dance and music not found even in China were handed down intact, the Korean government designated the ceremony as an Intangible Cultural Asset. But the ceremonial music of Seonggyungwan's Munmyo Jerye was not designated as a World Cultural Asset by UNESCO and I am not sure why this is so. This is perhaps because it is similar to that of the Jongmyo ceremony and by policy UNESCO does not give recognition simultaneously to identical or similar cultural assets from the same nation.

There are several trees on the grounds of Daeseongjeon. Of these, the two trees in front of Daeseongjeon are most notable. They are *cheukbaek* or western red cedars which, along with pine trees, symbolize the *gunja*, the most virtuous man in Confucianism. Because these trees are evergreens, they were thought to be appropriate in representing the Confucian spirit of *samusa* or 'mind of righteousness.' This is the reason why many of these trees were also planted on the grounds of a king's tomb. But these trees are oddly shaped. There is something unusual about the branches of both trees. If we look carefully, the tree on the right facing Daeseongjeon has three branches while the one on the left has five. These undoubtedly symbolize the *samgang-oryun* (Three Essentials and Five Relationships), the most important virtues of Confucianism. The Three Essentials refer to setting right the most essential of human relationships—father and son, king and subject, and husband and wife. More detailed prescriptions for human interaction, however, are found in the Five Relationships. *Oryun* (Five Relationships) delve deeper into human relationships, discussing in addition to the three relationships already mentioned between older and younger persons and between

Two trees in front of Daeseongjeon

friends. On a closer look at the five relationships, there must be filial piety from son to the father, righteousness from the subject to the king, distinction between husband and wife, hierarchy between senior and junior persons, and trust between friends. These Five Relationships were first designated by Mencius and have since become the most important elements of Confucianism. Among them, the concept of *hyo* (filial piety) in the first relationship and that of *seo* (hierarchy) in the fourth relationship form the two pillars of Confucian ethics. Since I have discussed this more thoroughly in another book, I will not go into any more detail here.

Confucianism places highest priority on the family, and of all familial relationships, that between father and son is considered to be the most important. Also, determining the hierarchy between persons based on their ages was also very important in Confucianism. Looking at modern

Korean society, we see that these two virtues still wield a great deal of influence. That Korea still remains a strongly patriarchal society and still has a culture that emphasizes devotion to one's parents is due to the influence of *hyo* (filial piety). The habit of comparing ages comes from the impact of *seo* (hierarchy). When Koreans meet for the first time, they first determine each other's age in order to properly frame the relationship. Even at school, students call upperclassmen *hyeong* (big or elder brother) or *eonni* (big or elder sister), terms used to call older siblings. This is a way of confirming the hierarchical relationship between seniors and juniors. Because of such social custom, the question most frequently faced by a foreigner in Korea is "How old are you?" Most foreigners are uninterested in each other's age. On the other hand, Koreans cannot have even a simple conversation until this issue has been resolved first. When we read Korean newspapers, the age of the subject of an article is always disclosed. This probably happens only in Korea. The problem with Confucian virtues is that they over-emphasize the duty of the lower person toward the higher person. In the father and son relationship, only the duty of the son, and in the older and younger person relationship, only the younger person's responsibility tend to be emphasized. Therefore, the Confucian doctrine forces absolute obedience of a younger person toward an older person. This does not mean that there is no word on the duties of the older person. A father must take care of his son with paternal love, and an older person must care for a younger one with benevolence. Confucian teaching is most beautiful when both sides make efforts to be mutually benevolent to one another.

These trees are not the only ones with significance in this area of the shrine. If we look with our backs turned to Daeseongjeon, there is a large pine tree in the front to the right. There is an interesting anecdote about this tree. A student at Seonggyungwan fell asleep under this tree one day and dreamed that he passed the state examination. Perhaps it was the dream, but afterward he actually passed the examination. News of the happening spread quickly, and soon all the students came to sleep under this tree. My personal opinion on this is that if you could pass the state examination just by sleeping under a tree, who would not give it a try. Beside the tree, we see a monument house. The monument inside is 600 years old and engraved on it is an explanation of how Seonggyungwan was established. The turtle serving as the foundation of the monument is exquisitely sculpted and is worth a good look. We have now basically seen everything to be seen in Daeseongjeon. Our next destination is Myeongryundang, the section in the back. When we go out through the small side door, we come to a courtyard and the Myeongryundang, but this is the courtyard we have already passed on our way into Daeseongjeon. Since the gate by which the king enters and leaves is closed, we had to come through the side door.

Seonggyungwan 2—At Myeongryundang (The Hall for Brightening the Ethics)

The Myeongryundang area follows a very simple layout. The main lecture hall, Myeongryundang, is the central building, and to its left and right are dormitories. There are also a large ginkgo and a few locust trees in the courtyard. We can find a gingko tree not only at Seonggyungwan but also at every *hyanggyo* because of old folklore that Confucius taught students under a gingko tree. The gingko tree here is over 500 years old and those found in the provincial schools also boast similar age. The reason why these trees are so old is that they were planted in conjunction with the construction of these institutions in the early Joseon era. This gingko tree in Seonggyungwan is so old that metal supports have been put in place to prevent its branches from drooping to the ground.

Ginko tree in the courtyard of Myeongryundang

The location of the dormitories on both sides in front of the lecture hall is a common layout for an institution of learning in the Joseon era. The Myeongryundang building, as seen in the picture, is a very simple structure. The building in the center was used as a lecture hall and the adjacent rooms on both sides were used by the headmaster or teachers. Over 400 years old, Myeongryundang is designated as a National Treasure. What attract our attention more than the main lecture hall are the dormitories on the east and the west. Both buildings together have less than 30 rooms altogether, and it is a wonder how 200 some students boarded here. The rooms are very small. They can barely fit two people lying down and I wonder how many students actually slept in each room. Once I showed these rooms to my teacher from the U.S., and he was curious how people could sleep in such small quarters. For a large-built American, it was an understandable question. I answered that the average height of Koreans during that period was less than 160 centimeters and therefore people probably had no problems living here. However, no matter how tightly people are jammed in, one can put only three or four in a room. I still wonder how they put up 200 students here. Even if the sleeping

Myeongryundang, Ginko trees, and dormitories on both sides

arrangement worked out somehow, how did they study? Since we do not know the exact situation at the time, a good answer is hard to find. Nevertheless, the dormitories here at Seonggyungwan were the largest in all of Joseon.

Let us put aside this question for now and look at the daily routine of the students who lived here. Because this compound is quite large, a drum was usually used to signal the hour. Everyone woke up to the beating of a drum before sunrise and then began morning study. Later, three drumbeats signaled the start of the joy of mealtime. A drum similar to the one used then still hangs by the east dormitory and the dining room is right next to it. Even now, this dining room is used when special events are held. It is interesting to note that there is an attendance book where a student marks off his name every time he enters the room for a meal. One mark for breakfast and one for dinner are totaled as one point. A student needs to accumulate 300 points to attain the qualifications to

Dormitory of Seonggyungwan   dormitory room

take the state examination. The intention of the point system is to assess the diligence of a student by calculating his attendance rate. We can understand this in the same vein as a university not giving credit for a course when a given number of lectures are not attended. However, once again, it is difficult not to wonder why attendance was taken at the dining room, since as long as a student lived here, he surely could not have avoided eating his meals in this room. According to folklore, the students were allowed only two days of leave each month. If this is true, almost all meals would have had to be taken in this dining room. Why attendance was taken in such a perfunctory manner remains a mystery.

Although outings were strictly limited, there seem to have been exceptions. This is conceivable, considering that although the residents were bright students studying for the biggest examination of their lifetime, they were nonetheless also ordinary human beings. One particular student who later became a great scholar would climb over the wall whenever the urge came and go drinking at a nearby tavern; it appears that he sometimes would not return for days. It is said that the king, unable to see this go on, personally wrote a letter to have him return to school. This student probably had a great future ahead of him and it seems that the king knew him personally. Therefore, the king wrote this student a letter urging him to return. I find this story both amusing and beautiful. First of all, I like the aplomb and the mischievous spirit with which the student jumped over the wall and headed to the tavern out of exasperation with the extremely strict lifestyle at school. I am also pleased by the attentive benevolence of the king who, rather than solving the situation with harsh punishment, personally wrote a letter to persuade the student to return. It is heartwarming to see such a display of mutual affection. As shown in this story, the state placed great value on the students here. Hence, one of the things that the king most feared was a protest by the Seonggyungwan students. There were several levels of protest, the most extreme type being a nationwide student strike. A number of kings of early Joseon liked Buddhism, but this was a religion that the Neo-Confucianists heavily disliked. One particular king in this period began to favor Buddhism and the Seonggyungwan students went on a strike to protest his pro-Buddhist attitude. In any case, I personally very much like the atmosphere of Seonggyungwan in which one can feel the cultural values of Joseon that valued its human resources.

After the morning meal, study at Myeongryundang begins. Lessons consist mainly of students memorizing aloud and then explaining the meaning of what they have learned. The students discuss and ask questions on the study material with teachers, and this is mostly done on a one-on-one basis. In the afternoons and evenings, review of the material and memorization of this are repeated. It is said the students were badgered not only with such repetitive study but also with countless exams. Since everything was paid for by the state, they could not afford to let the students slide on anything. In total, the students had to take more than 30 exams a month. An interesting anecdote related to the exams involves the stone under the tree that stands to the right facing Myeongryundang. Each time I visit here with my students, I ask about the use of this stone but never get a satisfactory answer. This stone is where students stood when they whipped themselves with a rod. After an exam, the students with poor scores would get up on this stone and hit their own calves. Because these students were earmarked to become important politicians in the future, perhaps such self-immolation was a way for them to develop self-discipline. If education is training oneself to do things independently, then this system of self-punishment is undoubtedly very educational. Then, when do the students here graduate? There is no established graduation date, but it takes about three and a half years to complete the entire program of study. But even after this period has passed, the student cannot graduate if he cannot pass the state examination. In other words, one graduates upon passing the state examination. However, a student cannot remain at the school, living on the bounty of the country, while waiting to pass the state examination. Students who have repeatedly failed to pass and have stayed for a long time can be dismissed, but the exact duration of stay that prompted a dismissal order remains unclear.

The front courtyard of Myeongryundang is large because the state examination is occasionally taken here. As mentioned before, on the day of the ancestral rites ceremony for Confucius, the king comes

Rod stone

here with the crown prince. He performs the ceremony and holds a meeting with the teachers and students in the front courtyard. This is done to encourage those who are to become competent government officials in the future. At the meeting, the king bestows rice wine to the teachers and students. It must have been a great honor for them to personally receive wine from the king. That the king personally participated in such an event shows the great extent to which the Joseon government valued Seonggyungwan. Along with such gatherings, occasionally the state examination is given here on an irregular basis. For that reason, this space is kept clear. Now such tradition is gone, and instead of state examinations, the courtyard is rented out to be used for wedding receptions. Next to Seonggyungwan is a center for Confucianism, and rental requests for wedding ceremony space are transacted in this building. This center, the headquarters of Korean Confucianism, is a small building. Looking at this building, we can feel the diminished power of Confucianism in modern Korea in comparison with its immensity during the Joseon Dynasty.

If Korean people today are asked about their religion, less than 2 percent will point to Confucianism. But if the question is rephrased to ask whether they find filial piety and other virtues of Confucianism important, more than 90 percent will agree. The efficacy of Confucianism as a religion has greatly faded in the present day, but Confucian values still possess tremendous influence over Korean society. This is why I assert that all Koreans are potential Confucianists. In some ways this is inevitable because Koreans are virtually the only people in the world that still ardently maintain the tradition of ancestral rites, hold clan meetings, and are genuinely interested in family genealogy books. Therefore, Confucianists who work as officers of this Confucian institution appear to think that Confucianism is still alive and well for the future. The reality, however, is not all that sunny. A few years ago, a book entitled "Confucius must die so that the country may prosper" became a bestseller and it made me wonder how Confucianists will overcome the bleak reality of Korean Confucianism that is implied by the title. There is a tendency by most Koreans to associate the term 'Confucianism' with something that is narrow-minded and antiquated. Such tendency is especially strong in the criticism that Confucianism advocates the patriarchal system too strongly while it neglects attending to women. I am very curious as to how Korean Confucianists will overcome this negative state of affairs. But regardless of the current situation, Koreans cannot live divorced from Confucianism. This is because the relationship between Koreans and Confucianism is like that of a fish to water. There are many great ideals in Confucianism. The problem is that these have not been successfully adapted to the modernized social mileau of today.

On Leaving Seonggyungwan

We have now seen the highlights of Seonggyungwan. The buildings we have not yet seen can be viewed briefly as we leave. In the back of Myeongryundang are two small buildings, and the nearer one is the school library. It is called Jongyeonggak, but as the national university library of Joseon, a country that worships learning, it is too small. I wonder how a library of such modest dimensions could have serviced over 200 students. My guess is that the size of the library has to do with the educational method of the day. The most important pedagogical method of Joseon was to memorize the classic texts, and there are only a few important Confucian classics. There were only about ten classics accompanied by many volumes of commentaries. Memorization of all

Jongyeonggak

these was the responsibility of the student. Therefore, although there was a great deal to study, the student did not need a lot of books. I think that this was the reason for not needing a large library.

On the right side behind the library stands a small building called Yugilgak, which was used to store bows and arrows. We may question the need for bows and arrows at a university, but to understand this, we must again return to the underlying principle of Confucianism. Confucianism is commonly thought to only emphasize studying, but this is only a partial picture of the whole. Confucianism views achieving *jungyong* (the mean or middle ground) as very important in order to strictly guard against leaning too much in one direction. Confucianism considers studying the classics as the most important task, but this does not mean that it has no interest in other forms of training. To guard against leaning too much toward literary

Yugilgak

learning, it also teaches that one must be proficient not only in academics, but also in the arts such as music, horsemanship, arithmetic, calligraphy, and archery. Only then can one become a *gunja*, the most virtuous man who possesses the characteristics of an ideal human being. Therefore, the reason for storing bows and arrows in this building is to guard the students from leaning too much toward book learning. The bows are displayed based on this principle of the mean, by which literary and military arts are considered equally important. It is a way of reminding the students not to neglect their physical training. Seen this way, there is flexibility inside Confucianism, but this does not seem to come through very well in everyday life.

As we come out of Seonggyungwan, leaving behind many thoughts on Confucianism, we see numerous buildings on the grounds other than the ones we looked at. But since they are not of great significance, let us be satisfied with taking a quick look around. Now we will visit the Buddhist temple Jogyesa, which is located not far from Seonggyungwan. Although Buddhism was harshly repressed during the Joseon Dynasty, it nevertheless greatly influenced the development of Korean religious culture. Buddhism in particular has left a rich cultural legacy with many relics. For this reason, to understand Korea you need to know Buddhism. Now we leave for Jogyesa to seek an in-depth understanding of Korean culture.

4. Jogyesa – The Headquarters of Korean Buddhism

In order to understand Korean culture from a religious perspective, it is necessary to have a multi-pronged method of approach. For example, to understand the structure of the Korean consciousness, you need to have prior knowledge of Confucianism and Shamanism. Confucianism is thought to have influenced the shaping of Koreans' social personality while Shamanism influenced the formation of their fundamental disposition. In comparison, the influence of Buddhism is hardly noticeable. This is because Confucianism was the state religion of Joseon, the last royal dynasty of Korea. However, this situation changes completely when we examine religious relics that have survived to the present. Approximately seventy percent of historical relics in Korea are related to Buddhism. Korean Buddhism was able to leave such an abundant heritage because it flourished for a full 1600 years on the Korean peninsula. To understand the religious culture of Korea, therefore, you need to know Buddhism. In this chapter, let us examine Korean Buddhist culture by visiting Jogyesa in downtown Seoul.

In Front of Jogyesa

Jogyesa is not that far away from Seonggyungwan and is adjacent to Insa-dong, which we will visit shortly. This temple compound holds the headquarters of Jogyejong, the largest sect among the various Buddhist orders in Korea. Different groups within Jogyejong fought over this headquarters for several decades and tried to take control of it with physical violence, but that is now all in the past; Korean Buddhism has become more mature. Such unpleasant conflicts arose for many reasons, but they certainly have some connection to the past 600 years of history that was forged by Korean Buddhism. We need to know this history in order to understand Korean Buddhism as it stands today, and an analysis of the roots of the name Jogyejong is a good place to start. 'Jogye' is related to the Sixth Zen Patriarch Huineng, considered to be the most important figure in Chinese Zen Buddhism. Although the Bodhidharma is recognized as its founder, Huineng is actually considered to be the first patriarch of Chinese Zen Buddhism. In any case, behind the temple that Huineng presided was a mountain called Mt. Jogye in Korean. By naming its order after this mountain, Jogyejong indicates that it is grounded in Zen Buddhism and upholds the mantle of the teachings of Huineng. Korean Buddhism does not shun sects that give priority to studying the classic Buddhist texts. However, it considers Zen Buddhism, which emphasizes sudden enlightenment independent of studying scriptures, to be superior. Hence, the order was named Jogye.

After arriving from China at the end of the 4th century, Buddhism enjoyed its status in Korea as the state religion until the end of the 14th century. However, with the rise of Joseon in the 15th century and that of Confucianism as the new state religion, Buddhism came under fierce persecution by Confucianists who were heavily disdainful of it. There were many types of persecutions during that time, but the demotion of the monks' social status from the highest class to *cheonmin* (the lowest social class) is the most telling example of the mistreatment suffered by Buddhism. When Korea became a colony of Japan in the early 20th century, Buddhism was finally released from its long period of oppression only to become subordinated to Japanese Buddhism and thus lose a significant portion of the unique character of Korean Buddhism. The most representative change was that many Korean monks married, following the custom of Japanese Buddhism. Korean Buddhism ushered in liberation from the Japanese imperialists in this altered state with the end of World War II. But liberation did not bring sunshine to Korean Buddhism. The first president of the Republic of Korea was a Christian who had no understanding or sympathy for Buddhism. To make matters worse, Korean Buddhism began to become embroiled in internal strife. Power struggles began between the majority of monks who have married and the traditionalist celibate monks. This conflict ended with the victory of the latter, but it was not the end of all strife. Fighting again broke out amongst the monks, now with the control of the order at stake. Interestingly, to win this fight, they had to take over Jogyesa. Therefore, Jogyesa became the scene of not a few violent struggles. But as Jogyejong has now found stability, we do not witness such commotions anymore.

It is easy for foreigners unfamiliar with Korea to think that the only sect in Korean Buddhism is Jogyejong. But in addition to Jogyejong, Korean Buddhism has about 100 denominations. Jogyejong is the largest denomination among these, and next in size in terms of size is Taegojong, which inherited the tradition of monks marrying during the Japanese colonial era. I will forego descriptions of other sects here since that would require more expertise. But I would like to mention one more sect called Won Buddhism. This sect is a new religion that was founded by Koreans and has significant influence in Korean society. Originally it was founded with no intention of being affiliated with Buddhism. The founder Sotaesan, however, brought it together with Buddhism and henceforth it took on Buddhist characteristics. Accordingly, I refer to this sect as Korean-style Buddhism. Let us talk about this religion at another time and focus now on Jogyejong. The nature of Korean Buddhism will be revealed when we understand Jogyejong.

Although we are visiting Jogyesa to understand Korean Buddhism, frankly, Jogyesa does not possess the beautiful appearance of a traditional Korean temple. To see truly beautiful temples, we need to go to provinces outside of Seoul. There are almost none in Seoul that are as presentable and refined. The fact that downtown Seoul lacks a good temple also has to do with the aforementioned history of Korean Buddhism. Because of the animosity toward Buddhism by the Confucian officials of the Joseon Dynasty, Korean Buddhists could not build temples in the capital city. Monks were forbidden to enter the capital, so building a temple here was unthinkable. This is why there are hardly any good temples to be seen within Seoul today. When we visit Jogyesa today, we will notice that it is not small. However, this was not always the case. Originally the scale dimensions of Jogyesa were very small, consisting only of one *beopdang* (dharma hall), the Jogyejong headquarters building and a few annexes. This was maintained until about ten years ago when nearby plots were bought and construction of additional buildings began, expanding to its present-day scale. The temple grounds continue to expand with no specific deadline. While indicative of the recovery of confidence and the advancement of Korean Buddhism, it is disappointing that Jogyesa does not possess the appearance of a traditional Korean Buddhist temple. But it is convenient to visit from downtown Seoul, so let us utilize this temple fully for an understanding of Korean Buddhism.

In Front of *Iljumun*

Korean temples begin with an *iljumun* (one-pillared gate), and at the entrance of Jogyesa we can see a big *iljumun*. Such an *iljumun* is not found in Buddhist temples in China or Japan. I am not sure of the reason for this, but the primary function of an *iljumun* is to mark the boundaries of the temple compound. The temple grounds begin from this gate. Thus, entering this gate indicates the leaving behind of the secular world. But this does not mean that we have completely entered the world of Buddha. At temples in other provinces, there is usually a distance of several hundred meters between *iljumun* and the main temple grounds. The name '*iljumun*,' or 'one-pillared gate,' comes from the fact that one pillar is used on each side to support the gate. There are a number of explanations for this, but my favorite is the explanation that it embodies One Mind, the most important concept in Buddhism. Buddhism asserts that all things in the universe come from this One Mind. On the path from *iljumun* to the *beopdang*, we must prepare our heart to meet the

Iljumun of Jogyesa

Buddha. Preparing the heart is nothing other than gradually washing away the filth of the greed-filled secular world. Korean temples usually have a flowing stream next to the path from *iljumun* to the *beopdang*. We must let this stream wash away all worldly desires and enter the world of Buddha with a cleansed heart.

Therefore, this gate is usually placed quite a distance from the main temple building. But the *iljumun* at Jogyesa is right in front of the temple because the temple is located in an urban area and has not been able to secure a large plot of land for its premises. As such, the temple lacks elegance. But what is more disturbing is that the gate is too big relative to the modest size of the temple. Originally the road into Jogyesa was so narrow that it could barely accommodate a car. This oversized gate was erected after the road was widened. There is nothing wrong with the gate itself, but it looks out of proportion relative to the buildings behind it. As soon as we enter the temple grounds through this gate, we face the main building—*beopdang*. Actually we meet the side of the *beopdang*. Such a layout is not found in a traditional temple. Although not found in Jogyesa, there are usually two or three more gates to pass through when you walk from the *iljumun* to the *beopdang* in a typical temple. Typically the first gate you meet is *cheonwangmun* (the gate of four devas) and inside this gate are figures of four burly warriors. Known as warriors who protect Buddhism, they were originally Hindu gods but were since also adopted by Buddhism. Under the feet of these warriors are mischievous-looking children. This was meant to show what happened to those who slander Buddhism and to scare people. But it is a bit strange to see Buddhism, a religion which emphasizes compassion above all, humiliate people in such a way. I wonder about this even more when occasionally I hear that some child was frightened by these warrior figures.

Four devas

After the *cheonwangmun*, you must pass through one more gate to enter the world of Buddha. This gate is ordinarily called *burimun* (gate of non-dualism), and this name has quite a philosophical subcontext. Therefore, it is difficult to explain. '*Buri*' means 'non-dual' and Buddhism asserts that seeing things dualistically is the root of all evil. Those which divide you and me, man and nature, heaven and hell, world of Buddha and world of humans, all arise from our dualistic mind. From the perspective of One Mind, all things are one. But we humans keep adhering to a dualistic mind, creating barriers that separate things and classifying all things as bad or good. Humans suffer because we see everything from the standpoint of the self (greed) rather than from the perspective of the whole. By transcending such a state in which we calculate and classify everything, we can enter the world of Buddha. The world of Buddha is a world without any more suffering. It is a world without birth, aging, sickness, or death. In other words, there is no need to be born again. After we are born, we suffer in life, shake in fear of death, and then inevitably die. Such suffering is beyond all imagination. But when we pass through this gate, such suffering should theoretically disappear, because we have entered the courtyard of the *beopdang* headed by Buddha. That is, we have entered the territory of Buddha. These gates have all been omitted at Jogyesa; as soon as we pass through the *iljumun*, we are in the world of Buddha.

Inside the Temple Grounds

On the temple grounds, upon entering the *iljumun*, we see the side of the *beopdang* and a small pagoda in front of it. In a Buddhist temple, a tap (pagoda) is usually placed in front of a *beopdang*, and this same format has been followed here. However, this pagoda is too small relative to the size of the *beopdang*, and also is not very well-made. It was probably placed here without much prior planning or deliberation. Koreans' sense of aesthetics has greatly deteriorated these days and we are not that good at making even our homes look beautiful. A temple is no exception. In that respect, we should not have high expectations for Jogyesa. But what we should note here is that a pagoda is typically erected in front of a *beopdang*.

What, then, is a pagoda? A pagoda is a place for preserving the corporeal remains of the Buddha after his cremation. That is why a pagoda is called the grave of the Buddha. Because the Buddha told his disciples not to create his likeness, the early Buddhists considered a pagoda with his remains in it as the embodiment of the Buddha and thus

Pagoda in the courtyard of Jogyesa

began to worship the pagoda. But after the Buddha's image was created and a *beopdang* to enshrine it was built, the object of Buddhist worship shifted from the pagoda to the *beopdang*. Without going into the details of Buddhist history, it is sufficient enough to know that the pagoda was very large in the early days of Buddhism. However, as worship of Buddha's image developed, the *beopdang* grew to be much larger than the pagoda. Originally only one pagoda was placed in the center of the front courtyard of the *beopdang*, but Korean temples began to build two pagodas as the pagoda became smaller and overshadowed by the latter. The most illustrative example of this practice is the case of Bulguksa in Gyeongju. In the front courtyard of Bulguksa are Seokgatap and Dabotap. Henceforth, this type of pagoda placement became something of a trend in Korean temples. Jogyesa made efforts to go along with this trend by erecting one small pagoda.

Speaking of pagodas, Korea has developed a unique building style.

Although the tradition of erecting a pagoda came from India, China, Korea, and Japan each has developed different pagoda traditions. The pagodas of these three Northeast Asian countries have similar shapes but are made from different materials. China liked to build pagodas with bricks, whereas Korea preferred making them from stones. Among stones, Korea liked to use granite, which was most readily available. Because granite is very hard, carving fine details on it must have been exceedingly difficult. Japan, in contrast, used wood to build pagodas. Although the materials were different, the pagodas were all similarly designed in the shape of a house. Simply put, a pagoda is a house built for the Buddha. Which pagoda then is the most ideal out of those built in the traditional Korean style? That is, which is the greatest pagoda in Korea?

Seokgatap

The greatest pagoda in Korea appeared far back in antiquity and it is Seokgatap in Bulguksa. Buddhism arrived in Silla in the mid-6th century and Seokgatap was built in the mid-8th century. Thus, the greatest pagoda appeared 200 years after the introduction of Buddhism to Korea. Bulguksa is a UNESCO World Cultural Heritage, and one of the reasons for this designation is that the greatest stone pagoda in Korea— Seokgatap—stands in its courtyard. In addition to Seokgatap, there is also

Pine tree in Jogyesa

Dabotap. Among Korean pagodas, Dabotap is a remarkably decorated pagoda that easily attracts the attention of first-time visitors. In contrast, Seokgatap, as if it were a minimalist work, is a statement in simplicity. With no ornamentation, it expresses perfection through proportion. There is nothing to remove or add to this pagoda—it is perfection itself. The simple is fundamentally the most difficult to make. No matter how long you look at this pagoda, you will not get tired of looking at it. After Seokgatap, there has been no other pagoda that surpasses it in the history of Korean Buddhism. Whatever pagoda we see in a Korean temple in the future needs only to be compared to Seokgatap. By comparing it with the best of its kind, the quality of that pagoda can instantly be determined. When applied to the pagoda on the grounds of Jogyesa, we can see that it lacks much in the way of artistic beauty. This pagoda certainly is not built in the style of Seokgatap. Its high and narrow spire is atypical within the tenets of traditional Korean style, and is more akin to the Japanese style It has been recently said that this pagoda will be replaced by one that is designed in Korean style.

Let us leave our thoughts on the pagoda for now and take a look at the main building, the *beopdang*. On the right side of the *beopdang* there is a pine tree with white branches that attracts our attention. Its white branches make this tree so rare that it has been designated as a natural monument. The branches turned white after the bark peeled away with the passing of time and the rarity of such a tree is probably the reason why it received this distinction. We look at this tree because we have to pass in front of it in order to enter the *beopdang*. The entrance for lay followers is always the side door. In contrast, the monks enter through the front door, and I have always considered this a little odd each time I visit the temple. Originally the motto for 'Daeseung Bulgyo,' or Mahayana Buddhism, was the principle of equality that did not recognize distinction between monks and lay followers; now when we visit a temple, oddly enough there is strict division between the two. But since monks believe themselves to be the masters of the temple, we as guests cannot object.

Inside the *Beopdang*

Beopdang literally means 'space for worship.' In Korean temples, the faithful prostrate themselves before the Buddha's image three times a day. At these times of reverential bowing, grains or cooked rice and fruits are placed on the altar, but tea was originally the most important offering. With the rise of the Joseon Dynasty, clean water came to be preferred over tea. Of course meats are absolutely forbidden. During worship before the image of Buddha, the monks mostly perform Buddhist invocations and bows. They confess that Buddha is the master of all sentient beings in the universe and promise to become enlightened no matter what happens. They also resolve to devote their all to the salvation of humankind, the main principle of Mahayana Buddhism. This consists of resolving everyday to carry out the most fundamental principle of Mahayana Buddhism, that is, to "attain wisdom from above and save the people from bellow." And finally the monks memorize '*Banyasimgyeong*

(*The Heart Sutra*),' a distilled version of the essence of Mahayana Buddhism. This sutra is made up of only 260 characters and contains the famous phrase '*saekjeuksigong gongjeuksisaek* (the matter is the form and the form is the matter, or being is nothingness and nothingness is being).' Often used in other ceremonies, this sutra, ending with the phrase "Let us go beyond to that world of enlightenment," is considered the favorite of Korean Buddhist monks.

While chanting invocations, Buddhist monks continuously bow before the Buddha image. The Semitic religions, beginning with Christianity, do not seem to think highly of such bowing. Korean Christians assert that the custom of bowing is equivalent to idolatry as defined in Christianity, and must be avoided at all cost. It is considered a violation of the first of the Ten Commandments— "Do not have any other gods before me." But an understanding of the true meaning of bowing will show that this religious act is unrelated to idolatry. Korean Buddhists usually bow three times, once to each of the highly important three treasures of Buddhism: the Buddha, his teachings, and the Buddhist community of monks and followers. The act of bowing in Asian religion signifies the complete giving of oneself. It also signifies an infinite lowering of oneself. It is the act of making humble the arrogant ego. To do so, you must lower the head because it is the most important part of a human being. When bowing while seated, Korean Buddhists turn up their palms as a sign of upholding the feet of Buddha. This shows the intention to place oneself under the feet of the Buddha and to pay utmost respect to the great teacher. Bowing is also a method of practicing self-discipline. It is not that easy to do in practice, but Buddhists do it hundreds to thousands of times. Doing so many bows is seen as a way to control the body, the source of desire, and focus the mind. In every case, the problem is always the ego. Overcoming the ego is the attainment of enlightenment, but this is the most difficult of human endeavors. Bowing is one of the methods to attain this goal.

Moktak

While chanting invocations, Korean Buddhists use a peculiar-looking instrument, a wooden gong called *moktak*. Sound is made by striking this round, hollow instrument with a stick during the performance of chanting. This *moktak* was of course brought in from China, but use of it during chanting is a practice found only in Korea, and nothing definite is known about its origin. What is known thus far is that its shape is taken from the outline of a fish. Why a fish? According to commonly-held belief of Buddhist practitioners, a fish does not sleep. Therefore, using the shape of a fish is a prescription for Buddhists to always be as awake as possible and to diligently practice self-discipline. No matter what its origin, *moktak* is an instrument that definitely helps in making the chanting go smoothly. This is so because just chanting can get boring, but chanting to the beating of *moktak* stimulates the chanter and also brings the congregation together in rhythmic unison.

The majority of Buddhist practitioners in Korea are housewives or elderly women, and Jogyesa is no exception. The male followers inside the *beopdang* are so few that they can be counted within ten fingers. In a recent survey of the educational level of Korean who profess to having a religion, over 40 percent of Protestants were college graduates while a similar percentage of Buddhists were primary school graduates. This indicates that Korean Buddhism has not been able to penetrate the

Three Budda images in Jogyesa's Dharma Hall

mainstream of society. Therefore, Korean Buddhism is sometimes self-mockingly referred to as 'housewife' or 'grandma' Buddhism. Moreover, Korean Buddhism is criticized as a religion that only seeks good fortune. But is there any religion that does not seek this out? One cannot say Buddhism is the only one that seeks blessing.

Directly facing the front entrance of the *beopdang* are three large images of the Buddha. Originally there were smaller Buddha statues but they were replaced in 2006 with these new larger statues because Koreans have a penchant for large objects. I worry that they are not a little too big for the size of this *beopdang*, but in any case the three figures represent the Buddha of the past, the present and the future. There are many things to discuss about the Buddha image, but let us only mention that this style of Buddha image originated 2000 years ago in India's northwest region, from the Gandhara culture of what is now a provincial area of Afghanistan. At the time, this region was part of a

Seoul

Taenghwa

country that was under the absolute influence of Greek culture. Buddhists were inspired by Greek sculptures of gods and began to create images of the Buddha in similar fashion. Such images of the Buddha were eventually brought into China by way of central Asia and transmitted to Korea and Japan in modified form. These at Jogyesa are of mediocre quality and not particularly exemplary. They seem to have been made in a generic style based on past images. Behind these Buddha images, it is a common practice to hang a painting called *'taenghwa.'* This painting depicts the Buddha giving a sermon to many disciples. Of the three

Lotus flower-shaped lanterns with name tags

Northeast Asian countries, Korea is unique in the hanging of such a painting. We can also see many lotus flower-shaped lanterns hanging from the ceiling. These are offered with the written names of family members to wish for good fortune. These lotus lanterns are a good source of revenue: the bigger they are, the pricier they get.

Outside the *Beopdang*

Let us now go outside the *beopdang* after one last look around inside. We did not look at the building closely as we were coming in, but this building was not originally constructed as a Buddhist sermon hall. This fact is not widely known, but this building was built as the *jeongjeon* or main hall when the founder of a new religion, firmly believing that he was an emperor, had a palace constructed upon 'taking the throne.' That is, this is like Geunjeongjeon of Gyeongbok Palace. Since temple buildings were originally copied from palace buildings, both are quite

Paintings depicting the life of Buddha

similar, but this building seems more like a palace when we look more closely at its details. In particular, the frame between the roof and the pillars is exactly the same as that found in a palace building. A Korean Buddhist temple rarely uses such a colorful frame, but this building has a very colorful one like that of a palace.

Viewing such exterior details of the *beopdang* is important, but it is also quite interesting to look at the pictures painted on the walls. Pictures are painted on the walls of the *beopdang* in Korean temples, rarely done in China or Japan. The motif for such a picture is usually the life of the Buddha. Generally, the Buddha's life is depicted in eight stages, but the paintings at Jogyesa divide the Buddha's life divided into a much more detailed 30 stages. The major scenes show how the Buddha was born, experienced the meaninglessness of life, became a monk, and after harsh ascetic training, attained enlightenment and founded an order of monks, expanded this order, and then entered nirvana. Since these paintings wrap around the *beopdang*, we can get an excellent understanding of Buddhism by looking at them one by one as we walk. But there are many pictures that are hard to fathom without explanation, so it would be best to ask for a guided tour from the information booth. There are now tours given in English, but I am not sure about the quality of the English or the method in which the commentaries are given.

After circling the *beopdang* like this once, you will notice other buildings nearby. The building in the far corner is called *Beomjonggak*, which is known to be uniquely Korean (there are similar buildings in China and Japan, but the interior composition is different). Inside this building are four Buddhist instruments, each of which is laden with symbolism and expresses the infinite spirit of benevolence in Buddhism. These four instruments are struck before dawn (around 3 a.m.) and in the evening (around 6 p.m.) during worship before the image of the Buddha. The instruments are struck in the order of *buk* (drum), *unpan* (cloud plate), *mok-eo* (wooden fish), and *jong* (bell). The subjects to whom each instrument's sound is directed differ slightly as well as overlap. Firstly, the drum sends out the gospel of Buddhism to all sentient beings, calling out, "hear this sound and come to the bosom of Buddha and be enlightened." 'Sentient beings' here indicate all living things other than plants. So even the smallest creature, as long as it has life and moves, is included. For example, ants are included as well as the mites that live off of plants. In Buddhism, all such sentient beings possess Buddha nature and therefore can become the Buddha and should be valued as such. This is why Buddhism forbids the consumption of meat. Killing a being that has the potential to become the Buddha violates the law of the universe. But there is no clear discussion on plants. In any case, striking the drum is a way of encouraging these sentient beings to make greater efforts to advance the evolution of their selves upon hearing the drum sound.

Next, the cloud-shaped metal plate is struck. This plate is called *unpan* (cloud plate) and its sound is directed at all sentient beings of the sky, referring to birds. That is, they are flying animals. The subjects for the drum sound were land-dwelling sentient beings, and now the subjects are sky-dwelling beings. Next in order is *mok-eo*, or 'fish made of wood.' It is carved in the shape of a fish with the belly hollowed out, the inside of which is struck with a stick. The sound is directed at fish living in the water. Imagine the number of fish living in rivers or seas! It is intended for fish to hear the sound and to find rest. Last is the bell. The bell is struck for the sentient beings living underground. Since there are countless organisms living underground, they should not be excluded from the list for salvation. In this way, all sentient beings in this world become subjects of Buddhist salvation. This aspect of Buddhist doctrine is markedly different from that of other religions. For example, Christianity and Islam are concerned from start to finish only with the salvation of

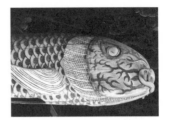

Mok-eo

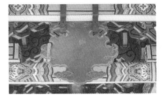

Unpan

Buk

Jong
Four instruments of Buddhism

human beings. In these religions, I have yet to hear a story about the salvation of animals. Animals are merely the 'other.' We can see how great and inclusive of a religion Buddhism is just by examining these four Buddhist instruments, which seem mundane just in appearance.

Typically all four instruments are found only at a large temple, and a small temple usually only has a bell. As in other temples, at Jogyesa they strike the bell at both the dawn and evening services. The bell is struck 33 times, a significant number in Buddhism. According to Buddhism, there are 33 heavens in the world. The 'world' here does not refer to the material world that we inhabit. It refers instead to the world of living souls. In this world, the highest realm is the Realm of the Buddha, where the Buddha lives. The other Buddhas discussed in Buddhism, such as Amitabha or Maitreya, each heads one of the heavens and saves people. The worldview of Buddhism is extremely complicated and difficult to understand in one sitting. Anyway, what we need to remember about this bell is that it is struck 33 times to enlighten all sentient beings living in the 33 heavens, once for each heaven.

Since we are talking about bells, the Buddhist bell is quite different from the bells of other religions. Usually a bell has a tongue inside that is swung to strike the interior side to make a sound, but a Buddhist bell is struck from the outside. Perhaps this is the reason for the deep sound of a Buddhist bell. When the sound of a bell reverberates deep in the mountains, it can travel for many kilometers. The sound of a Korean temple bell is renowned throughout the world. Among the three Northeast Asian countries, Korean bells have the reputation for producing the most weighty and beautiful sound. To produce such a high-quality sound, a Korean temple bell has a device not found in the bells of other countries. This unique device is a container placed above the bell. It is a device akin to a boiler vent that is set above the bell, filtering out noise and allowing the sound to spread out in both directions. Among Korean bells, the so-called 'Emile Bell' is considered to have the most beautiful sound in the world. This bell is currently displayed in the lawn of the National Gyeongju Museum. A tape recording of its sound is sold in the souvenir shop so that we can always appreciate it.

Emile Bell

Next to *Beomjonggak* is Geukrakjeon. In Buddhism, *geukrak* refers to heaven, and the Buddha in charge here is the Amita (Amitabha) Buddha. According to Buddhist teachings, one will automatically be reborn in heaven after death simply by reciting the *'namuamitabul'* chant ten times. Here *namu* means 'to take refuge in.' The person reciting this chant will be reborn in heaven unconditionally without regard to his or her religion. The word *'geukrak'* literally means 'ultimate pleasure,' so it is a place where there is only pleasure. When we enter this building, we see that there are numerous figures — ten officials standing in Chinese-style official uniform. These are the people who meet the souls of the dead when they enter the spiritual world, pronounce judgment on their deeds in their previous lives, and accordingly send them to the appropriate world of souls. They are the judges of the spiritual world. This is all we know about these people and nothing definite is known

Jogyejong Headquarters

about how they make such judgments.

Other buildings are not related to the tradition of Buddhism. Since this temple is the headquarters of Jogyejong, there should be a headquarters building, and this is located behind the *beopdang*. This building used to be quite dilapidated, but it has been recently rebuilt and transformed into a brand-new building. This shows the growing power of Korean Buddhism, and most likely there will never again be incidents of monks using violence to take over this building. To that extent, Korean Buddhism now has found stability. There is a museum of Buddhism in front of this building, a nice place to take a tour. Since many nice Buddha images are displayed there, I recommend a visit to those with interest in such things.

Who are the Monks?

I think we have now covered the basics of Korean Buddhism on our walk around the grounds of Jogyesa. But I sense there is something missing. It is about the monks, the main characters in a temple. Who are they? Why do they live so differently from us? What is their day like? The questions are endless. To define who they are, we first need to establish that they differ slightly from the clergy in Christianity. For the clergymen of Christianity and Judaism, there is strong emphasis on the priest's role of connecting God and man, but in Buddhism the monk's role as an intermediary between God and man is weak. Instead, the monk's role as a practitioner is much stronger. It is not that a monk does not take on the role of a priest, but the primary duty of a Buddhist monk is to practice meditation and to share the fruits of his work with the lay followers. Monks are not people who make a living by performing religious rites; however, such a priest-like role has become stronger in recent years. This is probably due to the growing accommodation by Buddhist monks of the requests of lay followers to perform incantations to bring good fortune.

Monks shave their hair. Whether in the East or the West, hair is thought to symbolize sexuality. Perhaps that is why Catholic nuns take care to cover their hair. The story of Samson in the Old Testament of how he lost his special power when his hair was cut probably came about in order to exemplify the symbolism of hair as power. Although it may not be true in all cases, when a person

Buddhist Monk

has all his hair cut off, his sexual attractiveness is substantially diminished. Especially with women, appearance changes drastically depending on how the hair is trimmed. But in leading a monastic life, hair is a nuisance and not very helpful. Moreover, the maintenance of hair requires a great deal of care. That is why it seems that the ancient Indians wanted to get rid of it from the beginning. The first thing that even Sakyamuni (the Buddha) did when he escaped the palace to devote himself to the spiritual path was to cut off his hair. This expressed his will to stop worldly desires before they arise. Korean Buddhist monks wear non-colored, gray attire. Gray is the middle shade between white and black. There can be various interpretations of this color, but it can be understood to mean that monks are not of the secular world. This is so because gray is neutral. According to Buddhist precepts, monks were originally not permitted to wear clothing made exclusively for their use. Instead, they were required to wear tattered pieces of discarded clothing that are sewed together. Some monks even took the sheets that had wrapped corpses to piece together and wear. They were tremendously austere. Furthermore, monks could possess no money and were restricted to only the most basic items such as a rice bowl. No one knows how many Korean monks adhere completely to such precepts today.

Although the monks normally wear gray clothing, at ceremonies they wear one brown sheet over their normal attire. What does this mean? The brown sheet is a modified version of the clothing worn by monastic practitioners in ancient India. Even now in India, there are Buddhist ascetics who wrap only a simple orange-colored monastic garb around their body. Since India is not cold, wrapping just a single sheet around the body does not pose a problem. But in China or Korea where there are distinct autumn and winter seasons, one cannot live wrapped in only one sheet. Therefore, the monks of this country wrapped the traditional monastic clothing over their heavier usual garb, and this monastic clothing gradually became smaller, with only a trace of it left today.

The monks appear to lead a life completely out of the ordinary. What kind of life do they live? It is common knowledge that they do not marry. They believe that there is something greater than getting married and having children. That is why they became monks. In India and China, monks did not get married, and Korea also followed in this tradition. By contrast, Japan permitted monks to get married and therefore is an exception. However, this does not mean that Japan Buddhism is not traditional. Japanese monks focused more on the ceremonial aspects of Buddhism than monastic practice. In comparison with the monks of neighboring China and Japan, Korean monks possess a unique quality. Because Buddhism in Japan is so heavily secularized, hardly anyone becomes a monk to attain enlightenment. In China, on the other hand, religious tradition has greatly weakened due to socialism. As a result, it is difficult to find monks engaged in traditional monastic practice. As discussed previously, Confucian ceremonies have disappeared in China to the point that the Chinese had to come to Korea to learn about them; it is likely that Buddhist tradition has disappeared to an even greater degree. Korea maintains a relatively close form of the original Buddhist traditions of Northeast Asia that first developed in China. For example, in Korea it is still possible to get a glimpse of the way a Buddhist monk gave a sermon in the temple at a given historical period. We can get such a glimpse inside the *beopdang* of Jogyesa. In front of the Buddha image is a stand for sermons, and we can see a monk go up on this stand on days for service and give a sermon. Such sermon giving is depicted in the books of the given periods used in Zen Buddhism, but monks are no longer seen giving sermons in China or Japan.

How, then, do monks spend their day? This has some relevance to the now popular 'temple stay,' so let us take a look. A temple stay is a short-term period of stay at a temple to experience the life of a Buddhist monk and is quite popular with foreign visitors. Monks usually wake up before dawn at around 3:30 a.m. They wash, then go straight to the *beopdang* to chant the Buddhist sutra for about 30 minutes. After this, they study until the morning meal. The studying can be learning the Sutras or practicing Zen. They eat breakfast at about 6 a.m. At this point I need to touch on the monks' way of eating, as it demonstratesthe spirit of austerity in Buddhism very accurately. Each monk has his own eating bowls, which consist of four pieces. The monks place the exact amount of rice, soup, side dish, and water to be consumed in separate bowls. This is done to prevent any waste of food. They must never leave anything uneaten, not even a grain of rice. After they have eaten, they must pour warm rice-tea in the bowls to swish them clean and then drink the rice-tea. In this way, even the tiny foodstuff stuck to the bowls are cleaned up and consumed. Finally, cold water is poured into the bowls to clean them and this water

Mealtime at temple stay

S e o u l

from each monk is collected in one container to be discarded. But if even a tiny speck of condiment is found in this water, the monk responsible is reprimanded. This is a way of preventing the waste of valuable food. Such an eating ritual is probably not found anywhere else in the world and shows the extent to which Buddhism emphasizes austerity and caring for the environment. Eating in such a way for one meal can be a far clearer picture of Buddhism than studying precepts in a book. But I also hear that such a way of eating is quite burdensome for some foreigners.

After the morning meal, the monks do their work, of which there are many kinds. The work may be managing the temple, learning from a master, reciting the names of the Buddha and Bodhisattvas (Buddhist deities) and praying, or practicing Zen. After each monk does his work, lunch is eaten at 11 a.m. in the same manner as breakfast. After lunch, the monks return to similar work, and then take dinner at around 6 pm. Although these days they eat three meals, only one meal was eaten a day in the time of the Buddha. Also, this one meal was taken before noon and nothing was eaten afterward until the next morning. This was part of ascetic practice, maintained in order to abstain from desires and to focus one's mind and energy on monastic practice. If such a regimen is required today, there will not be anyone wishing to become a monk, because it is too difficult for modern people to endure. The monks not only eat differently but also sleep differently from lay people. They go to bed a little after 9 p.m. Why do they sleep so early? This is also related to their monastic practice, for which the night is not the best time. Night is a period conducive to the passions, such as play and eating. We desire drinking and sex during this period. Therefore, the night is not a conducive time for those in monastic practice. It should be spent in sleep and one should wake up before dawn to devote himself to monastic practice with a clear head. But if we actually live like this, we will realize that it is quite a beneficial lifestyle. Most people who have done a temple stay seem to agree.

If the monks spend a day in such a way, how do they spend a year? A year in the life of a monk is similar to a school year. During the three months each of summer and winter, the monks study in the temple. In the three months between these seasons, they travel and have other masters check what they have learned. During the periods when they stay in a temple, the monks do not leave the temple grounds. Whether studying sutras or practicing Zen, for those three months they must devote themselves only to study. This custom began in India, was firmly established in China, and was continued in Korea—now the only country that still maintains this tradition. In *seonwon* (Zen centers) all across Korea at this moment, there are many monks with legs crossed in the lotus position practicing *chamseon* (Zen meditation) to attain enlightenment. Because Korean Buddhism places greater emphasis on practicing Zen than studying the sutras, there is a tendency of Korean monks to devote themselves only to *chamseon*. Of the many books in English depicting such aspects of Korean Buddhism, there is a fine book by Professor Robert Buswell Jr. entitled *The Zen Monastic Experience*. Since Professor Buswell actually lived as a monk in Korea, his depiction of Korean Buddhism is a very vivid one. Of Korean Buddhist writings translated into English, there is an anthology by Master Seungsahn, the Korean Buddhist priest who has been most successful in disseminating the teachings of Korean Buddhism internationally.

When we come back outside after touring the grounds of the Jogyesa, we will notice that there is something like a Buddhist town formed in the vicinity. This consists of many Buddhism-related shops on either side of

Buddhist stores around Jogyesa

and across from the main gate of Jogyesa. In these shops, they sell virtually everything and anything related to Buddhism. From books to incense, Buddha images, bells, garbs, the list goes on and on. If you want to remember Korean Buddhism, you can buy memorabilia at these shops. Even if shopping is not an interest, there is a rich assortment of items to see, so a visit here will be a good experience.

So we have now seen a general overview of Korean Buddhism. From Gyeongbok Palace to this temple we have seen the traditional culture of Korea. But let us take a break from all this learning and get some good food to eat. Touring the downtown area like this takes much time and gets you hungry. A good neighborhood to go for food is right next to Jogyesa, known as Insa-dong. Insa-dong is relatively well-known among foreigners and many foreign visitors come here. It also has many restaurants selling Korean food, and it is great for enjoying a variety of Korean cuisine. Located right across the street from Jogyesa, Insa-dong is very accessible. Let us go there now.

A Night in Seoul
— Insa-dong and Hongdae

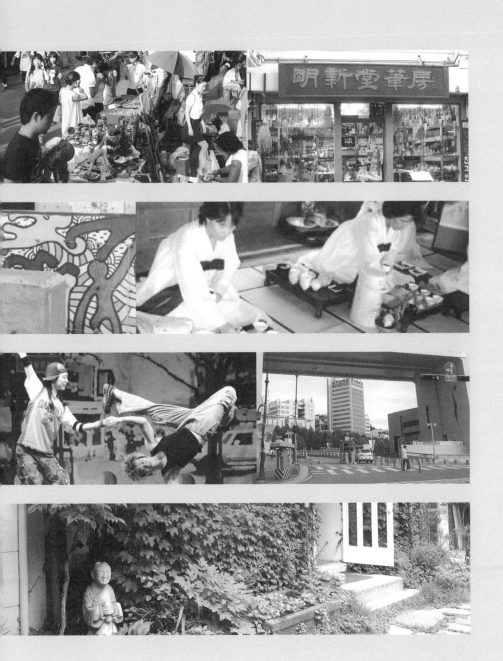

Chapter **4**

1. Where Tradition Still Breathes—Insa-dong

Unfortunately, with the exception of the palaces, there are not many places in Seoul that have retained the look of the Joseon Dynasty. This is because as I have mentioned throughout this book, destruction of Seoul began during the Japanese colonial period and virtually nothing of the city was left after the Korean War. Although Seoul is called a 600-year old 'old city,' the reality is that it remains difficult to find even traces of its original appearance. Many tourists say they had expected to find old Korea in Seoul, but were dismayed to instead encounter only a dense forest of apartment buildings.

However, there are still a few places in Seoul where you can get a glimpse of traditional Korea and the Insa-dong area is one of them. This area is a good one because not only can you feel a traditional aura but there is also a great deal of hearty food to be found. Nowhere, in not only Seoul but all of Korea, are there as many restaurants that serve formal Korean cuisine (the equivalent of formal haute cuisine, also mistakenly referred to as 'palace food') clustered together in one area. But although we still call this area a traditional district, it also has changed dramatically from the past. Before the 1970s, the area was studded with antique bookshops and curio stores as well as many tea houses that were frequented by older people. Now, it has lost much of its homespun charm and the old shops have been replaced by modern-style restaurants and cafés. Despite all this, Insa-dong is still regarded as the best place in Seoul to experience traditional Korea and thus attracts many visitors.

The Formation of Insa-dong

English-speaking tourists call Insa-dong 'Mary's alley,' although nothing certain is known about the use of the name Mary. Some say that 'Mary' is a variant form of 'many,' which would then mean there are 'many alleys' in Insa-dong. There actually are many small and narrow alleys in Insa-dong at present, but the number is nothing compared to what it was some 40 years ago. In the past, because there were still many alleys left intact, this area had the rich traditional ambience of the old days. The alleys seen here were of a similar form as those we saw previously in Bukchon. That is, where an ally appears to have reached a dead end, it turns on a sharp angle unexpectedly if you walk further on and takes you onto another alley, continuing like this in a 'twisting and turning' labyrinth of alleys. In those alleys you could find great hanok (traditional Korean houses) built by aristocrats at the end of the Joseon

Insa-dong street

Dynasty, while in the streets was a brisk trading business in antiques, making it possible to feel the atmosphere of the Joseon period at least partially. But now, as said before, the charm of the past has mostly faded, and rather than coming here to see the past, it is more accurate to say that people now come to enjoy the atmosphere of the past. But even now you can find all sorts of things, from 12th-century Goryeo celadon to popular items of the 1970s, being sold here. As such, Insa-dong can be seen as a place where you can find a mixture of the traditional and the modern.

Insa-dong has many specialty shops dealing in old books, calligraphy items, and art galleries. The reason such shops are concentrated here is directly linked to their tradition that dates back to the Joseon Dynasty. During that era, there was a government office located here called Dohwawon that handled paintings and calligraphy. Naturally, trade of paintings and works of calligraphy probably began to take root in this neighborhood. As a result, Insa-dong is still a home to many shops specializing in paper, brushes and ink used for traditional art and calligraphy. But the situation is different for antique shops. This is because they came into this area in the early 20th century. The collapse of the Joseon Dynasty simultaneously brought about the demise of the aristocrats living in Bukchon, whose household furnishings began to show up in Insa-dong. The collapse of the family fortunes necessitated selling their valuables and moving to a different district. Those who were interested in buying these goods were the Japanese who had begun to enter Korea. A market was thus formed in Insa-dong and many antique shops sprung up. Then, after Japan lost the war in 1945, the opposite phenomenon occurred. That is, the Japanese began to sell their Korean antiques as they prepared to leave Korea. This caused the Insa-dong antique market to become larger, and the main customers at this time were the U.S. soldiers who began entering Korea.

Tremendous amounts of antiques were sold at the time, and there is a related anecdote that I would like to share here. Among the many antiques sold were rare old books, and because it was a time when Koreans were uninterested in their own culture, they did not pay much attention to the uncontrolled buying and selling of such items. When a rare book was sold, the price charged was based not on an appraisal of the book's value but on its physical weight. They looked at a book not by its contents but as a stack of paper. This is something you will definitely not see nowadays, because such books or antiques of truly high value are rarely sold. There are two reasons for this. First, so much has already been sold that there is not much left that is of high value. Second, Koreans now have incomparably greater appreciation for their culture and highly value old relics. The drastically decreased number of antique shops is also a related reason. This decreased number is because of strong government regulation that was imposed beginning in the mid-1970s. With tougher regulations, the government aimed to crack down on illegal activities such as tax evasion and production of replicas that had become rampant in the business. At that time Korea lacked an effective tax system befitting of a developed country, and thus tax problems were also pervasive. Such blatantly illegal transactions created a sea of problems, some even leading to murder, and forced the government to clamp down on the antiqueware businessmen. As a result, most storeowners left Insa-dong to set up shop in the north side (Jangan-dong) of Seoul. Even now, there are lots of antiques being sold in this area, so people who are interested should go take a look.

What Shops Are in Insa-dong?

What kind of shops will we find when we visit Insa-dong? Let us take a look. There are over 500 shops here and over thirty percent of them are restaurants and tea houses. Most serve Korean food and traditional tea. There is no other neighborhood in Seoul with so many traditional tea houses concentrated in one place. There are many different traditional teas, but green tea is probably the most representative of these. Tea culture is highly developed in neighboring China and Japan, but this is not so much the case in Korea. The reason is simple. Tea was originally intimately related to Buddhism. Monks drank tea to clear the head during monastic practices or as a condiment to accompany conversations. Monks could not drink liquor. Korea also had a highly developed tea culture until the end of the 14th century because Buddhism was the state religion until this time. But when the state religion was changed to Confucianism in the final royal dynasty, Joseon, this Buddhist custom was put aside. The Confucian aristocrats preferred liquor over tea not only in their daily routines but also when performing ceremonies. As a result, by the end of

Traditional tea house

19th century, the culture of tea drinking was being handed down only among a small number of Buddhist monks and had almost entirely disappeared from the daily life of the common people. It was not until the latter half of the 20th century that, influenced by the developed tea culture of

Japan, Koreans began to pay attention to their own traditional tea culture. From then on, a custom of drinking traditional tea was gradually formed, and many tea houses were opened in areas such as Insa-dong. Going to a good tea house and drinking traditional Korean tea is an excellent cultural experience. What makes Northeast Asian tea different from western coffee is that unlike the latter, you can drink tea for an extended period of time. A serving of tea leaves with water poured on can be used for three or four rounds of tea drinking, and thus you can enjoy talking and drinking tea for an extended period in one sitting. Tea drinking is very simple in Korea. You first warm your tea cup with hot water and then simply pour tea and drink, repeating the process as often as needed. Compared with this, the tea ceremony of Japan is very complicated and intricate. It has many rules that must be followed, such as kneeling and turning the cup. In response to the Japanese art of tea drinking, Koreans assert that there is no need to make tea drinking so complicated as long as you do not drink it lying on your back. This accentuates the free-spiritedness of Koreans. But this is not to say that Japanese tea drinking is inferior to that of Korea. The two are simply different.

There is also much to say about Korean food, but since it has been discussed in another book, I will bypass further discussion of it here. But if there is one thing I can mention, it is that finding authentic Korean cuisine in Insa-dong is not an easy task. The reason is that the food originally eaten by the Joseon aristocrats was very elaborate, and replicating this today would not be commercially viable. It would require too much care and effort to be suitable for mass consumers of today. Another reason is that such traditional culinary culture had not been properly transmitted to the successive generations, and Japanese and western food culture has been mixed with Korean to the extent that it became difficult to demarcate the boundaries of Korean cuisine. In addition to this, the manner in which Korean food is served is very poor. At times you will see food served with too much formality, and at other times served in a rude manner. I believe that this lack of appropriate manner may be due to Koreans having lived under Japanese rule and then indiscriminately taking in western culture without a good knowledge of their own culture. That is why when I go to Insa-dong, I mostly seek out and eat at inexpensive places rather than the expensive, full-course Korean cuisine restaurants. I experience more of Korean ambiance from such inexpensive restaurants.

After restaurants, art galleries, antique stores, old book shops and *pilbang* (oriental stationery stores) make up the bulk of the shops in Insa-dong. In particular, there are about 80 art galleries and no other neighborhood in Seoul has this many. About forty percent of all art galleries in Seoul are said to be located here. The number of old book shops has dwindled compared with the past, but a shop like the Tongmungwan is still here. This book shop has a history that goes back over 80 years, and is considered the oldest book shop in downtown

The oldest bookstore in Insa-dong

Seoul. Being the oldest in Seoul means that it is also the oldest in Korea. There are also many oriental stationery stores that sell calligraphy paper and brushes. About ninety percent of such stores in Seoul are located here. That the government

office in charge of paintings in the
Joseon Dynasty was located here
probably has a lot to do with this
concentration of *pilbang*. Among
the *pilbang*, one was visited by
the Queen of England several
years ago. Thus, a *pilbang* is a
shop that effectively represents the
spirit of Insa-dong. In addition,
there are also shops that sell
embroideries, knits, brassware,

Pilbangs

naturally dyed clothes, traditional masks, and countless other types of
hand-crafted items that make wonderful souvenirs.

From Korean craftwork, you cannot leave out ceramics. There are not
many expensive ceramics sold these days, but in the past, high-priced
celadon such as Goryeo *cheongja* (celadon) of the 12th and 13th centuries
would periodically appear on the market. Now, many modern-style
ceramics are sold instead. In the old days, Korea together with China was
considered the world's best maker of ceramics. From the 11th~12th
centuries to the 16th century, spanning the Goryeo and Joseon Dynasty,
Korea (along with China) made the best porcelainwares in the world. The
best among them were the Goryeo *cheongja* and Joseon *baekja* (white
porcelain). Even in China, Korean *cheongja* was considered the best in
the world. In Europe, it was not until the early 18th century that they first
succeeded in making porcelain of such caliber in German Saxony. But
now Europe makes the best porcelain in the world. Japan, of course, is in
the same league. Its power greatly weakened after the invasion by Japan
in the 16th century, Joseon was unable to further develop its ceramics

production technology. Instead, the ceramics production technology of Japan began to grow in leaps and bounds. Of course, the Korean ceramic makers kidnapped by the Japanese during the war (1592~1599) contributed greatly to this development.

Along with these craftwork stores, you will find a number of shops selling *hanbok* (traditional Korean clothing). In the modern age with the influx of western influences, Koreans have drastically altered their traditional living style. They no longer live in the houses or wear clothes of the past. Relatively speaking, Koreans are much more loyal to eating their traditional food. They continue to consume a diet based on rice, soup, *kimchi*, soy sauce and bean paste. Diet is typically conservative by nature, so it is very difficult to change completely what one eats. And although most Koreans now live in western apartment housing, they continue to maintain the traditional *ondol* method of heating floors, and thus can be seen as a preservation of tradition to some extent. But clothing is a completely different story. For the first time in their history, Koreans have completely discarded their own attire and began to wear those from a different culture. They fell in line with the westernization of the world and began to wear western clothes. Up to the 1980s, you could still occasionally see people wearing *hanbok*. Especially during traditional holidays, it was considered customary to wear *hanbok* and many people wore the traditional attire at least for those times. For this reason, *hanbok* was even referred to as 'folk attire' at the time. But this had changed by the end of the 1990s; Koreans stopped wearing *hanbok* even on traditional holidays. Today we are in a strange situation where it is almost impossible to see someone wearing *hanbok* during traditional holidays unless they are entertainers on TV. Koreans have completely alienated their own clothing from themselves.

There is now a movement to resist this neglect of *hanbok*, which focuses on modifying it for daily wear suitable for a modern lifestyle. Traditional Korean clothing is somewhat inconvenient for a western lifestyle. This includes the fact that the pants and sleeves are too wide and that the clothes are too difficult to put on. Thus, a few *hanbok* designers began to make a new style of *hanbok* that fixes such inconveniences. The *hanbok* you find in Insa-dong today are the results of these efforts. In these, the beauty of traditional *hanbok* is preserved while modifications are made for convenience and comfort. But despite these efforts, the new *hanbok* did not receive much welcome from the Korean public. The government tried to promote wearing *hanbok* by giving free admissions to royal palaces and such, but did not achieve much success. If we take this as a benchmark, Koreans appear to have not yet fully recovered confidence in their own culture. It is interesting to see that, although they themselves do not wear *hanbok*, Koreans always include it among the cultural items representing Korea. Furthermore, schools teach that *hanbok* is very beautiful clothing. In this aspect, the thoughts and actions of Korean people are playing in separate ballparks. We know that *hanbok* is beautiful, but we wear only western clothes. In any case, one of the fun things about coming to Insa-dong is that you can see assortments of quite beautiful *hanbok*.

New *hanbok* house

There are also a surprising number of *tteok* or rice cake houses in Insa-dong and its vicinity. Rice cakes occupy a special position in Korean food culture. First of all, only a few countries make cakes from rice. China and Japan also make rice cakes but they are different from the Korean *tteok*. The identity of Korean rice cake can be seen from its relationship with cooked rice. If cooked rice is everyday food, then rice cake, used for celebrations or ancestral rites ceremonies, is considered food for special occasions. This is because you do not get to eat rice cakes everyday, as they are usually prepared for celebrations or ancestral rites ceremonies. A rice cake is thus a delicacy. There are many different types of rice cakes, but basically you grind rice into flour, cook with steam and then eat. But why are there so many rice cake houses in Insa-dong? We have learned previously that Seoul, as the former capital of Joseon, was divided into Bukchon and Namchon. The two sides were separated by the Cheonggyecheon stream running through the middle. Bukchon was famous for rice cakes while Namchon was renowned for alcoholic beverages. It is said Bukchon's fame for great rice cakes arose when court ladies who had worked in the royal kitchen settled here and began making and selling rice cakes. Perhaps that is why the history of rice cake houses here is quite long. A good way to experience Korean culture is to eat rice cakes. And since *tteok* is quite affordable, you should have some when visiting Insa-dong next time.

Leaving Insa-dong

We have now seen most places in Insa-dong, but I wish to recommend that, when in Insa-dong, you should explore the alleys. One of the fun places you will discover, although it has no particular connection to Korean culture, is the knife museum. It is a *kal*, or knife, museum and there are about 5,000 knives on display here. It claims to be the largest of its kind, but I am not sure if this is true. There are not only diverse types of Korean, Japanese and Chinese knives but also those from movies such as *Return of the King and Rambo*, which add to the fun. There is also a good museum for learning about Korean folk culture that I wish to introduce. It is called *Mokin* (Wood Figure) Museum and here they collect and display small human figures made of wood as folk craftwork, which were used as accessories. These works help you get a better understanding of Korean folk craftwork. But what is great about this museum is that from the rooftop you can get a bird's eye view of Insa-dong. There are tables and chairs for drinking tea on the rooftop, so you can have a nice chat over tea while enjoying the view.

There are not only quite a number of tea houses selling traditional tea, but also more than a few coffee houses. The most famous are Starbucks and The Coffee Bean and Tea Leaf. Although initially there was some opposition to these shops coming in to Insa-dong, they eventually had little trouble finding a home here because Insa-dong is a commercial area by nature. But there is something we should note about the Starbucks here. Its display sign is spelled in Korean and there is a rumor that this is the only Starbucks in the world with the sign written in the local language. It is said that because Insa-dong represents Korean traditional culture, Starbucks made an exception to company rules as a show of respect and allowed the

Mokin museum

'Starbucks' written in Korean

sign to be in Korean. But the font design of the Korean characters falls far below acceptable standards. I wish they had used a better calligraphic style. (When I visited China in 2007, however, I discovered a Starbucks sign that was also written in the local language.)

At the end of Insa-dong, there is a park called Tapgol Park, the first public park to be built in Seoul. Its history goes back about 100 years and it is said to have been built at the suggestion of an Englishman who was serving as a state advisor at the time. There is a notable pagoda in this park. It is a ten-story structure constructed in the 15th century. Originally this park was the site of a Buddhist temple called Weongaksa in the 15th century, and the pagoda is a relic of that time. This pagoda displays the beauty of Joseon craftsmanship, and when you look over it slowly, you will see how well it is made. That is why it is designated a National Treasure. Such a great work of art was made possible because the early Joseon Dynasty was a period in which a new and fresh framework for culture was being established. However you may be disappointed when you actually go see it. To prevent acid rain damage, it has been put under a glass cover and its magnificent form cannot be seen from a distance. But if you are interested in Korean Buddhist culture, this pagoda is a must-see because there is almost no pagoda in the Seoul area designated as a National Treasure.

Weongaksa Pagoda

Also in the vicinity is an alley called *Pimagil*. Here *pima* means 'to avoid a horse,' and the horse referred to is that which was ridden by a high government official in the Joseon era. During that period, when a high government official rode his horse to go to work in the morning, junior officials and commoners had to bow their heads and wait until he had passed by. In order to avoid such inconvenience, lower-ranking officials began to travel by alleys and from that time, this alley was called *Pimagil* or Horse Avoiding Way. At the time, it is said that there were many taverns for common folks along this street, and inheriting that tradition, now there are many down-to-earth eateries for average people. Some are too down-to-earth and can be a bit short on cleanliness, but if you want to appreciate the backstreet scenery of a big city, there is no better place than this alley. It is because when you enter here, it feels as if you have travelled twenty years back in time. (However, it is rumored that this alley will also disappear soon, to be bulldozed by urban redevelopment.)

Pimagil

One of the better ways to enjoy Insa-dong is to go there on the weekend. Vehicular traffic is closed off on Saturdays from 2 p.m. to 10 p.m. and on Sundays from 10 a.m. to 10 p.m. On Sundays, a small market called *Jangteo* (Cultural Marketplace) is held, and there is much to see. Among others, there are people playing traditional musical instruments, writing and selling calligraphy, and selling antiques and curios. The only downside may be that on Sundays there are so many people that you may find it too crowded to walk around unhindered.

If Insa-dong is seen as an enjoyable place with ties to traditional culture, there is another place, although with little connection to tradition, where culture is alive. It is the Hongdae Area. While Insa-dong is frequented by people in their forties and older with stable jobs, the Hongdae Area is where college students and young people hang out. The streets of the Hongdae Area have created a unique culture found no where else in Korea, let alone in Seoul. Let us go to Hongdae Area now.

2. Deviation from the Norm, Freedom, and Streets Full of Youthful Spark – Hongdae Area

So far, we have only talked about districts in Seoul that are related to traditional Korea. But ending a trip to Seoul with visits only to these areas without seeing the young and modern side of Korea would be a shame. With only descriptions of the traditional aspects of Seoul, it may appear to be an ancient city, but Seoul is also an incredibly dynamic place. With just a single trip to the south of the Han River, you can see this for yourself. But because Gangnam is an exceedingly commercialized area, we need not deal with it in this book. Where, then, should we go to experience Seoul's young culture? Daehangno, the Sinchon area, and the neighborhood in front of Hongik University are usually mentioned as representative watering holes of young culture. Itaewon is also an exotic place, but we will exclude those places as they are not areas that only young people frequent. Of the three places mentioned above, I think the Hongik area has the most unique brand of youth culture. Why? It is because in terms of having a definite and characteristic culture, Daehangno and the area around Sinchon are not as developed as Hongik. These two areas seem to give the impression that only eating and drinking cultures are developed. Indeed, why else would the streets in front of Yonsei University in the Sinchon area be called "Let's-eat alleys"?

Let us first go to Daehangno, of which the literal translation is 'University Street.' The name comes having been the site of the College of Arts and Humanities of Seoul National University until the college moved out in 1975. The street currently does not retain any relations to Seoul National University, but given its proximity to a number of other private universities nearby, the area still bustles with young university students. Daehangno is home to many small theaters, more so than any other place in Korea. Although this makes it seem like a very cultural space, only a handful of these theaters are actually capable of staging decent plays or musicals. Also, the theaters are hard to find squeezed amidst countless restaurants and bars. Such a phenomenon is the result of the indifference of young college students to culture. The young students are more drawn to drinking and enjoying nightlife rather than attending cultural events. Daehangno is much better compared to Sinchon, where a cluster of universities in the area make it the focal point of students from Yonsei, Sogang, Hongik, and Ewha Womans Universities. There is virtually no place to enjoy a bit of high culture at all. Sinchon is filled

B-boys at Daehangno

with beer and *soju* halls, aiming to satiate the primal instincts of young people. Daehangno at least has plays and musicals, however coarse or crude they may be.

Amidst the increasing commercialization of the Daehangno area, there are people who are trying to protect and revive theater-

S e o u l

Fashion street in front of Ewha Womans University

going culture. Because rising rent costs and the growing indifference of young students make it difficult for artists to survive here, many theaters have moved to the outskirts of the area for cheaper rent. There is no such phenomenon in Sinchon. Dubbed 'fashion street,' the streets in front of Ewha Womans University are full of beauty salons and clothing stores. It is impossible to reach the Ewha campus from the Ewha subway station without passing through the fashion streets. Once out of the Ewha subway station, it is difficult to imagine that the world's largest women's university is located somewhere within the dense forests of hair salons and clothing shops. There is no concrete reason for this, but it certainly is a strange phenomenon. The Ewha University area has become one of the 'must-see' places in Seoul for foreign tourists, especially among Chinese tourists. But this is because of Ewha being considered the center of Korean fashion and not for the academic environment of the school.

Yonsei University, located just one bus stop away from Ewha Womans University, is different from its neighbor in that it is famous for its streets

"Let's-eat alleys" in Sinchon

filled with beer halls and restaurants. There are almost no culture zones whil a highly diverse group of alcohol businesses are gathered together in one place. Over 100,000 people pass through Sinchon everyday, flocking into the area mostly to drink. What university in the world has such a massive drinking complex right in front of its campus? Yonsei is one of the most prestigious universities in Korea, and all you can find in the surrounding area are massive beer hall complexes. This clearly shows how much Korean university students love to drink. As mentioned several times in previous chapters, Koreans rank among the top as far as drinking, singing, and dancing are concerned. Students are no exception, and they love to drink and then go to *karaoke* afterwards. However, pubs are not the only formative feature of Sinchon. Another characteristic element is the so-called 'motel zone,' where several dozens of love hotels are crowded along the streets between Ewha and Yonsei. The all-too-obvious cycle of alcohol, *karaoke*, and love hotels is located directly in front of a university campus—which is supposed to pursue the search for truth instead of such worldly values. How can we explain this reality? This is part of the reason why the Daehangno and Sinchon areas have been excluded from this book. However, if we go a bit further west, things become a little different. We will now move on to the Hongdae area near Hongik University.

Why Hongdae (Hongik University)?

Hongik University is famous for its arts program, which is regarded as the best in the country. A diploma from the Hongik University College of Arts would earn you enough respect to fare well in Korean artist circles. Thus, many aspiring students of art naturally came to this area and set up their studios, creating a unique, creative ambience. Compared to mainstream convention, what these young artists pursued was experimental and very much free-spirited. In other words, it is the rise of counter-convention against conventional art. Because they favored such counter-cultural elements, like-minded artists in genres other than visual art also began to congregate in this area. Of them, underground musicians in particular came to become a vital part of what makes the Hongdae area so unique. The underground musicians are mainly followers of American rock, and they have proclaimed that they will not compromise their musical goals by giving into the temptations of commercial music and the glory that comes with popularity. They emphasize the fact that they pursue music that they truly believe in. The names of these bands are very interesting to the point of seeming almost grotesque. 'Thigh band,' 'Crying Nut,' and 'Hwang Sinhye Band' are some of examples. The American equivalent of 'Hwang Sinhye Band,' which was named after a famous actress in Korea, would be something

Main entrance of Hongik University

like 'Sharon Stone Band.'

But the above description of Hongdae is already ten years old; in recent years, the area has not been able to avoid the grip of capitalism. This is, in a sense, inevitable. Similar to the case of Insa-dong, there was little chance that capitalists — in a country like Korea that fully embraces capitalism — would pass by an opportunity to invest capital in a place full of profit potential like the Hongdae area. Thus, the innocence and pure creativity that once prospered in this quarter has been compromised in a sense. However, many cultural critics who are interested in the Hongdae area argue that it still retains its unique charm, which is not so easily lost. "The Hongdae area is like a stem cell. You cannot pinpoint exactly where, but it has very original technology that is full of indefinite cultural potential and possibilities in every corner of the streets," said Choi Geum-su, a Hongdae-based culture planner who runs an online arts magazine, 'neolook.com.' Choi's remark very well sums up the quintessence of the Hongdae area. Just like we humans do not know which part of a stem cell makes up which part of our body because research on this is still in progress, we do not know how the Hongdae area will continue to transform itself. In that sense, the Hongdae area is still in the making.

Hongdae culture—Alternative vs. Mainstream

There are many ways to describe the streets in the Hongdae area, but I believe that the terms 'young' and 'alternative culture' best fit the area's character. Alt. Space Loop and Ssamzie Space are two of the many examples of these keywords. These 'spaces' are in fact art galleries built in avant-garde fashion. On the way to Alt. Space Loop from the Hongdae Subway Station, there are many small shops full of interesting gadgets that are hard to be missed. Each shop seems to overflow with its unique character and disposition, as well as countless special items that are hard to be seen elsewhere. Among them are miniature versions of an old-fashioned desk and backless chair that are reminiscent of childhood as

A store in Hongdae Area

well as many kinds of small accessories—such items make it difficult to pass them by. These shops surely captivate young university students when even a middle-aged man in his fifties like myself is tempted to go inside for a look. What they sell here are like the rest of the Hongdae area—far from mainstream trends. Each shop seems to be decorated by the owners themselves, and its snug atmosphere and small physical dimensions do not overawe but instead make customers feel at home. The owners of these shops tend to personally make the items shown on display, which makes the shops even more unique. The price range is not high, but that does not mean that the quality has been compromised. When I went there on a field trip with my students (all of whom are female because I teach at a women's university), I had to practically rush them out of shops because they otherwise showed no intention of leaving.

Free market in Hongdae Area

These shops clearly represent the Hongdae spirit, but we could say that the way in which transaction takes place is still conventional. The shop is a place for the owner to choose what he or she wishes to sell, and in this sense, transaction mostly flows in a single direction. Nobody but the owner is allowed to sell. As opposed to these shops, there is an even more 'alternative' place in the Hongdae area where the boundary between seller and customers becomes fuzzy and both parties become equal participants in the act of buying and selling. Everyone is invited to this 'free market' to share whatever they have to offer. The 'free market' is held every Saturday from 1 to 6 p.m. between March and November in the Children's Park just across from the main entrance of Hongik University and is not to be confused with the similar-sounding 'flea market.' Technically, everyone can bring their personal creations and sell them here. The items to be sold must be the creative work of the seller. In order to keep the process orderly, those who wish to sell must apply for a space on the selling floor and also have themselves and their works reviewed by the organizers of the free market. This is where the experimentalism of Hongdae comes alive. A chance to showcase one's works in the conventional way is limited to only a few. On the other hand, the free market provides an opportunity for poor, unknown artists to interact directly with the public. It allows future artists to test out their artistic ideas and see firsthand how these are received by the public. The free market also features performances by underground bands and mime artists, adding spark to this already exuberant atmosphere.

The Hongdae area is home to galleries that are committed to exhibiting works of art that continue to push the limits of mainstream art. In keeping with some experimentalist spirit, Alt. Space Loop and Ssamzie Space are only two of many galleries that mostly deal with the works of non-mainstream artists who do not cater to commercial tastes. As a natural result, many young anonymous artists enter the fray, while the most avante-garde and talented of these become success stories. Alt. Space Loop was established in 1999 for contemporary Asian artists who do not submit to the influence of mainstream capitalism-dominated Western art and instead are devoted to preserving and developing Asian artistic traditions. Alt. Space Loop is highly evaluated as a space in which young like-minded Asian artists who are not shaken by the Western paradigm create uniquely Asian art. Although it was officially opened in 1999, cooperative efforts of the artists began much earlier. Their works were quite ahead of their time, and by the time personal computers began to appear on the market in the 1980s, they had already opened an electronic café, integrating the computer into their artwork.

Alt. Space Loop hosts a number of international conferences and exhibitions each year to promote exchange among Asian artists and stimulate Korean domestic art circles. There was an exhibition of artists from Korea, China, and Russia on the day that I visited the gallery. The main theme was the integration of art with modern technology.

Alt. Space Loop Gallery

The artists took a picture of an object and transformed it into a completely different look by using digital technology. Some works exuded an air of dreams and phantasms, and it was difficult to tell whether the medium was painting or photograph. Each time I see a work of modern art, I marvel at the novelty and originality of the ideas as opposed to being amazed by the absolute beauty that is conveyed by great masterpieces. This time I was impressed by the brilliant ideas of young artists. What was interesting about the exhibition was that although Alt. Space Loop declares its protection of artists from capitalist influence, the exhibition that day was sponsored by Hewlett-Packard Company, one of the largest multinational corporations. In a capitalist society, capital seems to be something that is difficult to keep close as well as push farther away.

The second gallery, Ssamzie Space, had a similar objective but took a completely different approach. The founders of Ssamzie Space took a more active approach to nurturing alternative arts. Each year they choose a certain number of artists, provide them with a studio for one year, and hold an exhibition of their works at the end of the year. Such projects cost a large sum of money and without great passion and persistence is impossible to pull off such ambitious projects. Because we had contacted one of the artists in residence in advance, we were able to meet and chat with him in person and see his works. A young artist based in Paris, he also created images by retouching original photographs with digital technology. His studio reminded us of a recycling center filled with scraps and junks, a fitting metaphor because whenever he finds something on the street that could be used for his work, he promptly brings it to the studio. In addition to studios for the artists in residence, Ssamzie Space has three floors of exhibition space. Words are not enough to describe

The interior of Ssamzie Space

the originality of the place, and nothing is better than to actually go and see it for yourself.

In accordance with the slogan 'Introduction of the culture of alternative arts,' there are various festivals that take place in the Hongdae area, and a representative example is the Fringe Festival. The Fringe Festival is held each August, and as its name implies, it is a festival for those who are excluded from the mainstream. 'Fringe' here does not mean those marginalized from commercialized popular culture. Of course, it refuses popular culture that moves increasingly towards becoming a slave of capitalism, but it also diverges away from conservative and 'serious' fine arts. The Fringe Festival considers both popular culture and fine arts as mainstream, and is a party for anyone and everyone who refuses to be part of either one of these. There is no restriction on genres, thus inviting many underground artists from various genres including plays, dance, mime, music and arts. When we take a closer look at its details, the programs consist of many interesting titles. In 2007, the festival consisted of the following titles: opening festival, 'boisterous singing' for the music festival, 'under construction' for the visual arts festival, 'with one voice' for the performing arts festival, and 'free for all' for the ending street festival. Are these not all interesting names?

The students at Hongik University are not bystanders to what happens in the area. There are many streets whose districts have wall paintings, and these are works by the arts students of Hongik University. While they do consider their time spent in studios to be important, they also seek to create a much larger 'studio' for artistic experimentation by making the alleys and buildings near campus their canvas. Such attempts to break out of the ivory tower and interact with the community began well over a decade ago in 1993, and their efforts gave birth to streets full of mural paintings. The only downside of this might be the fact that these streets are scattered far apart, so it is impossible to appreciate all of their work in a single view. When I took a foreign visitor to see these wall paintings, he remarked that while he was happy to see these works, strolling along the small streets in downtown Seoul was even more interesting. He thought a walk through the small and old streets in Bukchon and Insa-dong was a very Korean experience, and said it was a pleasure to find such a place in the Hongdae area. Come to think of it, the Hongdae area possesses a unique brand of traditional Korean street culture that is nonexistent in other university quarters like Daehangno and Sinchon. In that sense, the district around Hongik University offers an opportunity for its visitors to experience both contemporary and traditional aspects of Korean culture. As you walk along the streets with paintings on the wall, you can also see on the way many interesting bars, restaurants and cafés that are worth a visit. There is a café where you can have a bottle of beer or a cup of tea with your feet dipped in water, a bar furnished in the style of late Joseon, and cafés where you can dress up like a princess and have your picture taken. These unique places add even more fun to exploring the Hongdae area.

Night clubs are an essential aspect of any discussion on the Hongdae area. Frankly, middle-aged people like myself are not part of the generation that appreciates the culture of the Hongdae area. We tend to prefer the more conservative and traditional Insa-dong district, and rarely ever meet in Hongdae. I first got to know the Hongdae area through Indie bands. The term 'Indie band,' which is the abbreviation of 'independent band' was in fact coined by Koreans who love to shorten everything. (Likewise, synthesizers are referred to as 'synthe' in Korea.)

Mural painting of Hongdae Area

These Indie bands are also called underground bands and strictly adhere to freer styles that commercialized popular bands can never dare to try. They were started by small groups of rock music fanatics who simply wanted to express their talent by playing music by themselves and for themselves. These groups start out by practicing by themselves, and later perform in small clubs—because they perform their own brand of rock music, their method of expression is very much free and uninhibited. Because they never intended to sell records or make profits out of their music-making, they could pursue their musical ideals without any restrictions. For that reason, their lyrics are composed in straightforward rather than metaphorical language, and often contain forthright language and sometimes swearwords.

During performances, perhaps it is due to the small stage size, but there is no distinct boundary between the stage and the audience. Also, there are few rules and virtually no sense of etiquette required during the performance and intermission, and the musicians engage naturally in conversation with the audience at any time. While stars who appear on television tend to think of themselves as members of a privileged class and try to distinguish themselves from the crowds, such thinking is hardly found among Indie musicians in the Hongdae area.

Crying Nut poster

The down-to-earth and humble attitude of underground musicians has won the hearts of many young people and led to a club cult boom in the area. There are even cases in which an Indie band, with the enthusiastic support of its college student fans, succeeded in making a debut on national television. The band Crying Nut is one of the best-known Indie bands in Korea, and even I know some of their songs. Crying Nut started off as an alternative band, but it was absorbed into mainstream culture after it gained popularity. There are two types of clubs in the Hongdae area although the distinction is not always clear-one a place for dancing, and the other a place for both dancing and watching individual bands perform.

The best time to enjoy Hongdae club culture is Club Day and Sound Day, which are held once every month. Given the number of clubs in the area, it is impossible to visit them all in one day. Also, entering each of these clubs ends up costing quite a bit of money. But Hongdae has alternatives for everything: Club Day and Sound Day are a creative way for young people on tight budgets to fully enjoy the unique ambience and culture of the area. Once every month, with just one ticket which costs ₩ 20,000 (approx. 15 USD), you can have an unlimited access to all participating clubs for one night. If we first look at Club Day, it is the last Friday of every month, and people can go around each of 13 clubs and dance through the night. Each club has a different music specialization, so you can choose one that suits your taste and meet people with similar musical interests.

I am not an ardent fan of pop or rock music, but I decided to participate in Club Day as part of my field trip. I was not comfortable with the fact that I had to go out so late at night, and the atmosphere certainly did not suit the taste of a middle-aged man. The entrance was free once you bought the ticket—not a paper ticket but a neon florescent stamp on the wrist—at the first club you visited. After wandering about for a bit, we went into a club called 'Hodgepodge,' a pun on a similar-sounding Korean phrase that means 'wasting.' This club, which used to one of the most popular 'it' places a few years ago, now no longer exists. Clubs, too, seem to be ephemeral beings.

Inside, it was dark and filled with cigarette smoke and bodies, making it difficult to move around. People moved continuously to the rhythm of somewhat slow-tempo music. I marveled at how they could dance to music with such slow tempo. I am not too familiar with American popular music and cannot recall what type of music was being played then, but I remember constant repetition of simple rhythms. I could not feel myself get into the music because the rhythm was not fast. When I expressed how I felt to a student who was with me, I was promptly told that one had to be there until 6 or 7 in the morning to truly feel the energy of that club. I was chastised for my impatience. According to the student, after moving your body in groove with a slow rhythm like this for a few hours, you feel really uplifted. But being unable to stay in such a smoke—filled, noisy place until 6 in the morning, my group and I had a beer and left for another club.

While Club Day is meant to be a special day for dancing (and music), Sound Day is a day for music, when you can see diverse bands at a steeply discounted admissions price. On every third Friday each month, with a purchase of a single ticket, you can go to about 10 live music clubs. In each club, diverse styles of music are played—much of which you normally do not have a chance to encounter, including jazz, rock, hip-hop, techno, electronic, and crossover. To be honest, I am not familiar with the complex categories of American popular music. But I needed to experience this Sound Day at least once in order to write this section, so I took a day and went with a group of my students. One of the clubs was featuring a well-known pop singer and so we went there. By the time we arrived, the club was filled with people all the way up to the front entrance and it was not easy to get inside. This singer was popular with young women, but not with the middle-aged people like me. Inside the club, as expected, there was hardly any space to stand and you could not even see the singer's face. But when I heard the song, it was no different from what I had heard on the radio and I lost all desire to stay. It was too crowded for my liking, so we decided to go to another club. This place was a famous club called Evans, and it was also very crowded and difficult to find seats with a good view of the band. The music being played was rock and it sounded too loud for the smallness of the space. The entire audience was very much into the music and was moving in rhythm. Here too I felt my age. After hitting the club circuit like this and as the night deepened, not only did I became more convinced that this place is not to my taste and but also wanted to go home. But my students wanted to explore more, so I left them and headed home alone.

As I contemplated the night on my way back home, I realized that the best thing about Hongdae clubs is that you can experience music that you cannot easily encounter on broadcast media such as TV and radio. Broadcast content is consumed by the public and if there is even the slightest controversy about violating the sentiments of such a mass audience, it may be censored. Therefore, it is not easy to meet diverse genres of music thorough broadcast media, but it can be found here at the clubs in the Hongdae Area. However, this does not mean that Hongdae clubs cater only to underground music. As

Club Evans

mentioned earlier, bands that got their start here have gone on to star on TV music programs. Representative of such acts is the previously mentioned band Crying Nut. Of their songs, several are extremely popular and frequently requested in *karaoke* clubs. This band is no longer 'underground' but has become 'upperground.' Crying Nut's popularity grew to the point that even military enlistment of its members became big news. There are posters for various bands playing at Hongdae clubs and performing centers, and I recently saw one for Crying Nut. This is how I found out that they had completed their military service and were back playing music. Anyway, Sound Day is great for hearing music that you would normally not encounter on broadcast media, but what is even better is that after the performances are done, you can stay late to dance and enjoy more music.

Other Points of Attraction

We have so far seen the main attractions of the Hongdae Area, but there are many other points that have not been covered. The most important of these is the b-boy performance. There is a considerable b-boy following in Korea these days because Korean b-boys are among the best in the world. As I have touched on previously during the discussion of Shamanism, Koreans are one of the few peoples in the world who show great aptitude for singing and dancing. Koreans can sing and dance anytime and anywhere. Although there may be other factors, I believe that the reason Korean youths have been able to win the world b-boy championships so often has to do with the spirit of ecstasy that runs deep within the Korean people. The history of b-boy dancing in Korea does not go back very far in Korea, adding up to little over a decade. At the time they came into being, b-boy street dancing did not attract the attention of mainstream performance organizations. Breakdancing was thought of as something that young troublemakers, not good in school and full of animosity toward society, got together to do in the streets to let off steam. But when these b-boys began to win international competitions, the attitude of society toward them changed and b-boys began to attract the attention of the general public. Gradually, many more dance crews were formed and b-boy dancing came out of the underground into the upperground.

Now its popularity is such that there are a number of theaters that are designed exclusively for b-boy performances. Having several theaters opened in Seoul devoted to just one type of performance is unprecedented in history. For example, Nanta, which is rooted in traditional Korean drumming but has found great success by modernizing the old art, has only one or two theaters in downtown Seoul. But b-boy dancing already has four theaters, and they are all profit-making performing centers. This shows the extent of the current b-boy popularity. That is why expectations are mounting for b-boys to create the next *hallyu* (Korean wave).

Of b-boy performances, the most famous one is found in the Hongdae Area. It is one of the oldest among b-boy shows in Korea, and has not only dancing but a storyline similar to that of a play. Called 'The Ballerina Who Loved a B-Boy,' it is about a ballerina with no interest in breakdancing who by chance encounters b-boys performing in the streets and gradually comes to understand the b-boy culture. The storyline itself is unoriginal, but the setup of classical ballet meeting breakdance, the icon of street culture, is quite interesting. Apparently, putting a storyline to b-boy dancing like this has not been done anywhere else in the world, and the 'high culture meet low culture' plot is also unique. Neither ballet

"The Ballerina Who Loved a B-Boy,"

nor breakdancing has any cultural relationship with Korea, and that the two came together in Korea to achieve this success is quite a novel phenomenon. I had seen a b-boy performance with a similar theme at a theater in a different district and had not seen this particular show in Hongdae. But for this writing, I made time to go see this show at the Hongdae Area b-boy theater. Surprisingly, the theater was located in the basement floor of a very nice building. B-boy dance, treated as underground art not only in the U.S. but also in Korea, has really come a long way. The regular performing team for the show was Extreme Crew, one of the best in Korea that won the 2007 B-Boy World Cup held in Germany. For those who want to experience the dynamism of Korea, I recommend taking in this b-boy performance. The dancers' routines are close to superhuman and one of the team members does a move that no one else can do in the world. You will not regret seeing this show.

Another cultural package in the Hongdae Area that I would like to introduce is the Four Seasons Drama Gallery. This is a gallery created by Director Yun Seokho—whose TV drama 'Winter Sonata' was a big *hallyu* (Korean Wave) hit in Japan—while filming the TV drama 'Spring Waltz' in the Hongdae Area. Director Yun made a series of dramas based on the four seasons, the other two being 'Autumn Tale' and 'Summer Fragrance,' and probably created the gallery to commemorate these dramas. Inside, there are various props from the dramas on display as well as recreated mock-ups of the sets used during filming. There seem to be many Japanese visitors. For someone like me who has hardly seen any of Director Yun's work, this place may not be that meaningful, but it is a great place to visit for many Asians who are ardent fans of Korean dramas. I would also recommend Sangsangmadang (the Garden of Imagination), which is a representative example of mixed cultural

Four Seasons Drama Gallery

medium in the Hongdae Area. Each floor of a large building is equipped with a different medium, including a movie theater specializing in independent and non-mainstream films, a theater for alternative performing arts, craft shops and galleries that sell handmade works of non-mainstream artists, and art galleries—all designed to accommodate the people who create alternative culture. It is worth a visit because an entire building of about 10 floors, including the basement, is used for the sole purpose of promoting alternative arts. It best embodies the spirit of Hongdae Area.

One of the most novel places I found while exploring the Hongdae Area is called Ice Bar. I first learned of this place on a website about the Hongdae Area and went there without much expectation, but it turned out to be a surprisingly interesting place. Its official name is Sub-Zero, probably because the temperature inside is actually below zero degrees Celcius. The interior seems even colder because it is furnished entirely with ice. There are winter coats and even fur-lined boots for customers to wear. The inside was rather strange-looking. As can be seen in the pictures, the tables and chairs were all made of ice. Therefore the temperature must always be maintained at five degrees below zero. It is like having a drink at the North Pole. This is the only bar of its kind in

Ice Bar, Sub-Zero

Korea, one more reason to visit Ice Bar. But it was early February when I visited, and having weathered the cold outside, the cold that waited for me inside was not that exciting. I remarked to a staff member there that I should come again in the summer, and I was told that there are so many people in the summer that you have to wait in line. How refreshing and cool it must be to step inside from the sweltering summer heat. This bar's novelty was proven by the articles covering the wall, written by CNN, Reuters, NHK, and Hongkong and Chinese news stations. At least for me, of all the places I visited on the streets of the Hongdae Area, this was the most memorable.

Although this area overflows with alternative culture, restaurants make up the overwhelming majority of shops. Crowds of people come here so it is only natural that there are many restaurants. What is unique is that so many diverse eateries and pubs are concentrated in this area. From American fast food to the cuisines of Japan, China, France, Italy, Mexico, Thailand, India, and the Middle East, here you can enjoy food from all over the world. But of course, Korean restaurants predominate. This area is famous for charcoal-grilled meat where you sprinkle some salt on strips

Japanese pubs and Chinese restaurants in Hongdae Area

of beef, grill them over charcoal at the table and then eat. Also, it is relatively inexpensive. After Korean restaurants, or more accurately 'pubs,' Japanese pubs are next largest in number. I enjoy going to this type of pub occasionally because, like everything else that is Japanese, they are clean and you can enjoy simple drinks and food. While exploring this area, I was greatly surprised by the increased number of Japanese pubs. I thought to myself that this type of pub must be expensive for college students, but at the same time I realized that Koreans now live pretty well. I also sensed that animosity toward Japanese culture has diminished greatly in the younger generation of Koreans. Putting up a large shop sign written in Japanese was unthinkable 20 to 30 years ago, but now it is accepted without much resistance. Anyway, in terms of food, the Hongdae Area may be the most international of all neighborhoods in Seoul. There are also cafés, not exactly in the Hongdae Area but right next to it, that have a great view of the Han River and its surrounding scenery. From these cafés, you can enjoy not only the Han River, but also a great view that includes the bridges, the National Assembly Building, the 63 Building, and others, albeit at the slight burden of over ₩10,000 per cup.

Leaving the Hongdae Area

I think we have now basically covered the Hongdae Area. One final comment I would like to make is that the Hongdae Area has two faces, one for day and the other for night. During the day, it is a place where daily life meets art. When you walk the streets during the day, you may be led to think that there are diverse works of art everywhere in these alleys. Some refer to the daytime Hongdae Area as 'the gallery with no roof.' But when nighttime comes and the colorful lights of the shops are

Street for Strolling

lit, young people ready to enter the sensual world of music and dance begin to congregate and the place becomes a world of escape and freedom. As such, in this area, art and pleasure coexist in the same manner as day and night.

I explored the area both during the day and the night, but at night it becomes a completely different place, to the extent that you doubt that these are the same streets from the daytime. Of the streets to explore, there are 'Street for Strolling,' 'Picasso Street,' and the 'Art Supply Shops Street,' around which art tutoring schools are clustered. Of course there is also 'Mural Street,' which I have mentioned already. The 'Street for Strolling,' when seen during the day, is not particularly scenic, with just restaurants lined up on both sides of the street. But at night, when the lights come on, this street is transformed into a different world. Also in its vicinity are art galleries that satisfy our cultural inclinations such as Alt. Space Loop, which we discussed previously.

The situation is similar for 'Picasso Street.' At night, countless street vendors line up to hawk accessories. As there seems to be no connection between Picasso and accessories, I have no idea why it is called 'Picasso Street.' That is just the way it is. During the day, this is a normal street. But at night, with all the vendor tables lit and the accessories looking as if they are shining from the reflection of all the lights, it is a pretty sight. This street also has a small park where Free Market and the Fringe Festival are held. On market and festival days, the street overflows with art. It occurs to me that perhaps the Hongdae Area is a place where you can enjoy a holistic life of maintaining grace through experiencing elegant art during the day and pursuing pleasure—becoming true to your sensual side—at night.

After Seeing Seoul

In this trip we have visited the most representative examples of Korean heritage that are found in Seoul. The Hongdae Area, of course, is an exception, but we have looked at just about all the cultural heritage sites related to the Joseon period. But as I write the conclusion, I cannot help but have some concerns and regrets. I feel as though we have only seen limited parts of Seoul, and so I would like to emphasize that this book does not explain all of Seoul. In that respect, there are many things in this book that are missing. Of course there was no need to discuss all of them, but as I conclude this book I would like to briefly touch upon a few of them.

First of all, one half of Seoul is missing from this book. It goes without saying that this is Gangnam. Gangnam is a new metropolitan area that has been developed since the 1970s. Therefore not many noteworthy cultural relics are found there. Instead there is modern culture, and of this, consumer culture is especially strong. This is exemplified by the leading fashion street in Seoul, Apgujeongdong's Rodeo Road, and the many expensive restaurants and bars found throughout Gangnam. The Teheranro area, also known as Teheran Valley, is also remarkable. If you want to see the high tech image of Seoul, just take subway line Number 2 from Samseong Station to Gangnam Station. High-rise buildings line both

Teheran Valley

sides of the wide avenue. But since this area is described in detail in travel guides and is not related to cultural heritage, it was not given mention in this book.

But on the other hand, this does not imply that we have seen everything to be seen in Gangbuk. We mentioned fashion just now, and when you talk about this subject you cannot omit Fashion Town of Dongdaemun (East Gate). This place. is truly a city within a city. It comprises dozens of large buildings, with shops numbering in the tens of thousands. If you want to witness the dynamism of the Korean people, this is the best place in which to do so. It opens at 10 a.m. and closes at 5 a.m. the next day. When you go there especially at around 2 or 3 a.m., you will see the entire expansive area brilliantly illuminated with no trace of the night. People are so diligent that you wonder whether they sleep at all. One famous western architect sought out this place as soon as he arrived in Seoul. He did so probably because here you can feel a city that is alive. The shops are open until dawn to service the retail merchants who come from the provinces. Provincial merchants arrive late at night in rented buses, shop until dawn and then return to their respective regions. Then, they start the morning bright and early by displaying and selling the goods that they brought from Seoul just hours earlier. These people seem to live without sleep. Koreans are people who live tenaciously. This is why I recommend coming here if you want to see the dynamism of the Korean people.

Another regret I had while writing this book was that I was not able to discuss the Samcheongdong district. This area, interpreted broadly, could be included as a part of Bukchon, and it is considered to be an area akin to Insa-dong in its good balance of tradition and modernity. Here, there are many art galleries and unique exhibition halls. In recent years, the number of small, cute shops selling accessories has continued to increase. There are of course many restaurants as well, so it is a popular dating spot for young couples. But I omitted this area from this book because I feel that a culture unique to Samgcheondong has not yet fully formed. Since this area is still in the process of developing, I feel that it is best to just watch and see the direction in which it is going. I also have some regrets about not having included museums. For a foreign visitor, visiting

View of Samcheongdong street

at least the National Museum of Korea and the National Folk Museum of Korea would be a good experience. But you can find good guides at the museums and so I felt that there was no need to explain them further in this book. In addition to these museums, there are numerous art museums, but these were also not included.

Other things that come to mind are traditional markets in Seoul and walks along the old fortress walls. Then there is the Han River for those who want to explore nature. There are many stories related to this river which runs several tens of kilometers. Not only nature but also history and culture flow along the edges of the Han River. Seoul's Han River is currently being reborn. Seoul envisions a coming of the Han River renaissance and has announced that it will create a new Han River that encompasses a harmonious coexistence of nature and culture. It will be better to write about the Han River in the next volume after its development plan has been completed. The Itaeweon area also cannot be ignored when one talks about Seoul. Especially for those who want to enjoy multi-national cultures, Itaeweon is the best place. It is good place to shop and is made better by the diverse types of restaurants found there. But this area is also well-explained in guidebooks, so I need not discuss it here.

Finally, it may be fun to tour Seoul solely on places related to *hallyu*. *Hallyu* has lost its steam somewhat lately, but it is still strong. Seoul is in the center of the *hallyu* phenomenon because countless TV dramas were filmed here. Amongst East Asian people, therefore, Seoul is referred to as "the city of desire." Although *hallyu* culture is important, it is not discussed in this book because it is not directly related to traditional heritage. There are many other things to see in Seoul, because it is such a huge city. I wish to conclude by introducing a great book, *Refresh Your*

Soul in Seoul, for readers interested in all things about Seoul. Because this book is published by the city, it is not sold in bookstores. Like what the title states, this book provides well-planned travel routes for Seoul. By using this book to set a basic travel outline and then reading my book to get more in-depth information, you will be able to see Seoul in a clear and organized way.